TRAGEDY AND THE WITNESS

Tragedy and the Witness

Shakespeare and Beyond

Fred Parker

https://www.openbookpublishers.com

©2025 Fred Parker

This work is licensed under the Creative Commons Attribution-NonCommercial 4.0 International (CC BY-NC 4.0). This license allows you to share, copy, distribute and transmit the text; to adapt the text for non-commercial purposes of the text providing attribution is made to the author (but not in any way that suggests that they endorse you or your use of the work).

Attribution should include the following information:

Fred Parker, *Tragedy and the Witness: Shakespeare and Beyond*. Cambridge, UK: Open Book Publishers, 2025, https://doi.org/10.11647/OBP.0435

Further details about CC BY-NC licenses are available at https://creativecommons.org/licenses/by-nc/4.0/

All external links were active at the time of publication unless otherwise stated and have been archived via the Internet Archive Wayback Machine at https://archive.org/web

Updated digital material and resources associated with this volume are available at https://www.openbookpublishers.com/product/0435#resources

Information about any revised edition of this work will be provided at https://doi.org/10.11647/OBP.0435

ISBN Paperback: 978-1-80511-443-7
ISBN Hardback: 978-1-80511-444-4
ISBN PDF: 978-1-80511-445-1
ISBN HTML: 978-1-80511-447-5
ISBN EPUB: 978-1-80511-446-8

DOI: 10.11647/OBP.0435

Cover image: Rembrandt, *Saul and David* (between c.1655 and c.1658), Mauritshuis, The Hague, https://commons.wikimedia.org/wiki/File:Rembrandt_van_Rijn_-_Saul_and_David_-_621_-_Mauritshuis.jpg

Cover design: Jeevanjot Kaur Nagpal

For Jan, who gave me the Greeks

Table of Contents

Preface	ix
1. Overview: Phaedra and the Nurse	1
2. Welcoming the Stranger	23
Hamlet's request	23
Antigone and the chorus	30
Telling the hero's story	34
Admitting the alien	38
3. Imperfect Witness	51
Representation as betrayal in Shakespeare	51
Heroes and megastars: seeing double	70
Fantasising the heroic: *The Wild Duck* and *The Master Builder*	75
Antony and Cleopatra	85
4. The Crime and Punishment Story	93
Phèdre	115
The Trial	120
Molora: a post-apartheid *Oresteia*	129
5. Giving Audience to Madness	139
'Witness me. See me.' Beckett's *Not I* and Kane's *4.48 Psychosis*	140
Othello, *Hamlet*, and maternal support	152
Playing and playing mad: Pirandello's *Henry IV*	166
Macbeth	182
King Lear	197
Bibliography	225
Index	233

Preface

A few words of orientation may be helpful at the outset. To begin with the subtitle: Shakespeare and beyond. The thinking in this book sprang from Hamlet's dying request for Horatio to tell his story, and the book leads up to sustained readings of *Macbeth* and *King Lear*. Along the way *Hamlet*, *Troilus and Cressida*, *Othello*, *Antony and Cleopatra*, and *Coriolanus* all make their contribution. So the book is a good deal concerned with Shakespeare, and in my mind never moves far away from matters which particularly illuminate Shakespearean tragedy, and which Shakespearean tragedy particularly illuminates. However, you will find that many pages are given over to other works, usually of tragic drama, some of which are discussed at length and some only briefly touched on, and that I move between these works—of different kinds and from different periods—with irresponsible lightness. Part of the reason for that has to do with the book's genesis as a series of introductory lectures on Tragedy given to final-year undergraduates at Cambridge. In those lectures I wanted to suggest the range and variety of the topic, to stimulate curiosity, and to share my enthusiasms for works that seem to me of inexhaustible interest. Although this book has developed a long way beyond those initial lectures, those motives remain. But I have also come to find this method of multiple juxtaposition no bad thing as a way of thinking, a way of suggesting the coherence of the topic without policing its borders. The gods have not so taken my wits away that I suppose myself to be offering a general theory of tragedy, whose forms are famously various, mutable, and resistant to definition. But through these juxtapositions I try to bring out what Wittgenstein might call a 'family resemblance' with regard to the importance of witnessing in tragedy, so that observations about any one particular work become more resonant when set within this larger field of relations. However, that being said, if your main business is resolutely with Shakespeare, you will find the greatest concentration of Shakespearean material in Chapters 3 and 5, and may wish to go straight to those.

I should also say something about the main title: *Tragedy and the Witness*. This book is not directly about the task of bearing witness to events in real life that could be called tragic; it is not about historical or personal testimony, immensely important though that topic is. My focus rather is on figures within tragic theatre who stand next to the one in anguish, and on the dynamic relation between the one in anguish and the one who listens or watches. The protagonist needs in their suffering to feel that there is someone who can enter into their state of mind, who can find words that speak adequately for them, so that they may be released from that vortex of estrangement which threatens them. But the kind of anguish with which tragedy deals is not easy to find words for, not easy to communicate or to sympathise with, and the task of bearing good witness is fraught and problematic. The person in anguish who seeks to speak their pain before others—who appears in the theatre, so to speak—puts themselves at grave risk, for to be misheard or misrepresented is a betrayal that exacerbates the original sense of estrangement, perhaps to the point of madness. It is this area of risk and danger with which I deal.

The task for the audience in the theatre is an extension of the task of the audience-figures within the play, and you will find that I like to suggest this congruence between them (as Shakespeare also sometimes does). But the situations are not, of course, the same. The figures within the plays who react to the protagonist model for us possible responses that are often imperfect or tendentious, although all too human, and which we are invited to go beyond. It is not only that we are safer in the theatre, as is often said, or even that we see more, but that we have the resources of theatre itself to draw on. The play itself is an extension of that task of representation, of telling the protagonist's story, which falls to figures within the play, but what theatre represents need not be deferential to the givens of the reality-principle, the givens of that world which often denies to the protagonist's anguished inner life any home or voice or recognition. In the playing-space of theatre the world of the play can be shaped by the needs and fears and fantasies of the inner life, can bear witness to the reality and exigencies of that life, yet without our losing sight of the world's existence as a separate and independent entity. What is felt within the play as an intolerable conflict, or a violent subordination, may be felt in the theatre as a co-presence which is the very stuff of drama.

It is a worry to me that this emphasis on the specific dynamics of theatre, and on personal relation and the inner life, may seem to slight the political or societal forces that create so much of tragedy. A reading which displaced the world we share by the world of the imagination would only duplicate the estrangement of the protagonist. But here I can plead that it is precisely the task of the witness to make connection between those two worlds. Although I am not offering to generalise about all situations or works of art that might be called tragic, there are at least some forms of political violence which mirror failures of personal relation or are understandable in terms of those relations: xenophobia toward the alien; tyranny fuelled by paranoia; an unending vengefulness for a hurt which baffles adequate representation. As I write this, the Furies of Aeschylus's *Oresteia* are raging through Israel and Gaza, and the proposition of Athene—that the Furies will remain implacably destructive unless and until they are properly listened to, and believe that they are properly listened to—may seem as persuasive as it is desperate.

Finally, I would like to thank all the students at Cambridge with whom I have discussed tragedy over the years. Coriolanus was a fool to think a man might be author of himself, and I well know how much of this book is essentially collaborative, arising from those discussions with students and from their sense of something vitally interesting in what they were working on and working out. Without them it would not have been written.

Unless otherwise stated, Shakespeare quotations are taken from *The Riverside Shakespeare*, 2nd edn, ed. by G. Blakemore Evans, et al. (Boston and New York: Houghton Mifflin, 1997).

Quotations from translations of non-English texts are occasionally altered to bring them closer to the original; this is noted where it occurs.

1. Overview: Phaedra and the Nurse

> The tongue is slow to free itself from bondage,
> Unwilling to release a secret buried
> So long in ancient silence. Once confessed,
> It leaves the deep heart's safety and returns
> No more. The gods alone determine then
> If good or evil follow.[1]

At the start of Euripides's tragedy *Hippolytus*, Phaedra is suffering from some dire anguish whose source she discloses to no-one. It is a malady, a fever, a delirium which is palpably consuming her life; she takes no food, and seems resolved to die rather than speak the nature of her trouble. The chorus of her serving-women speculate on the possibilities: is her 'wandering mind bewitched by Pan' or Hecate? Is she being punished for some reason by the gods? Is she consumed perhaps by jealousy? Or is this something to do with the unhappy compound which is woman's nature, epitomised in 'the wretched helplessness' and 'mad thoughts' that surface in childbirth?[2] Although eager to know, they have no answers. Even the faithful Nurse who helps Phaedra out into the playing-area does not know what afflicts her, for even to her Phaedra has refused to speak. Between the tragic figure and those around her there seems to be an unbridgeable gap.

But the Nurse tries once more, persistently and persuasively, in an attempt to save her mistress's life. 'Don't be silent, child'—and although Phaedra resists, there is something in her, or in the relation between

---

1   Johann Wolfgang von Goethe, *Iphigenia in Tauris*, trans. by John Prudhoe (Manchester: Manchester University Press, 1966), I.iii, p.12, slightly altered.
2   Euripides, *Hippolytus*, trans. by Rachel Kitzinger, in *The Greek Plays: Sixteen Plays by Aeschylus, Sophocles, and Euripides*, ed. by Mary Lefkowitz and James Romm (New York: Modern Library, 2016), p.544.

them, that moves her towards disclosure. When Phaedra reacts to the name of Hippolytus, the Nurse—midwife to this agonising labour—coaxes and presses her to say more of the dreadful thing (in Greek: *deinos*) that is destroying her, until she finally yields and begins to speak, though still obliquely, of the history of disastrous erotic obsession that runs in her family. Gradually, with immense difficulty, knowledge passes from Phaedra to the Nurse:

> PHAEDRA: Could you somehow say for me what I must say?
>
> NURSE: I am no prophet, able to see what's invisible.
>
> PHAEDRA: What is it they call "being in love"?
>
> NURSE: The sweetest thing, child, but full of pain.
>
> PHAEDRA: Yes, mine would be the painful kind.
>
> NURSE: What do you mean? You're in love? With whom?
>
> PHAEDRA: Whoever he is, the son of the Amazon —
>
> NURSE: Hippolytus?
>
> PHAEDRA: You spoke his name, not I.[3]

Phaedra's monstrous desire for her stepson, hitherto locked inside her, is now known to another person, out, exposed, in the open. Crucially, it is only through the other person that it can be spoken of: 'You spoke his name, not I.' From this moment of disclosure, and in particular from how the Nurse reacts to what she hears, the tragedy will unfold.

This book is concerned with material that is hard to speak about, and with the hazardous site of communication between the tragic figure and the onlooker or confidant, the one who listens and responds. Insofar as this communication succeeds, it makes possible an act of witness; insofar as it fails or falls short, it often intensifies or exacerbates the tragedy. The witness is therefore an ambivalent figure, with the potential both to relieve and to hurt.

This ambivalence is reflected in the ambiguity involved in the term 'tragedy' itself, as used to suggest both some catastrophic instance of suffering and harm, and the dramatic form through which that suffering is expressed, communicated, and in some sense managed.

---

3   Ibid., p.550.

1. Overview: Phaedra and the Nurse

The charged relation between protagonist and witness was built into the form from the outset. When tragic drama began in Athens, it observed a simple structural distinction. There were, on the one hand, the figures to whom tragedy happened, and on the other there was the chorus, who observe and respond to the tragedy that happens to or for others. Phaedra's Nurse begins as an extension of the chorus, although her response does not terminate in herself but dynamically affects the action; the energies released by her movement across the boundary underline that boundary's significance. Post-classical tragedy rarely retains a formal chorus, but the essential distinction often remains: there are those who suffer, and those who look on, offering commentary and/or support.[4] Even where a character is drawn across the divide, as when a protagonist speaks of themselves in the third person, or an observer is engulfed by the tragedy, the essential positions remain distinguishable. Perhaps the simplest, most fundamental description of tragedy that can be made (it is much less than a definition) is that it involves the representation or enactment of suffering before witnesses.

At the centre of this study are Shakespeare's tragedies, where the dynamic between protagonist and reporter or witness seems to me peculiarly rich. But discussion will range more widely, to the Greeks and to works by Racine, Ibsen, Pirandello, Beckett, and Kane, among others, setting this central dynamic within a wider field of relations. There is some danger in this kind of ahistorical approach, but by focusing on the question of communicability I hope to avoid appearing to essentialise what is to be communicated, or to suggest that these very different tragedies are all about the same thing or function in the same way. What renders Phaedra's desire unspeakable may be historically contingent, but the difficulty of communicating and reporting the unspeakable is less so, and the Nurse's perplexed and anguished reaction to what she

---

4   In an influential analysis, Robert Weimann distinguished the two playing-spaces of the Shakespearean theatre: the *locus*—centre of the dramatic illusion, the apparently real world in which the action unfolds—and the *platea*—populated by chorus-like figures who comment on the action from a position of some detachment, and who feel closer to and may even signal their awareness of the audience in the theatre. Thus for example Othello belongs to the *locus*, while Iago speaks frequently from the *platea*. See his *Shakespeare and the Popular Tradition in the Theater: Studies in the Social Dimension of Dramatic Form and Function* (Baltimore: Johns Hopkins University Press, 1978).

hears points up how it is not only cultural distance that makes the tragic figure hard to relate to. And by the end I want to suggest that it is our own fearful need to be properly heard and known, in areas of experience where that is improbable if not almost inconceivable, that can explain something of why tragedy matters to us.

Witnessing is the term I shall often use, not just in the sense of being present and observing, but of actively formulating a response that is in some sense adequate to the event: *bearing witness*. That term will also overlap with others. Hamlet, dying, implores Horatio to *tell his story*, and this version of the idea—that there is someone who can tell your story, put together an account of what has happened which you may recognise as your own—is potent. It speaks to our sense of ourselves as narrative-making beings, whose lives come to have shape and meaning in the stories that can be told about them. The ambivalence of witness reappears in the dual capacity of stories, on the one hand to make sense of, integrate, affirm, and commemorate, and on the other to simplify or objectify or misrepresent, as ownership and interpretive power are ceded to the story-teller. Later in the study I also draw on the concept of one's experience *being held by another*, in something of the sense of supportive 'holding' with which the psychoanalyst Donald Winnicott used the term. The positive function of finding that one's feelings can be held in the mind of another person is something Winnicott traced back to the early relationship between mother and child. The mother is miraculously attuned to the child's world of feeling in all its engulfing vastness, and the child discovers in the mother's response that those feelings can gain foothold in a stabilising external consciousness. Only in this way can the child begin to gain access to their own feelings, begin to know their own being. 'What cannot be communicated to the [m]other cannot be communicated to the self', is the widely cited dictum that arose out of John Bowlby's therapeutic work on early attachment.[5] The child's faith in communicability as possible, which may be more or less firmly rooted in experience, then becomes the model for our actual relations with others, as well as for our capacity to imagine how relations with others may go.[6]

---

5   Quoted in Bessel van der Kolk, *The Body Keeps the Score* (London: Penguin, 2014), p.121.

6   These insights have been strongly developed in recent therapeutic practice. The concept of 'mentalising' advanced by Peter Fonagy and his team, cited below, is a

The desire for sympathetic understanding—the desire to be properly heard—is so immediately recognisable that pointing to it may not seem to take us very far. What is it here that speaks in particular to the tragic situation, and even more particularly to the tragic theatre? Part of the answer has to do with the delicate nature of the kind of response that is involved. The supportive listener, the good witness, must in some sense feel what the subject feels, must not only observe but participate in the subject's mental state. And yet to function as a good witness she must not feel *as* the subject feels, but as one who stands outside the vortex of subjectivity, as a being who lives out in the world, and is therefore capable of 'holding' the feeling in connection with the world rather than being engulfed by it. The psychologist Peter Fonagy has written extensively on 'the patient's experience of another person having the patient's mind in mind';[7] he sees this as one of the cornerstones of clinical practice and a key element in the development of the self. Tracing this back to early child-parent relations, he writes this about the caregiver's mirroring of another's internal experience:

> For affect-mirroring to serve as the basis of a representational framework the caregiver must somehow indicate that her display is not for real: it is not an indication of how the parent herself feels. We describe this characteristic of the parent's mirroring behaviour as its 'markedness'. A display that is congruent with the baby's state but lacks markedness may overwhelm the infant. It is felt to be the parent's own real emotion,

---

salient example in the UK; versions in the US include the form of dynamic therapy (AEDP) developed by Diana Fosha. 'The roots of security and resilience are to be found in the sense of being understood by and having the sense of existing in the heart and mind of a loving, caring, attuned and self-possessed other, an other with a heart and mind of her own.' 'Dyadic regulation and experiential work with emotion and relatedness in trauma and disordered attachment', in *Healing Trauma: Attachment, Trauma, the Brain and the Mind*, ed. by M. F. Solomon and D. J. Siegel (New York: Norton, 2003), p.228. For an incisive summary of the importance of work in this field, see 'Getting on the Same Wavelength: Attachment and Attunement' in Bessel van der Kolk, *The Body Keeps the Score* (London: Penguin, 2014). An overview of Bowlby's work can be found in Mary S. Ainsworth and John Bowlby, 'An Ethological Approach to Personality Development', *American Psychologist* 46 (1991), 333–341. A fine general introduction to these ideas is offered by Margot Waddell's *Inside Lives: Psychoanalysis and the Growth of the Personality* (London: Karnac, 2002): a set of reflections and case studies by a therapist who draws on the whole range of insights arising out of the work in object relations, and is alert also to the analogies offered in creative literature.

7   Peter Fonagy and Elizabeth Allison, 'The Role of Mentalizing and Epistemic Trust in the Therapeutic Relationship', *Psychotherapy* 51 (2014), 372–380, p.375.

making the infant's experience seem contagious, or universal, and thus more dangerous. [...] The projection of fantasy to the outside world can be terrifying. The acquisition of a sense of pretend in relation to mental states is therefore essential.[8]

The element of marked *representation*, rather than simple duplication, is crucial, despite the danger of misrepresentation or inadequate representation this entails, and the 'sense of pretend' which this involves speaks suggestively to the great space of playing and pretending which is the theatre.[9]

Another part of what makes sympathetic understanding critical to tragedy is that the protagonist's experience is crucially hard to understand and hard to sympathise with. Its particular intensity—and often its intense particularity—place it at a distance from the world of common and communicable experience in which the witness lives. This has to do with the nature of the distress which tragedy deals with. The story of my pain that others tell, or that is tellable to others—a coherent, sense-making, familiarising narrative—may be blind to the jagged, incoherent, disorientating quality of the experience that is intrinsic to what is to be told. On the break-up of her marriage, Rachel Cusk wrote: 'Lately I have come to hate stories. If someone were to ask me what disaster this was that had befallen my life, I might ask if they wanted the story or the truth.'[10] The experience of catastrophe can feel desperately estranged from the normal forms of account-giving or narrative-making. Representation here feels like the enemy, alienating the person from her experience. This works in both directions: we can think of pain as beyond language, but we can equally say that the forms of discourse available in a culture may have no place for a particular emotion or quality of experience, rendering it mute or private or estranged or taboo. Where

---

8   Peter Fonagy, Gyorgy Gergely, and Elliot L. Jurist, *Affect Regulation, Mentalization and the Development of the Self* (London: Routledge, 2002), p.9.
9   Compare Martha Nussbaum's account of what is involved in empathy. 'Empathy is like the mental preparation of a skilled (Method) actor: it involves a participatory enactment of the situation of the sufferer, but is always combined with the awareness that one is not oneself the sufferer.' *Upheavals of Thought: The Intelligence of Emotions* (Cambridge: Cambridge University Press, 2008), p.327.
10 Rachel Cusk, *Aftermath: On Marriage and Separation* (London: Faber & Faber, 2012), p.2. Cusk went on to transpose aspects of her experience into her version of *Medea*.

this nevertheless strives to be heard—where Phaedra speaks out—there is crisis, perhaps catastrophe.

In Shakespearean tragedy, this estrangement is sometimes expressed as the sense of an inner life deeply recessed away from the world of others. To speak of interiority in the Shakespearean theatre, where only what is performed can be present to us, may seem paradoxical, but the paradox is exactly the point. 'Inwardness as it becomes a concern in the theatre is always perforce inwardness displayed: an inwardness, in other words, that has already ceased to exist.'[11] Shakespeare's *Richard II*, in particular, is acutely aware of the gap between the 'substance' of his pain and the gestures available for its communication to others. (Indeed, the gap is something he dwells upon and amplifies, as if caressing the wound.) Such gestures expressing pain can be no more than 'shadows' of the reality.

> The shadow of my sorrow! Ha, let's see.
> 'Tis very true, my grief lies all within,
> And these external manners of laments
> Are merely shadows to the unseen grief
> That swells with silence in the tortured soul.
> There lies the substance. (IV.i.294–99)[12]

The sense of estrangement—in Richard's case, of having his public identity as king torn from him—intensifies the desire for connection; Richard cannot speak enough of his grief, he is spectacularly full of words. Yet he insists that his words are empty, his grief cannot be apprehended by those around him. By making an exhibition of his pain he also makes it an enigma. His immediate audience, the usurping Bolingbroke and his entourage, are hostile, which gives his estrangement a particular edge—but if 'external' performance cannot connect with the inner life of pain, then the fear is that *no-one* can enter into the grief that 'lies all within'.

The modern understanding of psychological trauma offers some degree of analogy. Dori Laub worked for many years eliciting and

---

11 Katherine Eisaman Maus, *Inwardness and Theater in the English Renaissance* (Chicago: University of Chicago Press, 1995), p.32.

12 Quotations from Shakespeare are taken from are taken from *The Riverside Shakespeare*, 2nd edn, ed. by G. Blakemore Evans, et al. (Boston and New York: Houghton Mifflin, 1997), unless otherwise stated.

recording the testimonies of those who survived the Nazi concentration camps. Their experience was, in a precise sense, unspeakable; enormous obstacles were in the way of their telling the story of what had happened to them.

> Massive trauma precludes its registration; the observing and recording mechanisms of the human mind are temporarily knocked out, malfunction. The victim's narrative—the very process of bearing witness to massive trauma—does indeed begin with someone who testifies to an absence, to an event that has not yet come into existence, in spite of the overwhelming and compelling nature of the reality of its occurrence. [...] The trauma—as a known event and not simply as an overwhelming shock has not been truly witnessed yet, not been taken cognizance of.[13]

The victim of trauma cannot tell what they feel, because the dreadful thing has 'not been truly witnessed yet', least of all by themselves. Within Shakespeare, one might think of Desdemona's response to the terrible scene in which her husband has spoken to her, with brutal contempt, as if she were a sex worker in a brothel. 'How do you, my good lady?', asks the concerned Emilia, to which Desdemona can reply only, 'Faith, half asleep' (IV.ii.96–97). But if this makes the communication of anguish peculiarly difficult, it also makes the need to be heard peculiarly acute, since only through its communicability to another can the experience begin to be processed. 'If trauma is a crisis in representation, then this generates narrative *possibility* just as much as *impossibility*, a compulsive outpouring of attempts to formulate narrative knowledge'.[14] In the preface to his Auschwitz memoir *If This is a Man*, Primo Levi wrote:

> The need to tell our story to 'the rest', to make 'the rest' participate in it, had taken on for us, before our liberation and after, the character of an immediate and violent impulse, to the point of competing with our other elementary needs.[15]

That is: not barely telling, but telling in such a way that the listener *participates* in the experience, breaking down the divide between sufferer

---

13 Shoshana Felman and Dori Laub, *Testimony: Crises of Witnessing in Literature, Psychoanalysis and History* (New York and London: Routledge, 1992), p.57.
14 Roger Luckhurst, *The Trauma Question* (Abingdon and New York: Routledge, 2008), p.83, and see also pp.79–86.
15 Primo Levi, *If This Is a Man / The Truce*, trans. by Stuart Woolf (London: Abacus, 1987), p.6.

and witness. Until and unless this happens, the sufferer has not truly spoken. Communicability, the visible reflection of one's pain in the response of another, is key to therapeutic possibility, according to Dori Laub:

> Trauma survivors live not with memories of the past, but with an event that could not and did not proceed through to its completion, has no ending, attained no closure, and therefore, as far as its survivors are concerned, continues into the present and is current in every respect. [...] To undo this entrapment in a fate that cannot be known, cannot be told, but can only be repeated, a therapeutic process—a process of constructing a narrative, of reconstructing a history and essentially, of *re-externalizing the event*—has to be set in motion. This re-externalization of the event can occur and take effect only when one can articulate and *transmit* the story, literally transfer it to another outside oneself and then take it back again, inside. Telling thus entails a reassertion of the hegemony of reality.[16]

But Laub also emphasises the difficulty for the trauma survivor of doing this:

> This imperative to tell and to be heard can become itself an all-consuming life task. Yet no amount of telling seems ever to do justice to this inner compulsion. There are never enough words or the right words, there is never enough time or the right time, and never enough listening or the right listening to articulate the story.[17]

The analogy with tragic drama is a suggestive one, with regard both to the relation between protagonist and witness and to the idea of the drama itself as 're-externalizing the event'. But the analogy with trauma narrative breaks down after a point, even if drama is taken as, in a broad sense, a narrative mode. For trauma is inflicted by historical events, and the survivor struggles with the unresolved legacy of the past, whereas tragic drama does not, in general, deal directly with real-life events. Laub's firm assertion of 'the hegemony of reality' has greater traction in the therapeutic situation than in the theatre, in which the location of 'reality' is liable to become a question. (I shall come back to this towards the end of the book, in relation to how the tragic theatre presents madness.) And although within the fiction the protagonist is sometimes haunted by events from the past (*Oresteia*, *Hamlet*, a good deal of Ibsen),

---
16   Laub, *Testimony*, p.69.
17   Ibid., p.78.

this is by no means always the case. The tragic figure in Shakespeare is more often exposed to a generalised, archaic anxiety, a disintegration of identity, which perceived events may trigger but which they cannot altogether account for.[18] That Lear's children are uncompliant and ungrateful, that Othello's wife may have cheated on him, cannot in itself explain the totality of Lear's and Othello's collapse, the extremity of their grief and rage. This disparity—which is itself a source of terror—is another factor in why the story that is immediately available may fail to account for the protagonist's plight. Stoppard's joke in *Rosencrantz and Guildenstern are Dead* catches this nicely, as Rosencrantz bemusedly anticipates his questioning of Hamlet:

> To sum up: your father, whom you love, dies, you are his heir, you come back to find that hardly was the corpse cold before his young brother popped on to his throne and into his sheets, thereby offending both legal and natural practice. Now, why exactly are you behaving in this extraordinary manner?[19]

Rosencrantz and Guildenstern make poor witnesses (or therapists, or spies), but it is not clear that better are available, either in Stoppard's play or in Shakespeare's.

The witnessing on offer may not only be inadequate, it may also be felt as unwelcome, even dangerous, releasing and amplifying what was already toxic by bringing it into the light. If tragedy often stages the need for anguish to be seen and to be heard, it is also much concerned with the risks and dangers of exposure—a tension well expressed in Winnicott's famous paradox: 'it is a joy to be hidden, and a disaster not

---

18 If we retain the concept of trauma here at all, it will be by distinguishing between trauma caused by nameable past events and what Dominick LaCapra in *Writing History, Writing Trauma* calls 'structural trauma', a vulnerability more or less endemic to the human condition, or at least to a given cultural situation in which the participants are involved. Stanley Cavell, for example, has related the tensions in Shakespearean tragedy around knowing others and being known by others to the rise of scepticism in the seventeenth century, precipitating a newly acute feeling of living in a groundless world, or what he calls 'the withdrawal of the world' from an inflamed subjectivity that cannot bear to acknowledge its situation. See in particular his readings of *Othello* and *King Lear* in *Disowning Knowledge in Seven Plays of Shakespeare* (Cambridge: Cambridge University Press, 2003).

19 Tom Stoppard, *Rosencrantz and Guildenstern Are Dead* (London: Faber & Faber, 1968). p.36.

to be found'.[20] Let us return to Phaedra and the Nurse. Something in Phaedra could not finally resist the Nurse's appeal, could not suppress the hope that this mothering figure, so concerned for her welfare (and so unlike her own monstrously afflicted mother), might offer her the kind of supportive understanding which a mother ideally offers her troubled child. And so she is finally drawn to speak. But another part of her shrank from confiding in another, and the Nurse's immediate reaction suggests all too clearly why:

> *oimoi*, child, what can you mean? You've ruined me.
> Women, I can't bear it, I won't endure it
> and live. Hateful day, light hateful to my eyes!
> I'll jump, hurl my body down, be released
> from this life.[21]

This is hardly the reaction you want from your therapist, or your mother. So much for the Nurse's assurances of remedy and support. In a reversal whose vehemence is perhaps not without some trace of comedy—a comedy that would itself underline the gulf that separates her from Phaedra—the Nurse cries horror, cannot bear what she has heard, and flees the stage. Phaedra's love has shattered the cosmos, she exclaims: Aphrodite can no longer be conceptualised as divine but is 'something more than a god if she brings / destruction to this house, this woman and me'.

But this is not the end. A few minutes later the Nurse returns, having pulled herself together, and now offers a quite different account of the situation:

> There's nothing untoward, nothing strange
> in your feelings; a goddess has visited her rage
> on you. You're in love — why the amazement?
> Many of us are.[22]

Phaedra's passion, which moments ago was something monstrous and unbearable, is now redescribed as entirely human and familiar, not so

---

20 D. W. Winnicott, 'Communicating and Not Communicating: leading to a study of certain opposites', in *The Maturational Processes and the Facilitating Environment: Studies in the Theory of Emotional Development* (London: Karnac, 1990), p.186.
21 Euripides, *Hippolytus*, p.550.
22 Ibid., p.553.

extraordinary, something which Phaedra would do well to accept and submit to. Not to do so would be *hubris*, the Nurse adds. After her initial horrified reaction, this may sound far more sympathetic, perhaps even wise: the dreadful thing is not, as another translator puts it, 'beyond thought or reason'—in the Greek, outside of *logos*.[23] It can be spoken of and reckoned with, it can be dealt with and managed. However, the Nurse's attempt to manage it will prove disastrous: when she approaches Hippolytus as a go-between, the horror which she here denies flares up to engulf the play. Even before that catastrophic outcome, we can say that she is not a good witness, for her reassuringly normalising account fails to enter into, and hence properly to acknowledge, Phaedra's self-horror. Her familiarising redescription of the situation is in fact dangerous, as Phaedra immediately recognises: 'This is what destroys the fine cities / and homes of mortals: words spoken too well.'[24] For the Nurse is drawing what was locked within Phaedra out into the world with a rhetorical fluency that promises the encounter can be readily managed and survived. Phaedra sees such reasoning as sophistry, a cleverness with language that only opens the door to deeper uncertainties. The Nurse's pragmatic rationalism, which seems so worldly-wise, is out of its depth here, and that makes it dangerous.

A little schematically, we can say that the Nurse's two reactions to Phaedra's disclosure represent the opposite poles of tragic witness. On the one hand there is the repudiation of the shocking, atrocious, anomalous thing as unbearable. On the other there is its comprehension under familiar, naturalising terms of reference that deny that the dread and horror go all the way down—whether out of an impulse to comfort the sufferer, or to protect the witness, or out of incapacity to recognise how radically disturbing the situation is, or out of our need and desire to make sense of things. The Nurse's alternative to repudiating Phaedra's condition is to familiarise and appropriate it. Each of these contradictory reactions is humanly understandable, but each makes for deeply imperfect witnessing. For I take the good witness to be one who both enters into the depth of the protagonist's being and yet is not engulfed by it, and so can carry report to the outside world in terms which the world can understand.

---

23 *exo logou*, line 437.
24 Euripides, *Hippolytus*, p.554.

Of these two poles of imperfect response—repudiation and rationalisation—I spend most time in this study upon the second, the attempt to bring the protagonist's condition under *logos*, under the terms of 'thought and reason'. This response may be adopted not only by characters within the drama but by the spectator in the theatre or the reader in their study. One perennial form this takes is the story of suffering as consequence, the story of tragedy as one of punishment following crime—or if not crime, then some mistake or mis-step or deficiency or weakness that brings about disaster. Phaedra does not easily lend herself to such accounts, since her passion is so clearly something visited upon her against her will. Nevertheless, among the chorus's speculations is that she may have offended some god by failing to offer due sacrifice (which is in fact the case with Hippolytus), and we can, if we wish, emphasise her speaking to the Nurse as the fatal mistake which leads to catastrophe. Even here, then, a version of the punishment-for-wrongdoing story is available, and in many tragedies it is front and centre. It is facilitated at one level by the simple fact of dramatic coherence—in most drama, actions plausibly follow one another, implying a chain of cause and effect—and at another, by our deep tendency to construe pain as punishment, and to arrive at intelligibility through the attribution of blame or the identification of error. The desire to find 'poetical justice' in the outcome of tragedy may sound like the quaint delusion of an earlier age, but much modern discussion still adheres, albeit in subtler ways, to the project of diagnosis, to uncovering the logic of catastrophe and so, in a weak sense, its justification. For to speak of the logic of catastrophe is to discover the law that the sufferer has broken. Tragic drama strongly acknowledges and even embraces the power of this explanatory model, but I want to suggest that it often does so by way of testing it to destruction. This idea gets emblematic expression in Kafka's story 'In the Penal Colony', in which the condemned are executed by the automatic working of a machine which, over twelve hours, incises the law which they have broken ever deeper into their flesh. The proponent of this method finds the machine to be a thing of beauty, an exquisite and admirable feat of engineering; he also alleges that at some point in the process the victims' agony turns into a state of ecstatic acceptance, as the law penetrates their bodies. However, the machine's glory days are past, it has fallen into some disrepair, and in the story it malfunctions altogether, mangling and shredding its victim when called on to incise the injunction 'Be Just'—the imperative which tragedy finds to be hugely problematic. Kafka's fable literalises the logic of the crime-and-punishment story as mechanism, a mechanism which fails to deliver the satisfactions which it promised. Both the promise and the failure inflect how the story appears in tragedy, which lies finally beyond its reach. This is the topic of my fourth chapter.

The other common form that rationalisation takes is well exemplified by the Nurse's words above. There is 'nothing strange', nothing extraordinary in Phaedra's feelings. Hers is in fact a common case, the Nurse suggests, offering her the shelter of the common human condition. She means this kindly, but we note that Phaedra receives it as an undermining, a betrayal. Such generalisation falls short of—and so insults—the protagonist's radical estrangement, the intense particularity of their condition, its unprecedented and incommensurable quality. Criteria brought from the world of external normality do not adhere to the mode of being in which the protagonist finds themselves. If what the witness sees is only too familiar, or all too human, then the witness does not fully see into what is there, and this exacerbates rather than assuages the sense of the protagonist's estrangement, of a horror too extreme for communication. In Shakespeare, the precarious specialness of the protagonist is often expressed in terms of an equivocally heroic figure who moves in a post-heroic or unheroic world, populated by onlookers who do not recognise anything very exceptional in the case. The death of fathers is a common occurrence, Gertrude reminds Hamlet: 'why seems it so particular with thee?' (I.ii.75). Iago, more tactically, takes a similar line with Othello about female infidelity as an everyday occurrence in Venice, so common as to be banal (III.iii.201–04). Lady Macbeth assures her husband that 'a little water clears us of this deed' and can wash 'this filthy witness' from his hands (II.ii.64, 44). These normalising responses are liable to generate a convulsion, a counter-reaction, an insistence in fact on filthy witness. Something in the protagonist or the play rises up in protest, as if to insist that the thing be otherwise understood, as if to stun the normalising voice into silence. The Nurse's assurance that Phaedra's passion falls within the common run of things was offered in denial of her initial horror: but the horror turns out to be far stronger than the voice of denial.

A kind of parable that bears on this can be found in Sarah Kane's *Blasted*. Ian is by profession a reporter, who sends in to his newspaper salacious copy about 'shootings and rapes and kids getting fiddled by queer priests and schoolteachers'.[25] He does so with professional detachment or indifference, and also with an eye to the appetites of his readers; when thus reported, terrible things are rendered eminently consumable, reducible to the commonplace, 'nothing strange'. This mundane, degraded world is smashed apart by an insistent knocking on the door and then a bomb blast that transforms a familiar and somewhat sordid hotel-room into a war zone. The nameless soldier who enters the torn-open space carries with him the real experience of atrocity—atrocity done to his beautiful girlfriend and atrocities he himself has in turn committed. He describes these with appalling, wholly unprocessed specificity. He says that Ian, as a reporter, should be able to do something for him; like Hamlet to Horatio, he asks Ian to tell his story. 'You should be telling people.' 'At home I'm clean. Like it never happened. Tell them you saw me. Tell them ... you saw me.'[26] The task of the true reporter, the true witness, is to carry the reality of the horror into the clean space of home, and to make a living connection between those two worlds. But this is not something that Ian's mode of reporting can reach to. 'This isn't a story anyone wants to hear.' 'I'm a home journalist, for Yorkshire. I don't cover foreign affairs.'[27] And so— for it feels to be in consequence of this refusal —the soldier rapes and mutilates Ian, repeating on Ian's body the atrocities of which he spoke, communicating his pain to another person in the only way that seems available. To the great discomfort of the audience, he does so onstage. The violence of the play—the savagery of its staging—works as an extension of the violence of the soldier. Ian's suffering body becomes a kind of witness to, or at least manifestation of, a horror that otherwise defied representation. Or perhaps it still defies representation, for Kane's requirements notoriously push what is practicable in the theatre to or beyond its limits. (Stage direction: 'He eats the baby'.[28]) It is perhaps, as Samuel Johnson said of the blinding of Gloucester, 'an act too horrid to

---

25 Sarah Kane, *Complete Plays* (London: Methuen, 2001), pp.47–48.
26 Ibid.
27 Ibid.
28 Ibid., p.60.

be endured in dramatick exhibition, and such as must always compel the mind to relieve its distress by incredulity.'[29] The play doesn't work, we may say, its staging of horror is crude or overwrought or alienating. But could this be the audience member's version of the Nurse's initial reaction? Both entail fleeing from the playing-space.

How does tragic drama which recognises these difficulties nevertheless offer good witness? I shall be proposing two lines of thought. The second chapter lands on the idea of offering hospitality to the foreigner, stranger, or alien figure, where such hospitality is both problematic and urgently required. It is problematic because it destabilises the existing order, the boundary that separates insider from outsider, us from them. In a classic study, the anthropologist Mary Douglas associated the idea of pollution with 'hybrids' or 'improper mixings' that blur the category boundaries on which all cultures necessarily depend. The foreigner who knocks at our door may herself embody such an improper mixing, as someone not at all like us who nevertheless evokes an affinity with us, and taking her in will in any case create such a mixing even if it was not there before. Most cultures treat such mixings as taboo, according to Douglas, with ritual procedures for excluding them or cleansing society from them: yet there may also be extraordinary rituals in which the taboo object is treated as the source of value and power, incorporated within the culture to regenerating effect.[30] There is some analogy here (at the least) with those tragic dramas in which the protagonist is presented as beyond the pale—repellent, abject, damaged, destructive, bizarre— and yet the drama urgently conveys to us that it is *this* figure above all that we need to relate to, *this* figure into whose experience we need to enter. A radical reorientation of the mind is asked of us; to figure this as the offering of hospitality to the alien or foreigner points to the deep connection of the psychological with the political in this area, each being understandable as an aspect of the other. In some plays this

---

29 Samuel Johnson, *Johnson on Shakespeare*, in *The Yale Edition of the Works of Samuel Johnson*, vol. VIII, ed. by John H. Middendorf, et al. (New Haven and London: Yale University Press, 1958–2018), p.703. With his next sentence, Johnson suspends that impulse to repudiate: 'Yet let it be remembered that our author well knew what would please the audience for which he wrote.'

30 Mary Douglas, *Purity and Danger: An Analysis of Concept of Pollution and Taboo* (London: Routledge, 2002). See especially ch.10.

is more than a figure of speech, the obligation and the cost of giving shelter to the stranger being the actual dramatic situation of the play; I end the chapter with examples from Aeschylus and from Albee. At a time when the politics of xenophobia is so much in evidence, the fundamental challenge embodied in this situation needs little underlining. Xenophobia is phobia aroused by the *xenos*, the stranger or foreigner who must be included in the host-guest relation, for *xenos* indicates not so much a person as a field of relation. It is a word that means equally stranger, guest, and host; none of those ideas are held safely distinct from the others. Affording hospitality to the stranger joins my other overlapping terms—witnessing; telling someone's story; psychological 'holding'—as ways of indicating this book's particular focus.

My second line of thought takes up the long final chapter, and has to do with the apprehension of madness in the theatre. All Shakespeare's heroes from Hamlet to Antony are at some point described as mad (and Coriolanus might easily have been, with his assertion that it is he who banishes the citizens of Rome). These figures seem to have lost their hold on the reality of the world as perceived by others; this has been loosened or displaced by the pressure of their more intense vision of things. 'Madness' here is an onlooker's term, secure in its own sanity; although from the protagonist's point of view we can also see how the gap between what they know has to be the case and what happens in the world is intolerable, is maddening. (*How can it be* that royal Lear's messenger has been put in the stocks? *How can it be* that everything about Desdemona shows her to be good and true when Othello knows her to be false?)

As those examples suggest, the inner world of the protagonist is not to be corrected by any simple reality check: for it has its own vital reality. The witness who acknowledges that indefeasible inner reality stands friend to the protagonist in a way that an unsympathetic, inhospitable world does not. But, like Phaedra's Nurse, such witness is double-edged, for it offers a prospect of external validation, of a foothold for fantasy in the world, that may prove treacherous or illusory. Its ambivalence is exactly that which Macbeth finds in the assurances brought to him by the weird women he encounters, assurances which 'cannot be ill; cannot be good' (I.iii.131). Winnicott's good enough mother was able to intuit and support the young child's needs and fantasies; such magical support belongs only to that particular relationship in that early phase of life, but we perhaps never quite banish its memory or the hope of its reactivation. Phaedra's Nurse, like the weird women in Macbeth, feeds such buried hope, gives reality to the protagonist's feelings through the promise that those feelings can be held and known in the mind of another. But—again like the weird sisters—the bridge that she seems to offer between mind and world leads nowhere; it breaks off over the void, abandoning the protagonist in a place of unbearable exposure.

What interests me is the degree to which the drama itself mimics such support, participating in the protagonist's vision of things, supplying a world which—up to a point—corresponds to the protagonist's inner world of fear and desire, a world no longer hidden, but now *realised*. If the protagonist is afflicted with madness, it might also be said that in certain cases the play likewise goes mad.

What I mean by that will be explored in the final chapter, but I can give a simple example here, one which conveniently connects with my other category, that of giving hospitality to the alien. At the end of Aeschylus's trilogy the *Oresteia*, everything hangs on whether the Furies—ancient and terrible goddesses of vengeance and resentment—can be accommodated within the modern city of Athens, rather than repudiated as utterly alien to the cause of civilisation. That this question can even arise depends on their being present to be negotiated with, and this in turn stems from Orestes' killing of his mother in the previous play. Although this act was commanded by Apollo, after committing it Orestes is seized with horror; he hallucinates the Furies coming for him. The chorus understand this as a mental aberration, a fit of madness brought on by the traumatic act of killing. But Orestes repudiates this rationalising interpretation: 'You can not see them, but I see them.'[31] And when the next play opens, we see them too: the Furies, astonishingly, are now the chorus, physically present in the theatre, occupying the space of witness. What had been understandable as a deranged fantasy, an expression of guilt and remorse, is now a theatrical reality. If Orestes was driven mad by the horror of the killing, the play itself now participates in that madness.

---

31 Aeschylus, *Oresteia*, trans. by Richmond Lattimore (Chicago: University of Chicago Press, 1953), p.131.

That may sound like an extreme way of putting it; theatre is just doing what theatre does. But that is the point: if tragic theatre offers itself as a representation of the world, it also offers itself as creating the world of the play, a vision not immediately subject to testing by the reality principle. Whether we believe that Furies exist, or whether Aeschylus's audience did so in their daily lives, or what it would mean to say either of those things, is not the question; what matters is that the Furies are shockingly present to us (assuming the play works), that we feel and recognise their electrifying threat as part of our present experience, beyond any possibility of rationalising them as allegories of remorse or signs of psychological breakdown. We see as Orestes sees, or more precisely we participate in the mode of being into which he has entered or has fallen. A comparable moment in Shakespeare would be the appearance on stage of Banquo's Ghost. Again, to one side we hear a rational voice, that of Lady Macbeth, insisting that this is a medical matter, an aberration from the real, familiar enough, capable of being understood as 'a thing of custom' (III.v.96), and so plausibly manageable. But *we* cannot call the bloody figure that we see on stage Macbeth's mere hallucination.

For the sake of clarity, I have given here the simplest example of how a play can participate in madness: hallucination given theatrical reality. I mean, however, something that goes beyond this simple case. There is no supernatural apparition in *Othello*, and *Othello* the play does not participate in Othello's delusion that Desdemona is unfaithful. But it does participate in his alarm that there is something monstrous and hidden at the heart of things which, once uncovered, poisons life at its roots. This alarm is the basis of his delusion, which attempts to give that feeling 'proof', to find for it an object in the idea of Desdemona's infidelity. We share in his alarm, I believe, not in a way that can be converted into a truth-proposition about life (let alone about Desdemona), but still with the kind of strong feeling that verges on cognition, and discovers its immediate object, its grounds for fear, in the play itself, with all that makes it so disturbing. In this sense at least, the play participates in the state of mind that generates Othello's madness.

In the examples I look at most closely—*Macbeth* and *King Lear*—madness sustains or protects some vital demand of the mind which the given environment will not accommodate. In being thus open to madness, by going mad in sympathy, the drama bears witness to the imperatives of the protagonist's inner life. But to say that is also to say that the drama cannot rest in madness. If the idea of good witness involves entering into (rather than diagnosing) the sufferer's experience, it also involves placing that fully entered-into experience in the shared world, bringing it back home—even if home no longer feels quite like home as a result. It makes connection between the two worlds. Now it is plain enough that tragedy commonly brings the protagonist's mental world into collision with an external world that resists or denies it—a collision frequently catastrophic for either or both parties. The question I explore is what might allow us to feel this collision also as a connection—such that the theatre experience mediates between, placing in bearable relation, those disparate modes of being which cannot be held together within the action. Here I think about the quality of grief or pathos which the play generates. Gillian Rose's concept of 'inaugurated mourning' is helpful here, for the way that Rose links such mourning to the possibility of representation.[32] If the source of grief in tragedy is the finitude that baffles the mind's desires and demands, one possible response is what Rose calls 'incomplete mourning', which repudiates limit and likewise repudiates representation, finding nothing in the world that answers to the intensity of its subjective life. It remains in melancholia or madness. By contrast, inaugurated mourning has an end, finds an object; it grieves over the misfit between inner imperatives and the given world in such a way as to honour both—acknowledging the *necessity of grief*, and thereby performing the work of witness. Thus, to mourn what is incompatible with human community is to imagine or create a mode of community which accommodates it. Such mourning undoes the absoluteness, the implicit violence, of sheer opposition (as between mind and world, or self and other, or madness and sanity). Between the Nurse's dual responses of repudiation and appropriation, there is created a difficult middle ground. By this way of thinking, making tragic theatre aspires to a mourning that may begin outside the walls of the city, for what is alien, illegitimate, and homeless, but by giving form and representation to anguish imagines a place for it within a reconfigured economy that is both psychic and civic.

---

32   Gillian Rose, *Mourning Becomes the Law: Philosophy and Representation* (Cambridge: Cambridge University Press, 1996). See especially pp.20–26, 35–39.

A final point. I have pitched this argument throughout in terms of bearing witness to the protagonist, the figure of the suffering tragic hero. That is mostly how it works in Shakespeare, as in much other tragic drama—but not all tragedies have a central protagonist of this kind, and to speak of the protagonist's inner or mental world fits some plays much better than others. In truth the tragic protagonist is always, I think, a gateway into a mode of being to which she or he is peculiarly susceptible, which flows into them or out from them or into which they fall, and which is felt as something that extends beyond their individual consciousness or situation. To bear good witness to this is not to attend only to a discretely other person, but involves an element of recognition. We enter the theatre prepared to be the witnesses to another's plight, to see whether we can bear and 'hold' the protagonist's experience, but that relation turns out to be reversible, and we may find before the end that it is the play that is 'holding' something in us, that it is our plight to which witness is borne.

2. Welcoming the Stranger

> As when sore blindness of heart cometh upon a man, that in his own country slayeth another and escapeth to a land of strangers, to the house of some man of substance, and wonder holdeth them that look upon him ... (*Iliad* 24.480–82)[1]
>
> Does any here know me? — *Lear* (I.iv.226)[2]

Hamlet's request

The tragedy of *Hamlet* nears its end. Gertrude, Claudius, and Laertes all die in swift succession, victims of the poisoned cup and the poisoned rapier, and Hamlet too is dying. With his last energies, he addresses the horrified onlookers, and tries to tell his audience something, something that would make comprehensible the terrible thing before them. But this cannot be: so he bequeaths this task to his one close friend.

> You that look pale, and tremble at this chance,
> That are but mutes or audience to this act,
> Had I but time — as this fell sergeant, Death,
> Is strict in his arrest — O, I could tell you —
> But let it be. Horatio, I am dead,
> Thou livest. Report me and my cause aright
> To the unsatisfied. (V.ii.334–40)

Hamlet's request epitomises the difficulty and the challenge which tragedy presents to those who witness it. The difficulty: those around him are appalled and silent. What has happened here is so disturbing as to baffle any adequate response. The onlookers are like mute actors

---

1   Homer, *The Iliad*, 2 vols, trans. by A. T. Murray (London: William Heinemann, 1976) II, p.599.
2   Quotations from Shakespeare are taken from are taken from *The Riverside Shakespeare*, 2nd edn, ed. by G. Blakemore Evans, et al. (Boston and New York: Houghton Mifflin, 1997), unless otherwise stated.

©2025 Fred Parker, CC BY-NC 4.0   https://doi.org/10.11647/OBP.0435.02

in a play, and the consciousness of theatre—'mutes or audience to this act'—blurs the boundary between the onstage onlookers and the actual audience, mute also, who find ourselves included among Hamlet's addressees. Can we give audience of a more adequate kind? Might the difference made by theatre make that possible? Hamlet asks that words be found, report be made, witness be borne.

Horatio begins by rejecting this office; he would rather drink from the cup and follow his friend into death, rather identify wholly with Hamlet than endure the pain of being the survivor and the witness. But that is something Hamlet will not allow:

> O God, Horatio, what a wounded name,
> Things standing thus unknown, shall I leave behind me!
> If thou didst ever hold me in thy heart,
> Absent thee from felicity a while,
> And in this harsh world draw thy breath in pain
> To tell my story. (V.ii.344–49)

Like his father before him, from the threshold between life and death Hamlet lays upon his survivor the obligation to make right a bleeding wound in the fabric of life. The threat is of misrepresentation, or of a failure of representation. Confronted by this pile-up of killings, the onlookers will surely suppose that Hamlet's known madness has flared, once again, into the homicidal and bizarre. And at the level of theatre, the sensational last scene and the spectacular final carnage might seem to belong to a much cruder and simpler Elizabethan tragedy than—surely?—the play of *Hamlet* truly is. Horatio's task is to put aside such misunderstanding by explaining to the onlookers about Hamlet's task of revenge, giving his bewildered hearers that knowledge of the plot which we as Shakespeare's audience already possess.

But as the history of commentary on *Hamlet* shows, it is far from obvious that any account, however well informed about the plot, will remove all shadow of 'things unknown'. Many attentive responses to the play stress its ambiguity, its openness to interpretation, even to the point where interpretability itself becomes a large part of its subject; and others divide in crucial ways on the mix of light and darkness, of sympathetic and disturbing elements, in how Hamlet is presented and in how his development or non-development across the course of the tragedy should be played.

These uncertainties remind us that what Hamlet asks of Horatio is something profoundly difficult. In fact, he makes three overlapping requests: report me aright (affirm my true identity), report my cause aright (as if I were a plaintiff or defendant come to trial), tell my story (give a coherent narrative shape to what has happened to me). These are not synonymous, but the final request comprehends the others: Hamlet's culpability or innocence can only be assessed through a true understanding of his story; and personal identity, it can be argued, is realised only through narrative. 'To answer the question "Who?" [...] is to tell the story of a life. The story told tells about the action of the "who." And the identity of this "who" therefore itself must be a narrative identity' (Paul Ricoeur).[3] Taken together, what Hamlet asks for expresses a complex of desires: to be commemorated—which would give, for once in this play, a bearable idea of what happens after death; to be vindicated (the rescuing of Hamlet's 'wounded name'); even, to be affirmed as a hero, someone of whom stories are told after they die. Lying beneath all these is the yet more fundamental human need: *to be witnessed*—to be properly heard and understood by others, sympathetically and supportively but also truly, in a way that reflects the obscure depths of the self. Even in the normal conditions of life, this need is not so easy to meet. But when we approach the domain of tragedy, the need to be witnessed becomes both acutely urgent and acutely difficult.

For tragic figures are figures *in extremis*, whose anguish or state of being are extraordinary, awe-full, heart-stopping, jaw-dropping, existing at or beyond the limits of normal human communion. In the strong sense

---

[3] Paul Ricoeur, *Time and Narrative*, 3 vols, trans. by Kathleen McLaughlin and David Pellauer (Chicago: University of Chicago Press, 1984–1990) III, p.246. The quotation continues: 'Without the recourse to narration, the problem of personal identity would in fact be condemned to an antinomy with no solution. Either we must posit a subject identical with itself through the diversity of its different states, or, following Hume and Nietzsche, we must hold that this identical subject is nothing more than a substantialist illusion, whose elimination merely brings to light a pure manifold of cognitions, emotions, and volitions. This dilemma disappears if we substitute for identity understood in the sense of being the same (*idem*), identity understood in the sense of oneself as self-same [*soi-même*] (*ipse*). The difference between idem and ipse is nothing more than the difference between a substantial or formal identity and a narrative identity.'

of the Shakespearean word, they are 'strange'.[4] Their estranging presence threatens rupture to the circulation of sympathetic understanding. Thus Hamlet addresses his pale and trembling onlookers as 'mutes', whose silence confirms that what confronts them is *unspeakable*. Or Lear, entering with the dead Cordelia in his arms, rebukes the stunned onlookers as 'men of stones', incapable of the infinite outcry which the occasion demands (V.iii.258). Or at the re-entry of the self-blinded, self-polluted Oedipus, the chorus recoil in fascinated dread. 'Where am I carried to?', he demands of them, and they reply, 'To a terrible place—unspeakable—unwatchable'.[5] To tell the story of such figures, to report their experience aright, would be to find words for the unspeakable. It would be to find a way of connecting the figure of extremity with the community, of accommodating the most disturbing experience within an act of *communication*, within in-some-way-adequate speech and in-some-way-adequate representation.

The challenge of such a task lies at the very heart of tragic theatre, which might be most simply described as the representation of suffering before witnesses. This is peculiarly visible in the Greek theatre, with its formal distinction between protagonist and chorus, but the same dynamic between those involved in disaster and those who stand at one remove is reworked in all kinds of ways in Shakespeare's tragedies. It also extends to the theatrical event itself, where we gather as a community to watch an action of exceptional threat, danger and destructiveness. In the institution of the tragic theatre in Athens, this astonishing ambition was writ large: suffering and calamity were staged as part of a festival designed to affirm and strengthen the civic community.[6]

The audience's response has been traditionally said to be one of fear and pity. The interest of that formula lies in how much the looseness of its terms leaves open, for both fear and pity can equally be distancing emotions or experiences which draw us in. What I fear can be your otherness, your alarming opacity to my understanding, but my fear can

---

4   Paul Hammond, *The Strangeness of Tragedy* (Oxford: Oxford University Press, 2009), brings out the resonance of this concept in Shakespearean tragedy and beyond.

5   Timberlake Wertenbaker's translation: *Sophocles: Oedipus Tyrannos, Oedipus at Kolonos, Antigone* (London: Faber & Faber, 1997), p.41; line 1312 in the Greek.

6   See Simon Goldhill, 'The Great Dionysia and civic ideology', in *Nothing to Do with Dionysos?: Athenian Drama in Its Social Context*, ed. by John J. Winkler and Froma Zeitlin (Princeton, NJ: Princeton University Press, 1998).

also recognise how the terrible case might become my own—or, more fundamentally still, the possibility that it is already my own, in some sense not easily acknowledged. 'Pity' could be a feeling that rests on distinctness and separation, an emotion that stems from a privileged position of safe spectatorship. But pity could also mean what Yeats believed the pathos of tragedy must involve, 'a drowning and breaking of the dykes that separate man from man'.[7] Between those poles of estrangement and participation, the experience of tragedy makes its way. The compassionate liberal reader or spectator will want to feel tragedy as an overcoming of otherness and separation, a revelation of human connection: but tragedy troubles that desire, insists upon an experience that resists confident communication or assimilation.

The presence of another person, a witness, is crucial. Report me aright, Hamlet demands of Horatio, tell my story, find words for my anguish, my extremity. Only you, another person, can do this for me. It is not only the poison that prevents Hamlet from telling his own story, but something intrinsic to his predicament. As the figure in extremity, Hamlet cannot simultaneously speak *of* his extremity with the access to normative language and common experience which report or story requires. After listening to the player's moving speech about the death of Priam and the grief of Hecuba, he bitterly reflects that—fantastically articulate though he is—he by contrast 'can say nothing'; nothing, that is, that would express and communicate the quality of his plight (II. ii.569). This accords with what he told Gertrude at the start, that no possible manifestation of grief could denote him truly.

> GERTRUDE: Thou know'st 'tis common, all that lives must die,
>   Passing through nature to eternity.
> HAMLET: Ay, madam, it is common.
> GERTRUDE: If it be,
>   Why seems it so particular with thee?
> HAMLET: Seems, madam? nay, it is, I know not "seems."
>   'Tis not alone my inky cloak, good mother,
>   Nor customary suits of solemn black,
>   Nor windy suspiration of forc'd breath,
>   No, nor the fruitful river in the eye,

---

7   W. B. Yeats, 'The Tragic Theatre', in *Essays and Introductions* (London: Macmillan, 1961), p.241.

> Nor the dejected havior of the visage,
> Together with all forms, moods, shapes of grief,
> That can denote me truly. These indeed seem,
> For they are actions that a man might play,
> But I have that within which passes show,
> These but the trappings and the suits of woe. (I.ii.72–86)

Hamlet wants to say that he is no hypocrite; but what he actually says is that the hypocrisy of 'seeming' is for him inescapable. (Performing in the theatre, there is of course nothing he could ever do that would not be an action that a man might play.) His anguish is so 'particular' to him, so subjectively consuming, as to be incommensurable; there are no common terms that would permit it to be shared or even imagined by others. This is why his attempts to speak his pain are always liable to become theatrical, hyperbolic, equally accusing and self-accusing. Or as T. S. Eliot's Harry puts it in *The Family Reunion*:

> This is what matters, but it is unspeakable,
> Untranslatable: I talk in general terms
> Because the particular has no language.[8]

Hence the need for a witness who might nevertheless speak adequately for you or of you; hence the intensity around the idea of being truly witnessed, truly known.

What the protagonist wants in wanting this is a kind of reflexive or two-stage process: to think that my pain can be turned into story or spectacle that makes it visible to others, is to be able to apprehend my own pain in a way I cannot do simply by suffering it. As Hippolytus feels in Euripides's play, you cannot just do this by yourself.

> *pheu*, I wish I could look at myself standing
> here. I'd weep then for the hardship I suffer.[9]

---

8   T. S. Eliot, *The Family Reunion*, ed. by Nevil Coghill (London: Faber & Faber, 1969), p.83.

9   Euripides, *Hippolytus*, trans. by Rachel Kitzinger, in *The Greek Plays: Sixteen Plays by Aeschylus, Sophocles, and Euripides*, ed. by Mary Lefkowitz and James Romm (New York: Modern Library, 2016), p.572. *Pheu* is a cry of anguish.

At this moment, Hippolytus stands falsely accused of raping his stepmother; he is threatened with exile and his father's curse, and perhaps also entangled by his horror at Phaedra's contaminating desire. If he could be his own audience, if he could apprehend himself as other for one moment, he would weep, but he has no-one to tell his story, and he does not try to tell it himself. There is a plot reason for this—he has vowed to keep silent—but like the poison which cuts Hamlet short, this stands for a more fundamental sense in which the sufferer *cannot* speak their own pain from a position of isolation, cannot weep for what they feel, or convey all that is atrocious in their situation. It must first be borne witness to by others—or, failing that, the sufferer is left with the challenge of imagining himself as another, as at one moment Lear also does:

> I am mightily abus'd; I should ev'n die with pity
> To see another thus. (IV.vii.52–3)

What Lear and Hippolytus imagine at those moments is the solace of an impossibly perfect correspondence, where they would be perfect witnesses to their own anguish because they could see it as another's. But in the nature of the case, the actual witness or onlooker can hardly have such total access to the sufferer's experience in extremity, and what they can say may not displace the sense of something left unspeakable. Hamlet may hope that Horatio will report him aright, but he has spent much of the play energetically demonstrating to others that they cannot gain access to 'the heart of my mystery' (III.ii.366). Coriolanus pushes away all 'report' of his nature and his actions, however sympathetic or admiring, as false to his essential being (I.ix.41–55; II.i.162–69; II.ii.66–77). When Edgar witnesses the meeting of his blinded father with the mad king, and hears Lear teasing Gloucester with his blindness, his response is curiously precise. 'I would not take this from report; it is, / And my heart breaks at it.' (IV.vi.141–42) No imaginable report can match what *is*, what now confronts Edgar in its unbearable particularity, and although he tries hard to bear witness, to reflect and comment on catastrophe somewhat in the manner of a tragic chorus, his attempts here and elsewhere exhibit a flinching awkwardness, or else break down into a near-stupefied dismay.

Antigone and the chorus

In Greek tragedy the situation of the chorus is, on the face of it, simpler. The chorus are, in principle, witnesses rather than participants. They usually belong to some kind of class of people disqualified from full agency—women, slaves, foreigners, sometimes elderly men—and this reinforces their structural position in the drama as non-participants in the action, who are to some extent insulated against the danger and affliction taking place. Instead, they watch and they respond. With rare exceptions, after their first entry they remain present throughout, and so they witness everything that happens in the play. It is true that they cannot, therefore, tell of the atrocity that happens off-stage, but this is often reported to us by another figure who plays no part in the drama except that of witness: the messenger who delivers the 'messenger-speech', another recurrent formal feature of Greek tragedy. In these speeches, when the messenger tells of the self-blinding of Oedipus, the dismemberment of Pentheus by his mother, or the suicides of Antigone and Haemon, the dreadful event is recounted in a performance of virtuosic intensity. This virtuosity both vividly evokes the horrifying scene and assures us that the messenger is undamaged by what he has witnessed, as the lightning runs through his protected body, so to speak, to be earthed among the listening community.

This function of mediation through a climactic act of witness is echoed in a more dispersed and generalised way by the chorus throughout the drama. What the protagonist says and does is turned by the chorus into story, as they reflect upon it, connect it with other stories, seek to give it form and shape, link it with general maxims, and—often, though not always—regard the protagonist with pity. Their mediating capacity is felt, too, in their dual role as figures within the frame of the action (elderly citizens, serving-women, etc.) and as those who sing and dance for Dionysus in the great choral odes which punctuate the play, and which formally create the time and space for a full response. These broadly cautious, sensible, normative figures are intermittently transfigured by the energies and music of the dance, another form of lightning or potential excess that is captured in the patterns and symmetries of form and safely transmitted to the community. The chorus, like the messenger, have the function of both responding to and transmitting extremity.

But how adequate is this act of witness, how safely is the lightning earthed? What I have written above about the function of the chorus is broadly true, but the exceptions and qualifications are at least as significant. For one thing, the dichotomy between sufferer and witness is not always as clean and safe as I have made it sound. In certain plays by Euripides in particular—*Hecuba* and *The Trojan Women*—it disappears completely.[10] In these plays the chorus are Hecuba's companions, overthrown and enslaved at the fall of Troy as she has been; her anguish is reflected in theirs, and in *Hecuba* they are moved to join her in her act of terrible vengeance on Polymestor and his family. These plays write large the vulnerability which is often an aspect of the chorus's marginal status as women and/or slaves. And in plays by Aeschylus and Sophocles as well as Euripides, there are moments when the putative safety of the formal divide between actor and chorus breaks down: intensely powerful passages of antiphonal lament or outcry when actor and chorus speak or sing together in lyric metre. These exceptional moments suggest how the witness-position may be more properly fearful than secure, at risk of being invaded and overwhelmed by what is borne witness to, with no certain immunity against infection.

For another thing, Greek tragedies are as much concerned with the resistance of extreme anguish to being witnessed as with its assimilation. The messenger-speech describing Oedipus' self-blinding is then followed by the appearance of the blinded Oedipus himself, in the condition that the chorus flinch from as unwatchable and unspeakable. 'I can't look at you. / And yet, so many things to ask, to learn, to examine. / [...] How I wish I'd never known you.'[11] If the horror of Oedipus's self-revelation and self-blinding seemed to have been acknowledged and contained by

---

10 I am indebted to Wai Chee Dimock's account of the 'breakdown of immunity' in these plays. She takes Euripides' plays of the Trojan War as portraying the kind of universal catastrophe epitomised by war (large-scale natural disaster being another) which overwhelms distinction between the more and the less affected. 'Witnessing and suffering are here one and the same.' 'After Troy: Homer, Euripides, Total War', in *Rethinking Tragedy*, ed. by Rita Felski (Baltimore: Johns Hopkins University Press, 2008), pp.78–79.

11 Sophocles, 'Oedipus Tyrannos', in *Sophocles: Oedipus Tyrannos, Oedipus at Kolonos, Antigone*, trans. by Timberlake Wertenbaker (London: Faber & Faber, 1997), p.40.

the messenger speech, that is deeply unsettled when he emerges before us. Can we, after all, cope with *this*? And more generally, the story the chorus tell can sometimes seem crucially to fall short, or to miss the essential quality, of the plight confronting them.

Take, as one strong example, a passage in the *Antigone*. Antigone has been convicted of burying her brother against the law of the city, and is being taken to her death. As she is brought in for the last time, the chorus weep for her, and she appeals directly to them to see her go her last journey. She both desires and stands off from their acknowledgement and their pity, and the exchanges between them turn on whether her extraordinariness can be reached by their sympathy. They lament that she is making 'her painful way' to the chamber of death where all come to rest. But she insists how her death–she is to be entombed alive–is not like the death of others, but radically singular; there will be no wedding-hymn for her, she says, excluded from the normal relations of life, for Hades will be her husband. The chorus reply by accepting her uniqueness but casting it as praiseworthy: it is by her own choice that she goes to her fate, descending alive into the world of death. Antigone responds by doing for herself what the chorus would more normally have done, and seeks some companionship in a mythological parallel: with Tantalus's daughter Niobe, 'the Phrygian stranger', who also endured a life-beyond-death, entombed as rock or stone, yet still endlessly weeping. 'And men tell / how / under the incessant beating of rains / and snow / she dissolves in her grief, / tears flow from her stony brows.'[12] This attempt to see herself as another, which elicits the image of freely flowing tears, is gently qualified by the chorus, for they point out that Niobe was a god and descended from a god, whereas Antigone is a mortal. Yet they put this in a wholly supportive way: 'Still, it is good to have it said of one who is mortal that her lot was equal to one of the gods, not only in life, but in death as well'.[13]

This would seem to be an entirely sympathetic way of, in Hamlet's terms, telling her story. But what is remarkable is that Antigone hears in their words only mockery and derision.

---

12 Sophocles, 'Antigone', in *Sophocles: Oedipus Tyrannos, Oedipus at Kolonos, Antigone*, trans. by Timberlake Wertenbaker (London: Faber & Faber, 1997), p.121.
13 Ibid., p.121.

> *Oimoi.*
> Now they laugh at me.
> I'm to be reviled.
> In the name of the gods of my father, can't you wait until I am dead?
> Must it be while I stand here before you!
> City, city
> and you, its well-born citizens.
> Streams of the river Dirke
> Thebes: sacred grove,
> rich chariot ground,
> be my witnesses now. See:
> how no friend weeps for me [...]
> an alien among the living and alien among the dead.[14]

Their pity and praise seem to reach her not at all, but terribly to intensify her sense of herself as essentially alien. Now only the landscape—the river and the grove—might bear witness to her plight, and this soon gives way to a lament for her utter and absolute estrangement:

> No weeping, no friend,
> no marriage song.
> The road is prepared.
> My mind reels —
> no more glances
> on this light, the hallowed,
> quivering face of day ...
> no tears over my fate,
> no friend,
> mourning,
> no.[15]

To describe herself as unwept and friendless is to set aside the chorus's tears as well as the existence of her sister Ismene and her fiancé Haemon. Her fierce loyalty to the dead has taken her outside the community of the living. Is this ... wilful? self-indulgent? masochistic? Such psychologising judgements miss, or flinch from, the immense and uncanny power of the passage in the theatre, just as Creon fails to take the measure of Antigone when he enters and similarly rebukes her. Throughout these exchanges Antigone has been chanting or singing with the chorus in lyric metre,

---

14 Ibid., p.121.
15 Ibid., p.122.

in a quasi-antiphonal lament known as a *kommos*. Such passages occur when the main actor is carried beyond the normal boundaries of the self by the intensity of their anguish. Intertwined with the chorus yet also standing out against them, Antigone sings her own death-song in reproach of those around her, as someone compelled and condemned to bear witness to her own pathos. This self-lamenting is essentially endless (as Creon complains), with no prospect of finding release in common sympathies. For it is the lamenting itself that estranges her from the fellow-feeling whose absence she laments, 'an alien among the living and alien among the dead'.

Telling the hero's story

If the witnessing figures within the play struggle to find words that connect with the sufferer's plight, perhaps art can help: the creative imagination's power to 'hold [...] the mirror up to nature' (Hamlet's phrase, hoping that theatre might hold the solution to his perplexity; III.ii.22). There is a famous case in Book 8 of the *Odyssey*. Odysseus is feasting with the Phaeacians as their shipwrecked guest, and is as yet incognito. But now the bard at the feast sings of the fighting at Troy, and includes in his song the actions of the great Odysseus.

> He sang how one and another fought through the steep citadel
> and how in particular Odysseus went, with godlike
> Menelaos, like Ares, to find the house of Deiphobus,
> and there, he said, he endured the grimmest fighting that ever
> he had, but won it there too, with great-hearted Athene aiding.
> So the famous singer sang his tale, but Odysseus
> melted, and from under his eyes the tears ran down, drenching
> his cheeks. As a woman weeps, lying over the body
> of her dear husband, who fell fighting for her city and people
> as he tried to beat off the pitiless day from city and children;
> she sees him dying and gasping for breath, and winding her body
> about him she cries high and shrill, while the men behind her,
> hitting her with their spear butts on the back and the shoulders,
> force her up and lead her away into slavery, to have
> hard work and sorrow, and her cheeks are wracked with pitiful weeping.
> Such were the pitiful tears Odysseus shed ...[16]

---

16   Homer, *The Odyssey*, trans. by Richmond Lattimore (New York: HarperPerennial, 1991), pp.134–135.

Here Odysseus hears his story truly told by another, told in such a way as to release in him those 'pitiful tears'. Hearing his story permits a kind of self-realisation: after this song Odysseus can declare his identity to the Phaeacians, and tell what we take to be the true story of his travels, rather than the false tales which he tells elsewhere. At the same time, this is not a moment of simple self-affirmation: Odysseus 'melted', and those pitiful tears speak of the grief at the heart of his victory, of the distance travelled between heroic Odysseus then and reflective Odysseus now. Odysseus weeps both for himself and for himself-as-another, and Homer's extraordinary simile underlines this, vividly connecting him with a figure who is in every respect his opposite—a woman, bereaved, a captive, and a loser. Those pitiful tears are not the tears of self-pity, but connect the exceptional figure with a wider community of grief. All of which becomes possible when the tragic story is well told by another.

Within tragic drama, the encounter with such an ideal chronicler-artist is rare. But there is something of the artist about Richard II, so that he can imagine the effect of his story on others, and instruct his queen in its delivery:

> In winter's tedious nights sit by the fire
> With good old folks and let them tell thee tales
> Of woeful ages long ago betid;
> And ere thou bid good night, to quite their griefs,
> Tell thou the lamentable tale of me,
> And send the hearers weeping to their beds. (V.i.40–5)

Earlier in the play, but with his power already slipping away, Richard was keen that he and his companions should 'sit upon the ground / And tell sad stories of the death of kings' (III.ii.155–56). That model of tragic story-telling was still largely narcissistic: it was the death of *kings* that mattered, all stories conformed to Richard's own—and although the speech ended by reaching out to the dependency of a common experience ('I live with bread like you, feel want, / Taste grief, need friends'; III.ii.175–76), it did so largely in a spirit of hyperbolic bitterness that such a connection should be thinkable. The later speech is different. The unexpected tenderness of Richard toward his queen is part of this, for he is seeking to lead her out of her own grief and rage into some larger spirit of acceptance. This underlies the remarkable image he conjures up of the exiled queen as a gossip among other gossips, 'with good old folks' sitting by the fire, one in a circle of traditional story-tellers. Although this folksy image—not easy to reconcile with the convent to which she is bound—is soft-focus by comparison with the hard realism of Homer's war-widow, it shares the same impulse to ground the exceptional experience in the wider commonality which story-telling implies. The old folks are telling sad tales of long ago, of figures preserved in history and in legend, but these are also *their* griefs, it seems. And the queen's sad tale of Richard will 'quite' (requite) those griefs, in an act of exchange and repayment that also suggests the satisfying of a want. In consequence, tears flow, as they flowed from Odysseus, and as Hippolytus felt they would flow if only his inner life could be known by another.

There is still, though, some trace of narcissism in Richard's emphasis on 'the lamentable tale of me', or at least something problematic in a figure of suffering who does so much of the work of bearing witness to himself. This tends as much to reinforce as to overcome the sense of a great distance that separates him from others, as we saw with Antigone. That tension is even more strikingly apparent at the end of *Othello*, where Othello, like Hamlet, urgently requires of others to tell his story, but goes far beyond Hamlet in specifying just how that story should go.

> Speak of me as I am; nothing extenuate,
> Nor set down aught in malice. Then must you speak
> Of one that lov'd not wisely but too well;
> Of one not easily jealous, but being wrought,
> Perplexed in the extreme; of one whose hand
> (Like the base Indian) threw a pearl away
> Richer than all his tribe; of one whose subdu'd eyes,
> Albeit unused to the melting mood,
> Drops tears as fast as the Arabian trees
> Their medicinable gum. (V.ii.342–51)

This speech has been heard and played in very different ways, from Othello regaining his lost nobility of mind to Othello hiding the reality of his actions behind a cloud of rhetoric. It is a kind of confession, and its peculiar difficulties are partly suggested by what Coetzee has observed about the partiality or doubleness of first-person confession, in which the self which confesses can never be entirely gathered up into the self which is confessed; something necessarily remains untold.¹⁷ Coetzee's examples come from narrative (Rousseau, Dostoevsky, Tolstoy), and his observation is both sharpened and complicated by the context of theatrical performance. Sharpened, because the possibility of manipulation or self-deception is so clearly to the fore; we are aware that a much less favourable story might be told, that Othello is pleading from the prisoner's dock. And complicated, because seeing oneself as a character, from outside, readily feels in the theatre like a form of insight, and also because, at this late point in this almost unbearable scene, we as audience are longing for the kind of moving reconnection with Othello which the speech offers. If only someone else had spoken it! The strain comes from Othello having to be his own story-teller and even, beyond that, his own audience. At the end of the passage quoted he would seem to be stage-directing his own weeping, as the passage as a whole exhibits that shift from the first to the third person which characterises his moments of crisis.¹⁸ This shift may be evasive, but it also strives for that relieving ability to feel for oneself as another which Hippolytus desiderated. The tears that Othello speaks of (whether or not he is actually weeping) are intensely desirable, associated with what is 'medicinable' and healing, or—in language traditionally associated with tragedy—cathartic. Yet this reflexivity suggests that terror of infinite estrangement which is generating Othello's urgent need to believe that a story can be truly told about him, that he has not fallen utterly and forever beyond the circle of communal understanding. The repeated 'one who' presses to be heard as 'one of that familiar category of men who', while nevertheless being haunted by a dreadful singularity.¹⁹ If Othello is extreme in so richly elaborating the story which must be told by another, what this barely keeps at bay is his strangeness to himself, 'perplexed in the extreme'—a phrase whose lack of specificity brilliantly manifests that perplexity of which it speaks. The speech struggles to connect the noble Moor with

---

17   J. M. Coetzee, 'Confession and Double Thoughts: Tolstoy, Rousseau, Dostoevsky', in *Doubling the Point: Essays and Interviews* (Cambridge, MA: Harvard University Press, 1992), pp.251–293.

18   The reverse movement, from third- to first-person, is one of extreme anguish. 'That's he that was Othello; here I am' (V.ii.284).

19   This tension between the singular and the general also touches the passage's textual crux: Othello sees himself either as the base Indian, i.e. 'ignorant in the way that all Indians tend to be', or the base Judean, i.e. Judas Iscariot—whose crime is like no other.

the vile murderer; but that the murderer could weep over his victim—as Othello did over the sleeping Desdemona, weeping 'cruel tears'—is as much estranging as humanising.[20]

This duality finally rises to the surface at the end of the speech, as Othello finds a way of narrating his own suicide.

> Set you down this;
> And say besides, that in Aleppo once,
> Where a malignant and a turban'd Turk
> Beat a Venetian and traduc'd the state,
> I took by th'throat the circumcised dog,
> And smote him — thus. (V.ii.351–56)

The loyal Venetian kills the malignant Turk; Othello casts himself in both roles, but finds an irreconcilable polarity between them. The stranger, the foreigner, the alien, is identified only to be repudiated and killed: there is no living with what he represents.

Admitting the alien

Othello's final speech stands in striking contrast to the start of the play and the backstory we are there given of his acceptance into Venice. As he will do at the end, Othello tells his own strange and exotic story, tragic in all but its outcome, given the 'disastrous chances' of his life, his sufferings, wanderings, and adventures (I.iii.134). But here he has listeners who respond, and whose response is all that he could wish for. He is heard in the second place by the senators, who are duly appreciative, but before that he has been heard by Desdemona. In her response to his story, we may see a tragic protagonist's ideal audience.

> My story being done,
> She gave me for my pains a world of sighs;
> She swore, in faith 'twas strange, 'twas passing strange;
> 'Twas pitiful, 'twas wondrous pitiful.

---

20 'I must weep, / But they are cruel tears. This sorrow's heavenly, / It strikes where it doth love.' (V.ii.20–22) Samuel Johnson gives this note in his edition. 'I wish these two lines could be honestly ejected. It is the fate of Shakespeare to counteract his own pathos.' *Johnson on Shakespeare*, in *The Yale Edition of the Works of Samuel Johnson*, ed. by John H. Middendorf, et al. (New Haven and London: Yale University Press, 1958–2018), VIII, p.1045.

> She wish'd she had not heard it, yet she wish'd
> That heaven had made her such a man. [...]
> She lov'd me for the dangers I had pass'd,
> And I lov'd her that she did pity them.
> This only is the witchcraft I have used.
> Here comes the lady; let her witness it. (I.iii.158–70)

'Passing strange', 'wondrous pitiful'—Desdemona registers something very like the fear and pity aroused in the audience of tragedy. 'She wish'd she had not heard it; yet she wish'd ...': the dismay and disturbance which are almost denial give way to an acknowledgement of strange and unexpected relationship, a desire for closer connection. To say that this makes her a strong witness to Othello's story may be to stretch the term. It is not that she can vouch for the reality of the Anthropophagi. But it is because his story evokes in her that emotion for which 'pity' stands as an approximating term—the sense of a vulnerable humanity unlike but not utterly unlike her own—that Othello can find his strange adventures to be earthed in a recognisable (because recognised) humanity, and can discover opening in himself the capacity to love. There is a peculiar rightness in the way the speech ends with Othello calling Desdemona as witness to its truth, and to his truth. It was because of how she listened to him then that he can speak so confidently now. That he loves her for how she responded to his story should speak to us of the intensity of that need to be witnessed.

I will return in the final chapter to what makes Desdemona here the paradigm of the ideal witness, at least as Othello feels her to be. The point I want to underline now is that she is making connection with a foreign figure, an alien in Venice, that 'extravagant and wheeling stranger' of whom Roderigo speaks (I.i.136). The radical *strangeness* of tragic experience, threatening total estrangement, is what makes the task of the witness so challenging, and the scenario of greeting and accommodating the foreigner can exactly instantiate what is involved. We can find a cue for this in a passage early in *Hamlet*, where Horatio and Hamlet struggle to come to terms with the phenomenon of the Ghost.

> HORATIO: O day and night, but this is wondrous strange!
> HAMLET: And therefore as a stranger give it welcome.
>   There are more things in heaven and earth, Horatio,
>   Than are dreamt of in your philosophy. (I.v.164–67)

Admit the existence of the non-rational and the unknowable—that is the import of those final lines. But more interesting still is the simile with which Hamlet illustrates what he has in mind: *as a stranger give it welcome*. There is a special kind of hospitality that is given to the stranger who appears at the door, the foreigner or alien, precisely because they are not one of our own, and threaten our familiar frame of reference. To give welcome to such a figure—to find language for what they present us with, to let them in—is not to mitigate their strangeness, for it is 'as a stranger' that they are welcomed, but it does mean entering actively into relation with that strangeness.²¹

Hamlet offers this as a kind of ethical imperative, but self-evidently it is not without risk. Hamlet's companions urge him not to follow the Ghost, lest it draw him into madness or self-destruction. Desdemona's welcoming of Othello will not end well. Here is Toni Morrison, from *Jazz*, on the dangers of taking in the stranger:

> Hospitality is gold in this City; you have to be clever to figure out how to be welcoming and defensive at the same time. When to love something and when to quit. If you don't know how, you can end up out of control or controlled by some outside thing.²²

The City is Harlem; the speaker is the narrator of the novel, an observer and commentator, in love with the City for its energy and the plenitude of the life that it fosters, but also cautious about being drawn too completely in. 'I lived for a long time, maybe too much, in my own mind. People say I should come out more. Mix.' But, she reflects, if entering into relationship leaves one disappointed or betrayed, 'well, it can make you inhospitable if you aren't careful, the last thing I want to be'. So, the task is to be 'careful' or 'clever' in one's hospitality, avoiding the fate of

---

21 If Hamlet's parallel seeks to familiarise the encounter with the Ghost, it also holds as strange the idea of welcoming the foreigner. (One should hear at least as strong an accent on 'stranger' as on 'welcome'.) In her own discussion of 'welcoming the stranger', Sara Ahmed, writing with colonial encounters in mind, worries about the ethics of a welcoming that claims entirely to assimilate—entirely to *recognise*—the alien. 'There must be surprise', she suggests, of an enduring kind: 'the host must be surprised by that which is encountered as other within the home'. The encounters staged within tragedy, and surely often also between tragic drama and its audience, might be thought to richly meet that criterion. Sara Ahmed, *Strange Encounters: Embodied Others in Post-Coloniality* (London: Routledge, 2000), pp.149–154 (p.151).

22 Toni Morrison, *Jazz* (London: Chatto & Windus, 1992), p.9.

the couple at the centre of the story, each of whom is overwhelmed by an illicit, out-of-control passion triggered by their involvement with a third person. Cleverness with hospitality is a survival tactic, it keeps you safe on the streets, the narrator tells us. But it also seems to qualify the narrator as story-teller, able to maintain just the right kind of relation to the City to make possible the good telling of the stories of others.

The challenging task of giving hospitality to the stranger, which Hamlet and Morrison invoke as simile or analogy, forms the actual dramatic situation of certain Greek tragedies. In Aeschylus's *Suppliant Women*, there arrive at the city of Argos a large group of foreign women, refugees from Egypt, fleeing from the male cousins who would force marriage upon them. These women have an ancestral link with Argos, but their foreignness is emphasised. They apologise for their 'foreign voice', and wear 'Sidonian veils'[23] and what the Argive king Pelasgus calls 'fancy foreign robes' such as no Greek woman wears; to him they look 'more like Libyans than the women here', and they remind him of classes of women who are exotically barbarian—camel-riding nomads, or 'flesh-eating Amazons, who hate all men'.[24] Alien but not altogether alien, strikingly foreign yet remotely kin, they embody the stranger who has a claim on us. Appealing for sanctuary, they must be given shelter and taken in. To do otherwise would bring terrible pollution, for suppliants are sacred—protected by Zeus, who also protects the claims of the *xenos*, the stranger-guest.[25] Accepting them turns the potential curse with which they threaten Argos into the blessings which they then call upon the city. But to take them in is also dangerous. At the most

---

23 Aeschylus, 'The Suppliants', trans. by Gail Holst-Warhaft, in *Aeschylus, 2*, ed. by David R. Slavitt and Palmer Bovie, Penn Greek Drama Series (Philadelphia: University of Pennsylvania Press, 1999), pp.114–115.

24 Ibid., pp.118, 120.

25 Maurice Blanchot reflects on how, at great moments in Greek poetry, 'the suppliant and the stranger are one; both are cut off from the whole, being deprived of the right that founds all others and alone establishes one's belonging to the home.' Interestingly, Blanchot emphasises the encounter with the stranger-suppliant as a matter of speaking and being heard: 'The suppliant is, par excellence, the one who speaks. [...] The stranger, lacking all common language, is paradoxically the one who is present solely through his speech; just as it is when everything is lacking that the man engulfed in misfortune has the means to speak, for therein is his true measure. It is after speech— speech having arranged this space between two where men meet who are separated by everything— that life once again becomes possible.' *The Infinite Conversation* (Minneapolis: University of Minnesota Press, 1993), pp.93–95.

obvious level, they may draw destruction upon Argos from the violent men pursuing them, who at the end of the play are threatening the city with war. More subtly, what they represent in themselves is dangerous in its threat to existing civic norms. For they are women who repudiate the claims of men upon them and repudiate marriage, refusing to act as women should do. When the second chorus of attendants cautiously sing, 'Yet we'll never neglect the goddess of love [...] To the wily goddess all honour's due',[26] that prudent correction points up something problematic in the suppliants' militant virginity.

When these foreign women pass into the city, it is as if two barely compatible modes of being were being hazardously brought into connection. Their choric ecstasy of terror, their violent extremity of emotion, as when they contemplate collective suicide within the sanctuary rather than be taken by their pursuers, threatens its own form of pollution or radical disturbance to the order of things in the city. In this first play of the trilogy they are victims, but the audience know that in the myth they will come to spill the blood of their husbands. If the king Pelasgus speaks of an ethical choice between right and wrong, he more often speaks of ruin on either hand, a tragic dilemma. When the city, with carefully explicit democracy, unanimously choose to let them in, this would seem to be the right and necessary action—but even so, their entry into the city space is described as hazardous both to the city and to the women themselves. 'Everyone's apt to speak ill of strangers', they reflect, and their father agrees, 'evil tongues are ready for use — / it's easy to speak quick words of hate'.[27]

This tension involved in welcoming the alien has a perennial force in the context of tragedy. The theme is superbly treated in Edward Albee's *A Delicate Balance*, written in 1966—a work which deserves a permanent place in the repertoire. In this play, the middle-class American family of Agnes and Tobias is visited unexpectedly one evening by their 'best friends' from the club. Sitting at home, Edna and Harry felt an inexplicable loneliness and terror, so they come to their friends and ask to be taken in and to stay indefinitely, without further explanation, almost as a matter of course. The play then unfolds around the cost—or benefit—of opening the family home to these disturbing visitors.

---

26   Aeschylus, 'The Suppliants', p.148.
27   Ibid., pp.146, 147.

The family has its long-standing griefs and dysfunctions which, before the arrival of the guests, are just barely managed and contained. The one who manages and contains is Agnes, the wife and mother. In a bravura opening speech she unfolds what she finds 'most astonishing', and before coming to what is ostensibly her main topic, she elaborates at some length on

> that belief of mine, which never ceases to surprise me by the very fact of its surprising lack of unpleasantness, the belief that I might very easily —as they say— lose my mind one day, not that I suspect I am about to, or am even ... nearby ...
>
> TOBIAS: There is no saner woman on earth, Agnes. [*Putters at the bottles.*]
>
> AGNES: ... for I'm not that sort; merely that it is not beyond ... happening: some gentle loosening of the moorings sending the balloon adrift — and I think that is the only outweighing thing: adrift; the ... becoming a stranger in ... the world, quite ... uninvolved, for I never see it as violent, only a drifting.[28]

Out of this acute awareness of the possibility of chaos and estrangement, Agnes maintains order, maintains the home. Her elaborate syntax in these opening sentences, with their complex subordinations and meticulously retrieved suspensions, itself enacts her vigilant control over refractory material. Within the family home and history, that troubling material is represented by her resident alcoholic sister— irresponsible, mocking, and truth-telling—whom Agnes counters with ferocious hostility; her serially divorced daughter, whom Agnes inexhaustibly soothes and re-stabilises on her inevitable returns home; and the unresolved feelings of her husband Tobias after the death of their son, which have left them semi-estranged. This Agnes manages by 'making the best' of what remains between them, countenancing though never entirely overlooking Tobias's desire to minimise conflict, avoid difficult encounters, and generally let things be. Their way of getting on is perfectly illustrated by the play's opening, where Agnes's semi-challenging assertions of the imminence of chaos are punctuated by Tobias's wary deflations, as if to say, 'yes, I hear you, but let mundanity provide its securing ballast'. With these deflations she wryly plays along,

---

28   Edward Albee, *A Delicate Balance* (Harmondsworth: Penguin, 1969), p.13. Points of ellipsis as in original.

as if to confirm that madness, or 'becoming a stranger in the world', is for her only a hypothetical possibility.

And so the household is maintained, with a running accompaniment of tension, abrasiveness, and unreconciled loss that are not permitted to rise to a point of crisis. The arrival of Edna and Harry throws this into jeopardy. Best friends and (Albee makes clear) mirror-images of Agnes and Tobias, they present Agnes and Tobias with the infinite loneliness and fear that might afflict them—that now in fact lie in wait for them, were their defences to come down. As Edna puts it, they *only came where they were expected*. An almost-surreal intrusion into the realist drama, their strange, irrational fear and their claim to move in, so calmly asserted, threaten to bring the madness of which Agnes spoke. They disturb the delicate balance of the household, evicting the returning daughter from her room and requiring Agnes and Tobias to share a bedroom for the first time for many years. 'There was a stranger in my room last night',[29] as Agnes says to Tobias the next morning, in a phrase that links their intruder-guests with the strained relation between husband and wife. The visitors bring, as she puts it, the terror, the plague—and so, the question, which she insists Tobias must decide: should they be admitted or excluded?

Tobias's eventual answer comes in a long speech to Harry which Albee notates as an 'aria', an impassioned expression of his conflicting feelings, delivered with 'all the horror and exuberance of a man who has kept his emotions under control for too long'. I quote the final section, where Tobias returns to Harry's triggering question, 'You don't *want* us, do you, Toby? You don't want us here.'

> I DON'T WANT YOU HERE!
> YOU ASKED?!
> NO! I DON'T
>   (*Loud*)
> BUT BY CHRIST YOU'RE GOING TO STAY HERE!
> YOU'VE GOT THE RIGHT!
> THE RIGHT!
> DO YOU KNOW THE WORD?
> THE RIGHT!

---

29 Ibid., p.81.

> (*Soft*)
> You've put nearly forty years in it, baby; so have I, and if it's nothing, I don't give a damn, you've got the right to be here, you've earned it
> (*Loud*)
> AND BY GOD YOU'RE GOING TO TAKE IT!
> DO YOU HEAR ME?!
> YOU BRING YOUR TERROR AND YOU COME IN HERE
> AND YOU LIVE WITH US!
> YOU BRING YOUR PLAGUE!
> YOU STAY WITH US!
> I DON'T WANT YOU HERE!
> I DON'T LOVE YOU!
> BUT BY GOD ... YOU STAY!!
> (*Pause*)
> STAY!
> (*Softer*)
> Stay!
> (*Soft, tears*)
> Stay. Please? Stay?
> (*Pause*)
> Stay? Please? Stay?[30]

In modern America there is no Greek *xenia*, the Zeus-sanctioned right of the stranger-guest to hospitality, but Albee finds an equivalent: the right conferred by having been 'best friends' for forty years. If that counts for nothing in a crisis, if that can be set aside, then all human relations outside blood-relationship are revealed as hollow, void of obligation. This is a thought that Tobias has just voiced to Agnes with regard to their own marriage.

> If that's all Harry and Edna mean to us, then ... what about *us*? When we talk to each other ... what have we meant? Anything? When we touch, when we promise, and say ... yes, or please ... with our*selves*? ... have we meant, yes, but only if ... if there's any condition, Agnes! Then it's ... all been empty.[31]

And so letting in the stranger is an imperative, for Tobias no less than for the king Pelasgus in Aeschylus. But this is not something Tobias

---

30   Ibid., pp.103–104.
31   Ibid., p.96.

whole-heartedly *wants*, and every agonised line of his speech expresses the intense ambivalence in his feelings.

In the event, the invitation to stay (if that is what it is) comes too late. Harry has perceived that they are not wanted, and moreover has reflected that were the situations reversed, he would not want to take in Tobias and Agnes. More is being asked than is easy or perhaps possible to give. So Harry and Edna leave, despite Tobias's ultimately plaintive appeal that they stay, with its surprising implication that it is he who has become the suppliant, and will lose most by their going. It is a striking reversal. There has been some kind of failure; some kind of opportunity has been missed, as well as crisis averted; but something has also shifted in Tobias, and through him perhaps in the family, as a result of this encounter. The visitors having departed, the play ends with Agnes' affirmation of daylight—that after the madness and fearfulness of the night, 'Come now; we can begin the day'.[32] It is, I think, a powerfully open ending: a return to the status quo, perhaps, but perhaps also speaking of some possible new life arising from this encounter.

It hardly needs to be said that there is an immense distance between Aeschylus and Albee. Most obviously, the crucial unit of community has shrunk, from the city-state in the Greek play to the family home in *A Delicate Balance*. What was primarily political has become domestic and psychological. Nevertheless, the plays share a common dynamic. The suppliants bring danger to the community; yet they call out to be admitted. Their appeal is grounded in an ethical principle on which society depends—*xenia* in one case, long friendship in the other—while being strengthened also by some yet more fundamental connectedness. The strange foreign women are of Greek extraction; Edna and Harry are versions of Agnes and Tobias, and letting them in has implications for the level of intimacy Agnes and Tobias dare allow one another. The community cannot, therefore, offer sanctuary to these strangers without being itself affected, without acknowledging an affinity with what would otherwise have been merely and safely alien. And this is a fearful thing: as Agnes puts it, it means letting in the plague, the terror, the potential for madness.

---

32 Ibid., p.108.

Nowhere in tragic drama is this hazardous taking in more clearly dramatised than at the end and climax of Aeschylus's *Oresteia*. Orestes is newly arrived at Athens, and Athene speaks of the great danger and difficulty of deciding what to do about him. For he is both 'a suppliant pure and harmless', whom the city should admit and protect, and a mother-killer pursued by the Furies, ancient deities of implacable vengeance. If he is admitted and they are denied, their anger will bring plague upon the city. 'So stands the case', she declares to Orestes; 'either course, that you should stay / or that I should send you away is disastrous, and perplexes me'.[33] Like Pelasgus, she insists that this is a matter for democratic decision by the citizens, beyond the power of any individual to decide, whether king or god. But when the citizens come to vote, she urges upon them one crucial principle, that

> that they shall not cast out altogether from the city what is to be feared.[34]

It is a line of rich implication. What is to be feared is in Greek that which is *deinos*, a word that encompasses the terrible, the wondrous, that which strikes and fills with awe. What is to be feared is the mother-murderer Orestes, whose case is now to be judged—but it also includes the Furies, whose anger now threatens Athens. After Orestes' acquittal, which depends upon her casting vote, Athene's task becomes to accommodate the Furies within the city, to persuade them to accept a place of honour in Athens, with a limited but still powerful function in an economy that is at once civic and of the psyche. The vision she holds out is one of reciprocal connection: they will receive honour from the city, they will hold an interest in the city's flourishing. She invites them to 'live with' her (*sunoikian*) at line 833, a term refined when they actually pass into the city: Athene now refers to them as *metoikoi* (1011), a term they then repeat (1018), which for the audience links them with the metics or immigrant workers who held 'resident alien' status in contemporary Athens, living 'among' or 'alongside' (*meta*) the citizens without being wholly naturalised. Antigone went to her death as one not *metoikos*[35]

---

33   Aeschylus, *The Eumenides*, trans. by Hugh Lloyd-Jones (New Jersey: Prentice-Hall, 1970), p.40.
34   Ibid., p.55.
35   Line 852. George Steiner renders the word in Antigone's line as 'the half-breed, the hybrid stranger'. *Antigones* (Oxford: Clarendon Press, 1986), p.279.

among the living or the dead, an alien in both worlds, but the Furies for all their threatening strangeness will be accommodated within the city. A truly civilised society, like a truly integrated mind, must find room for 'what is to be feared'. As Rowan Williams puts it, thinking particularly but not only of the Greek tragedies, 'the city where tragedy occurs fails or refuses to know that it encompasses strangers. [...] What makes Athens the city as it should be, as opposed to chaotic and bloodstained Thebes, is that it seeks ways of accommodating the stranger.'[36] And he cites the welcome that Theseus gives to the exiled and polluted Oedipus in *Oedipus at Colonus*: 'I will never shrink / from a stranger lost as you are now.'[37]

At the end of the *Oresteia*, this movement towards acknowledgement mirrors the larger shift in how we apprehend the Furies. In the first two parts of the trilogy the feelings they embody were sensed as an ever-present source of threat and unease, a deep reservoir of resentments from the past, like the 'ancestral voices prophesying war' that Coleridge's Kubla Khan heard from far away. But in those plays they were inchoate and invisible, seen or hallucinated only by the second-sighted Cassandra and by the distraught Orestes after killing his mother. Now, in the final play, Aeschylus brings them on stage as the chorus, in what must have been felt as a stunning stroke of theatre: the choric figures who normally respond to and mediate the horror have now become its incarnation. And although the reactions to them are at first of horror and revulsion—the priestess is appalled, Apollo disgusted—what Athene does is to grant them hearing, to acknowledge them as great powers, and to persist in engaging with them as beings who are open to persuasion, *or can be rendered such if only they are granted the proper kind of attention*. When they finally lay down their curses and accept their offered role in the city, it becomes possible to think of them not as Furies but as the Eumenides, 'the kindly ones'. They are forces rather than persons, of course, so the point cannot be pressed too far, but what is suggested here is the potency of truly bearing witness to

---

36 Rowan Williams, *The Tragic Imagination* (Oxford: Oxford University Press, 2016), p.33.
37 'I was once brought up an exile, like you, and I faced all the dangers that beset a foreigner, and because of this, I would never turn away a foreigner like you now.' *Oedipus Tyrannos, Oedipus at Kolonos, Antigone*, trans. by Timberlake Wertenbaker (London: Faber & Faber, 1997), p.60.

what is alien or appalling, the potency of giving it representation, and by extension the potency of the tragic theatre itself.

Fear remains, however, and danger. The Furies are not wholly domesticated or assimilated or transformed. When Athene is setting out their role within the city, she amply acknowledges this:

> Mighty and hard to please
> are the divinities I make to settle here.
> All the affairs of men
> it is their province to manage.
> And he that encounters their anger
> does not know from where come the blows that assail his life;
> for crimes born from those of long ago
> hale him before them, and in silence destruction,
> loud though he boast,
> through their wrath and enmity grind him to nothing.[38]

Taking in the Furies includes knowing *this*: how precarious the civic achievement is, how fragile the accommodation with the irrational, with forces that may at any time powerfully begrudge their suppression or marginalisation in the interests of a wider economy. The Eumenides are still always also the Furies. And if to bear witness to the Furies— to acknowledge them within the orbit of the human, to report them aright—is to discover that they may be negotiated with, loosening their vindictive grip upon the present or upon the mind, it is also to ascertain with a new certainty the reality of 'what is to be feared'.

---

38   Aeschylus, *The Eumenides*, p.68.

3. Imperfect Witness

> Never trust a witness,
> By the time a thing is
> noticed, it has happened.[1]

Representation as betrayal in Shakespeare

Never trust a witness? The self-evident gap in time and in space between the thing itself and the notice taken by others can open a site of dynamic tension. In tragedy, this often means a shortfall in sympathetic understanding, but also something more than shortfall: one concern of this chapter is to highlight how Shakespearean protagonists find themselves threatened or betrayed by the way others see them. The onlooker's tacit claim is to be not in a deficit but a privileged position, able to see and to say how it *really* is with the protagonist. Often this is in ways that challenge the protagonist's exceptionality or even self-identity, a disturbance that may come to be at the very heart of the tragedy. For the first part of the chapter, the witnesses that I bring forward from within Shakespeare are of this hostile kind, inclined to reduce the central intensity to the terms of a knowing objectivity, essentially disallowing the heroic. Tragedy then arises out of the resistance this encounters, or the pain this inflicts. *Coriolanus* and *Troilus and Cressida* are offered as plays in which the gap between protagonist and onlooker is peculiarly excruciating, and which stand at opposite ends of the spectrum of the power-balance between them. Towards the end of the chapter, however, I think about a different mode of witnessing, for which I go (via Ibsen) to *Antony and Cleopatra*. Here the imperfectness of witness, its under-determination by its material, leaves it as free to affirm exceptionality, or even to bring exceptionality into being, as to undermine it. Throughout,

---

1   Kay Ryan, *The Best of It: New and Selected Poems* (New York: Grove Press, 2010), p.116.

although my immediate focus is on witness figures within the plays, I think also about the play itself as a form of witnessing, of our own position as spectators in the theatre: sitting not as observers of a given reality, but rather as attuned to—or implicated in—how the matter of the play is shaped and re-shaped, fluidly and dynamically, by the energies of representation.

The lines from Kay Ryan's poem quoted above suggest that the very act of noticing involves a time-lag; being skewed by retrospection, the story told by a witness is essentially unreliable. Jacques Derrida takes a similar thought and runs with it in *Memoirs of the Blind*, his essay on (among other things) the art of drawing. Following Baudelaire's suggestion that the artist is always drawing from memory, even when they have the scene or sitter in front of them, Derrida spins this into the paradox that it is the blind man who makes the best witness.

> In fact, a witness, as such, is always blind. Witnessing substitutes narrative for perception. The witness cannot see, show, and speak at the same time, and the interest of the attestation, like that of the testament, stems from this dissociation. No authentication can show in the present what the most reliable of witnesses sees, or rather, has seen and now keeps in memory.[2]

'Witnessing substitutes narrative for perception': implying that one displaces the other.[3] Derrida is interested in the 'dissociation' which this uncovers, the gap or tension between the thing itself and what is introduced with the attempt at representation.

> The child within me wonders: how can one claim to look at both a model and the lines [*traits*] that one jealously dedicates with one's own hand to the thing itself? Doesn't one have to be blind to one or the other? Doesn't one always have to be content with the memory of the other?[4]

---

2   Jacques Derrida, *Memoirs of the Blind: The Self-Portrait and Other Ruins*, trans. by Pascale-Anne Brault and Michael Naas (Chicago and London: University of Chicago Press, 1993), p.104. For Baudelaire's suggestion, see his 'Mnemonic Art' in *The Painter of Modern Life*. 'All true draughtsmen draw from the image imprinted in their brain and not from nature'. *Baudelaire: Selected Writings on Art and Artists*, trans. by P. E. Charvet (Cambridge: Cambridge University Press, 1981), p.407.
3   An alternative emphasis would be on how narrative enables understanding. This is the view taken by Paul Ricoeur in *Time and Narrative*, where Ricoeur sees narrative as gathering up time in such a way as to undo the abyss between then and now which informs the aporia of Ryan's poem and Derrida's paradox.
4   Derrida, *Memoirs of the Blind*, pp.36–37.

'Narrative' and 'memory' here stand for all that the artist or witness brings to their task from the stock of their own mind—as the product of their own hand, rather than a pure reflex of the eye. Derrida offers this as the speculation of his inner child: the child being, we may suppose, less inclined to automatically refer the drawing to a referent in the world, more likely to be alive to its own qualities as a drawing, 'the thing itself', and therefore to be struck by the incongruity between the model and the record that is generated.

These general reflections on the impossibility of unmediated representation or perfect witness acquire special relevance in the vicinity of tragedy. There is the obvious fact that suffering is not a matter of language, and to represent or report it in words is to translate it into a foreign medium. This is true even of simple physical pain, where we do the best we can with clumsy metaphor (is it a sharp pain or a dull pain?), and acutely true of more fundamental states of anguish, where terms of bridging comparison are likely to fail altogether. (What is it *like*... to lose a child? to have suffered violation? to receive a terminal diagnosis?) The difficulty is further compounded insofar as the anguish is felt as isolating or estranging, perhaps shocking or taboo, intrinsically likely to appal or repel the listener, or even as mysterious or appalling to the sufferer herself. It is often this kind of anguish with which tragedy deals. And given that by tragedy we mean in the first place the artwork which is a tragic drama, the question of representation is even more obviously in play. In one sense, theatre offers a way round the problem, for unless a play deals with contemporary life or recent history, there is no literal anterior reality to be represented or distorted. *King Lear* affects us as a present experience, not as a representation of ancient Britain. Yet for that experience to matter to us as it does, many people feel that some element of *recognition* is involved, that the story told is about something beyond itself; the problem returns in a subtler form.

The potential shortfall involved in theatrical representation in the area of tragedy is the subject of Luigi Pirandello's *Six Characters in Search of an Author*. In this ingenious parable of a play, the 'Characters', who wear the fixed masks of tragedy, are bound together by traumatic events from their past. These events have never yet been told, and, like Hamlet, they seek someone who will tell their story: they implore a company of actors to represent their personal tragedy as a play. The Actors agree, and begin to play the Characters, and to act out their tragedy. But the Characters are dismayed: the very act of representation seems to them to misrepresent their reality, to make of them something other than they are. The Father speaks courteously of the leading man's skill, but nevertheless

> it will be difficult to play me as I really am. It will be more like—apart from how I look—it will be more like how he plays the way I am, how he feels like me—if he does feel like me—and not how I myself feel inside of me. And it seems to me that, concerning this matter, whoever is expected to judge us should keep this in mind.
>
> DIRECTOR: Now you're worried about the judgements of the critics?[5]

The Father knows that disclosure will invite judgment, and that judgment based merely on what can be made manifest is likely to be harsh and misplaced. The Director's misunderstanding of what he means only underscores the gap between the site of pain and the project of representation. The Son makes a similar complaint to the Actors, with greater aggression and greater anguish:

> Somehow you still do not seem to understand that you cannot put on this play. We are not inside of you, and you actors are looking at us from the outside. Is it possible that we have to live in front of a mirror which, as if it were not enough, is not satisfied to freeze us in the image of our very own expression, but rather gives it back to us as an unrecognizable grimace of ourselves.[6]

How is an anguished inner life to be made manifest in the world? Pirandello's brilliant conception maps the difficulty of being properly known, and properly judged, onto the dynamics of theatre. When the Actors play out the matter of the tragedy, they show that they have failed to enter into the inner experience which is its source, and the distress of the Characters is exacerbated rather than relieved.

In Shakespeare's early tragedy *Titus Andronicus*, there is an unforgettable scene which presents the problem of tragic witnessing in its starkest form. We see on stage a bleeding woman, who moments

---

5   Luigi Pirandello, *Six Characters in Search of an Author and Other Plays* (London: Penguin, 1995), p.36.
6   Ibid., p.63.

before has been raped and mutilated, her hands cut off and her tongue cut out. She is encountered by her uncle Marcus, who makes a speech of some 45 lines. This is only the first half:

> If I do dream, would all my wealth would wake me!
> If I do wake, some planet strike me down,
> That I may slumber an eternal sleep!
> Speak, gentle niece: what stern ungentle hands
> Hath lopp'd and hew'd, and made thy body bare
> Of her two branches, those sweet ornaments
> Whose circling shadows kings have sought to sleep in,
> And might not gain so great a happiness
> As half thy love? Why dost not speak to me?
> Alas, a crimson river of warm blood,
> Like to a bubbling fountain stirr'd with wind,
> Doth rise and fall between thy rosed lips,
> Coming and going with thy honey breath.
> But sure some Tereus hath deflow'red thee,
> And lest thou shouldst detect him, cut thy tongue.
> Ah, now thou turn'st away thy face for shame!
> And notwithstanding all this loss of blood,
> As from a conduit with three issuing spouts,
> Yet do thy cheeks look red as Titan's face
> Blushing to be encount'red with a cloud.
> Shall I speak for thee? shall I say 'tis so?
> O, that I knew thy heart, and knew the beast,
> That I might rail at him to ease my mind!
> Sorrow concealed, like an oven stopp'd,
> Doth burn the heart to cinders where it is. (II.iii.13–37)[7]

Marcus goes on to develop the comparison with the Ovidian story of Tereus and Philomel, and to recall how exquisitely Lavinia sang and played upon the lute, as something she can no longer do, before offering to take her to her 'father's eye', concluding:

> Do not draw back, for we will mourn with thee.
> O, could our mourning ease thy misery! (ii.iii.56–57)

---

7   Quotations from Shakespeare are taken from are taken from *The Riverside Shakespeare*, 2nd edn, ed. by G. Blakemore Evans, et al. (Boston and New York: Houghton Mifflin, 1997), unless otherwise stated.

In this scene Shakespeare takes things to extremes—both atrocity, and the linguistic response to it. Marcus's expansive rhetoric seems grotesquely inappropriate to the reality before him. This is so even if we try to take its decorative excess as a register of shock, a compulsive filling of the void with words, or an attempt to re-imagine the horror which confronts him in the terms of an aesthetically bearable pathos. He must speak for Lavinia, who cannot speak for herself, but his words stand at an immense distance from her plight. 'O, that I knew thy heart' refers not just to Lavinia's knowledge of the perpetrators, but expresses the abyss that separates her condition from the person looking on. Her mutilation prevents her from communicating the story of her rape, but in its human and theatrical extremity, it more fundamentally prevents her anguish from being communicable. Although she visibly bleeds and Marcus volubly laments, this is still primarily a case of 'sorrow concealed', stopped up, incapable of expression or communication. The offer he makes at the end—'we will mourn with thee'—is hollow, for we have no access to the pain and grief that Lavinia must be feeling. And indeed the offered solidarity collapses in the next line, as 'our mourning' falls back into separation from 'thy misery'.

In this scene from his early work, Shakespeare sets out with horrible clarity the tensions around witnessing which he will explore again and again in his later tragedies. Marcus's speech tells us how Lavinia is responding to his lament for her. She turns her face away, which Marcus understands as being 'for shame', and she 'draws back' at the prospect of being exposed to her father's eye. Shame is a complex idea, but it might be the right word for Lavinia's feelings here, in the sense of feeling radically betrayed by how one appears to others—exposed, indeed, but also misrepresented. She is exposed, in the first and last place, to us in the theatre; Pirandello's implication of the theatre in the failure to tell the tragic story truly (a story also associated with an overwhelming sense of shame)[8] is relevant here also. Marcus's intensely visual descriptions of her damaged state heighten our discomfort as spectators, queasily fascinated as we are bound to be by the spectacle she makes on stage. (This is equally true whether the director opts for naturalism or stylisation in the staging.) Her distress comes to seem

---

[8] The Father was discovered to be unknowingly soliciting his own daughter in a brothel.

like a response to how she is being talked about and looked at now, by him, by us; she wishes to draw back, to be elsewhere, as if shunning the further violation inflicted by the attempt to represent her plight.

Much Shakespearean tragedy revisits this sense of threat in how one is seen and reported. Cassius's words to Brutus cast a long shadow over the tragedies that follow.

> CASSIUS: Tell me, good Brutus, can you see your face?
> BRUTUS: No, Cassius; for the eye sees not itself
>   But by reflection, by some other things. [...]
> CASSIUS: Therefore, good Brutus, be prepared to hear;
>   And since you know you cannot see yourself
>   So well as by reflection, I, your glass,
>   Will modestly discover to yourself
>   That of yourself which you yet know not of. (I.ii.51–70)

Brutus cannot know himself except as he is reflected in others' eyes. This may be straightforwardly true of his face, but when Cassius suavely moves from 'your face' to 'yourself', he makes a more disturbing claim. Cassius is an equivocal friend to Brutus, and this power of 'reflection' is an ambiguous one, for if the image of Brutus which Cassius reflects back to him is hitherto one that he knows not of, in what sense is it his? Cassius offers himself as a reflecting glass or mirror, but Richard II could not find himself in the mirror that he was brought, and the Son in Pirandello repudiates his image in the mirror held up by the actor as one that he 'can no longer recognise'. As Derrida puts it, 'the naked face cannot look itself in the face, *it cannot look at itself in a looking glass.*'[9] At this moment in *Julius Caesar*, a tremor runs through the ground; we feel the borders of Brutus' identity shift and blur. Never trust a witness. The identity of 'good Brutus', as something here repeatedly and pointedly *attributed* to him by Cassius, may, it is insinuated, exist nowhere except in attribution.

Although Cassius assures Brutus that he is no 'common laugher' (I.ii.72), there is something latently derisive in the dependency that opens up here. Another firm Roman, Coriolanus, feels himself positively mocked at the climax of his play by the eyes upon him. The embassy of his family led by his mother has persuaded him to make peace not

---

9   Derrida, *Memoirs of the Blind*, p.69 (his emphasis).

war, to abandon his implacable vengeance on the city of Rome and to acknowledge his human connectedness. As they approached, he already felt himself to be like a player who has forgotten his lines. 'Like a dull actor now / I have forgot my part, and I am out, / Even to a full disgrace' (V.iii.40–42). The final lines in Volumnia's long speech, the lines which seem to clinch her persuasion of him, threaten him with what *she* will say of him if he carries out his intention. 'I am hush'd until our city be afire, / And then I'll speak a little' (V.iii.181–82). He weeps and takes his mother by the hand, in silence—a silence explicitly marked, exceptionally, in the Folio text—as if he had indeed forgotten his lines. What is happening to him at this moment is not speakable. And for that reason, its meaning falls into the hands of those who look on:

> Oh mother, mother!
> What have you done? Behold, the heavens do ope,
> The gods look down, and this unnatural scene
> They laugh at. (V.iii.183–85)

Those who witness this will laugh at the spectacle he makes—his firmness of resolution all undone, the great warrior reduced to tears by a mother's plea, his course of action with the Volsci rendered absurd. He falls into 'the anguish of perceivedness',[10] to borrow a phrase from Samuel Beckett. The phrase appears in the notes to Beckett's work *Film*, and relates to his protagonist's dread of being caught full-face by the camera—that is, being forced to know that he is seen, or to see himself as he is seen. The camera, which we come to understand as pursuing him, entirely defines our view of him (he has no words). We, as the viewers of the film, are what he fears to confront, to acknowledge. In Coriolanus's lines, Shakespeare does something similar with the metaphor of the theatre, suggested by 'heavens' (the name for the Globe theatre ceiling, which could open) and confirmed by 'scene'. At this moment of extremity, Coriolanus feels himself to be a mere player on the stage, with all the derogatory connotations which that image often carries in Shakespeare, exposed to the derision or amusement of the gods who look down on him. In the actual theatre, no-one laughs; the imagined cruelty of theatre is more firmly held at a remove than with Lavinia. But it is commonly felt that although the scene ought to be moving—and is

---

10 Samuel Beckett, *The Complete Dramatic Works* (London: Faber & Faber, 1990), p.323.

in one sense extremely moving—we are nevertheless held at a distance, unusual in Shakespearean tragedy, from the protagonist's subjectivity. The tears that Coriolanus weeps are almost as strange to us as they clearly are to him; it is 'no little thing' for his eyes to 'sweat compassion', as he so characteristically puts it (V.iii.195–96).

A comparable sense of the threat in being seen is vividly posted at the start of *Antony and Cleopatra*. Antony's love is a thing of wonder and beauty, an emotion that transcends the concerns of politics and empire—if we listen only to his language. But the Roman soldier looking on is unimpressed; what his place among the spectators gives him is a perspective on the grand gesture that degrades and diminishes it.

> Look where they come!
> Take but good note, and you shall see in him
> The triple pillar of the world transform'd
> Into a strumpet's fool. Behold and see. (I.i.10–13)

'Behold and see' is offered as lethal to the claims of a heroic love. What we *see*, according to this Roman witness, is the all-too-familiar sight of an elderly man making a fool of himself over sex. This possibility that the heroic sentiment is jeopardised by what we see in front of us is activated at various other moments in the play, not least when the dying Antony is hoisted up the back of the Globe theatre to the musicians' gallery where Cleopatra awaits. The stage action bathetically counterpoints the intensity of the dramatic situation. Many productions shirk doing this, but Shakespeare's text explicitly requires it.

Clearly, this is one particular kind of seeing—seeing with the sound turned down, so to speak, uncomplicated by empathy—and the claim that this kind of (reductive) eye-witness determines what is true is highly questionable. The whole question acquires a further force from the nature of Shakespearean theatre. As the Chorus in *Henry V* reminds us, the gap between 'this cockpit' which we see and 'the vasty fields of France' which it may represent, the awareness that 'four or five most vile and ragged foils' are disgracing 'the name of Agincourt', is always available and near the surface (Prologue to Act I.11–12; Prologue to Act IV.50–52). Although all theatre can and perhaps must instate itself as ceremony, the ceremonial nature of Shakespearean theatre is far less securely contracted with its audience than we may suppose was the case with the tragedies played at the festival of the Great Dionysia or in the French neo-classical theatre or even in the naturalistic mode of Chekhov or middle-period Ibsen. None of these are shot through with the theatrical self-consciousness that Shakespeare repeatedly invokes. Another way of putting this would be that the collaborative basis of the kind of claim we are prepared to allow is never far from consciousness in the Shakespearean theatre (as also in much contemporary drama). The kind of question represented by 'will this boy-actor do as Cleopatra?' extends without a break into the more interesting kind of question represented by 'will a weeping Coriolanus do as heroic?' Will we allow that this familiarising representation connects us with the strange and extraordinary quality for which it stands, but of which it manifestly falls short?—drama being a present event as well as an act of witness to a reality not confined to the play-script. Which in turn touches on the question pressed by tragedy which Hamlet raises in connection with the Ghost: how is the figure in extremity to be accepted, to be borne witness to, in all its strangeness?

Charles Lamb had half a point, therefore, when he suggested that Shakespeare's tragedies are always diminished in the theatre, that his protagonists are degraded when exposed to the gaze of the community.

> So to see Lear acted—to see an old man tottering about the stage with a walking-stick, turned out of doors by his daughters in a rainy night, has nothing in it but what is painful and disgusting. We want to take him into shelter and relieve him. That is all the feeling which the acting of Lear ever produced in me. But the Lear of Shakespeare cannot be acted. [...] The greatness of Lear is not in corporal dimension, but in intellectual: the explosions of his passion are terrible as a volcano: they are storms turning up and disclosing to the bottom that sea, his mind, with all its vast riches. It is his mind which is laid bare. This case of flesh and blood seems too insignificant to be thought on; even as he himself neglects it. On the stage we see nothing but corporal infirmities and weakness, the impotence of rage: while we read it, we see not Lear, but we are Lear,— we are in his mind, we are sustained by a grandeur which baffles the malice of daughters and storms.[11]

We need not be persuaded by Lamb to give up on the theatre—a word which means, in its Greek derivation, the place of seeing—but we can still

---

11 Charles Lamb, 'On the Tragedies of Shakespeare, considered with reference to their Fitness for Stage Representation', in *Lamb as Critic*, ed. by Roy Park (London: Routledge and Kegan Paul, 1980), p.96.

recognise, as he does, the enormous tension involved in (crudely put) both seeing Lear and feeling with him. The simpler version of this—call it version A—is that seeing Lear's impotence cancels the grandeur which I feel when I identify with his subjectivity: theatre disallows and derides the heroic. What remains is Lear as the foolish fond old man, protected from mockery only by our compassionate fellow-feeling. The subtler version, version B, is that seeing Lear makes Lear's great rage (which to him is natural and inevitable) into something *strange*, a strangeness which is more challenging to bear witness to. A large part of what is dramatic in Shakespeare's tragedies is the contention between these two modes of response, taking place in the audience and sometimes also in the protagonist.

Othello's anguish, for example, is nowhere more powerfully expressed than in the idea he momentarily allows himself to entertain, of being seen—whether as cuckold:

> but alas, to make me
> The fixed figure for the time of scorn
> To point his slow unmoving finger at! (IV.ii.53–55)

or, in an equally nightmarish near-hallucination, as the murderer of his innocent wife:

> When we shall meet at compt,
> This look of thine will hurl my soul from heaven,
> And fiends will snatch at it. (V.ii.273–75)

Behind the terror of these lines lies the presence of Iago as, above all, an onlooker. He is the figure closest in position to the theatre audience, whom he can address directly, especially in the first half of the play. In Iago's cool appraisal all idealism turns to dross. The play threatens us with the possibility that if we look clearly at this great love, with a vision unclouded by rhetoric and the normal human appetite for self-delusion, we shall see as Iago sees. 'It is merely a lust of the blood and a permission of the will' (I.iii.334–5).

A comparable pressure is exercised in *Macbeth* by the presence of the witches, Macbeth's metaphysical spectators, the *seers* of the play. They open Macbeth to a terrible evil; but they also strike a grotesque, almost banal note. In their thrice-hail to Macbeth, their prophecy of his future greatness, there is a kind of mockery: they are the derisive gods that Coriolanus imagines, and in this play full of dramatic ironies, Macbeth is the victim of their cosmic practical joke. Of course, that is not how we experience his path to the murder of Duncan: in the first two acts the poetry makes us so extraordinarily intimate with his subjective experience that we can hardly *see* him at all. But the continual invocations of darkness and blindness—'the eye wink at the hand' (I.iv.52)—spring from a great fear as to what clear vision might bring. To say that Macbeth is fending off the true horror of his deed is true—he will not look again at Duncan's bleeding body—but we can press harder on the question of where, for him, the dread lies. Clear vision reveals Macbeth to be what, in the second half of the play, others see him as: a butcher, a tyrant, a coward racked with fear, a dwarfish thief, the kind of man who murders for personal gain. Undeniably, what these voices tell us has some truth. And yet, as a full account, it is also radically untrue to the being of acute moral sensibility and imagination that we encounter at the start of the play, whose motive to murder is always mysterious to himself. The real horror in *Macbeth* and for Macbeth lies not in the killing of Duncan, but in the fact that Macbeth should be the killer—that is, in the bottomless incongruity that has opened up for him in the fabric of things. 'Nothing is but what is not' (I.iii.141–42). He is appalled at the person that he is because he is not that person, and the consequence is an anguish condemned to experience, with a kind of ferocious tenacity, an intolerable dualism.

> Can such things be,
> And overcome us like a summer's cloud,
> Without our special wonder? You make me strange
> Even to the disposition that I owe,
> When now I think you can behold such sights,
> And keep the natural ruby of your cheeks,
> When mine is blanch'd with fear. (III.iv.109–15)

The gap between his experience and what the person standing next to him sees, who in this case is even his wife, makes Macbeth a stranger to himself.

From *Hamlet* onward, Shakespeare's tragedies dramatise the tension between what the protagonist feels to be the case and the situation as it is likely to appear to others. 'Does any here know me?': Lear's question—which he trusts, though a little fearfully, to be rhetorical—echoes through the plays (I.iv.226). That tension is intensified by the urgent desire to be witnessed, which exists alongside the anxiety that what the witness sees will be condemning or degrading... or simply, agonisingly, inadequate. And this dynamic between the protagonist and onlookers within the play is reflected also in the relation between the play and ourselves as spectators in the theatre. Part of what Shakespearean tragedy asks us to endure is the terrific co-existence of this double perspective.

Only perhaps in *Troilus and Cressida* is this tension collapsed, and the spectator's cold vision comes close to determining entirely what can be felt. Cassius's thesis, that a person's identity depends on being reflected back to them by others, is elaborately set out more than once in the play, most extensively in Ulysses's argument to Achilles that what Achilles is—a hero, a great warrior—depends entirely on how he is regarded. His essential qualities are not his own but lie in the hands of others:

> No man is the lord of any thing,
> Though in and of him there be much consisting,
> Till he communicate his parts to others;
> Nor doth he of himself know them for aught,
> Till he behold them formed in th' applause
> Where th' are extended. (III.iii.115–20)

The attempt to persuade Achilles back to the battlefield, where his great qualities can be manifested, extends itself into a sinister vision in which only the perpetual and ceaseless performance of Achilles by Achilles can keep him from collapsing into the void that awaits at every moment. Achilles tries to resist this: he has reasons, he says, for his 'privacy'. But in another quietly terrifying speech, Ulysses replies by demolishing the very notion of privacy. His system of surveillance—the 'watchful state'—sees everything, even thoughts before they are uttered.

> The providence that's in a watchful state
> Knows almost every grain of Plutus' gold,
> Finds bottom in th' uncomprehensive depth,
> Keeps place with thought and almost, like the gods,
> Do thoughts unveil in their dumb cradles. (III.iii.196–200)

Disturbingly, Ulysses' thesis is largely confirmed by the mode of the play. The great figures of the *Iliad* are presented to us as narcissists, braggarts and buffoons, in an extreme demonstration of Lamb's anxiety about theatre's power to diminish and degrade. Although we understand this as parodic, it is with an uneasy sense that the parody may have rendered the original inaccessible. Those nearest to the chorus position—Pandarus and Thersites—give commentaries that are routinely cheapening and cynical, and these come close to determining how we too see the action. When Cressida arrives in the Greek camp and finds herself 'kiss'd in general' (IV.v.21), Ulysses declares her to have revealed herself as lascivious and whorish. These are qualities, he says, that could be plainly seen in her body language:

> There's language in her eye, her cheek, her lip,
> Nay, her foot speaks; her wanton spirits look out
> At every joint and motive of her body. (IV.v.55–57)

This is clearly a misogynistic projection, but it nevertheless threatens to be determining; Shakespeare allows only a weak resistant presence to Cressida's subjectivity, to the Cressida projected upon. She has some lines during the kissing scene, though not many, and although in these she seeks to deny the men, she does so in an idiom mirroring theirs: coerced, perhaps, or surely, but also capable of being heard as coquettish. Her love affair with Troilus is likewise desperately short of 'privacy': Pandarus repeatedly interrupts with his mocking, voyeuristic commentary. We, similarly, are often placed as lookers-on who make intimacy impossible, given the peculiarly external mode of apprehension which the verse and the staging promote in this play. In the scene of Cressida's infidelity with Diomede she is little more than a puppet, shrunk down to be so by the commentary of those who are witnessing the scene, for she is being watched by Troilus and Ulysses as one tier of spectators, who are themselves observed by the knowing, all-mocking Thersites. Nothing more wretchedly expresses Cressida's abjection than when she presents herself as others see her, as an all-too-familiar case:

> Troilus, farewell! one eye yet looks on thee,
> But with my heart the other eye doth see.
> Ah, poor our sex! this fault in us I find,
> The error of our eye directs our mind.
> What error leads must err; O then conclude,
> Minds sway'd by eyes are full of turpitude. *Exit*
> THERSITES: A proof of strength she could not publish more,
> Unless she said, "My mind is now turn'd whore." (V.ii.107–14)

There is some ironic bite in her final line: the 'minds swayed by eyes' include those of Thersites and Troilus, her secret watchers in this scene. They too are full of turpitude. But Cressida's trite couplets effectively extinguish her under the weight of generalisation: she is reduced to a typical example of female frailty led astray by the untrustworthiness of the senses.

Beyond the immediate ugliness of such categorisation lies a more troubling possibility: for we may think that *any* attempt to understand a situation of extremity must involve some element of generalisation. To claim to understand your situation is to recognise it as a situation *of a certain kind*; to tell your story is to use words whose appropriateness comes from their history of wider reference, and which associate your experience with that of others. 'I know how you feel' is the sympathetic version; 'we know what you're like', the more hostile. But either way, to thus 'understand' the person in extremity may be to deny or threaten the reality of their being. We have seen how Hamlet flares into anger when Gertrude suggests that his grief for his father is part of common experience. When Ulysses is expounding his argument to Achilles about the power of the observer over the agent, he sums up the implied threat in a single line: 'One touch of nature makes the whole world kin' (III. iii.175). Such homogenising vision disallows all claims to exceptionality.

Only at one moment is Cressida allowed a cry of full resistance, when a sudden fear grips her that she is being seen by Pandarus and Troilus as the hyper-sexualised Cressida of legend. Speaking frankly at last of her love, she reflects that she may have made herself vulnerable by such open speaking, and should be quiet: 'Stop my mouth'. But the men (and perhaps the audience too) hear this as flirtatious, a request to be kissed, on which Troilus duly acts. They are startled by her response:

> My lord, I do beseech you pardon me,
> 'Twas not my purpose thus to beg a kiss.
> I am asham'd. O heavens, what have I done! (III.ii.136–68)

Appalled by how her script has made her appear, she attempts to take her leave, as if to flee from what she will next be made to say and do, betrayed by a self which is not herself.

> TROILUS: What offends you, lady?
> CRESSIDA: Sir, mine own company.

> TROILUS: You cannot shun yourself.
> CRESSIDA: Let me go and try.
>   I have a kind of self resides with you;
>   But an unkind self, that itself will leave
>   To be another's fool. I would be gone. (III.ii.144–50)

One might say that she wishes she could disappear from the stage altogether. For her to express her love is impossible, given how Troilus and Pandarus are responding to her words and actions. But she cannot resist their account by insisting on a different version of herself. 'I am ashamed', she says, and the most she can do is register, for this moment, a radical duality in her being, an infidelity that is in the first place to herself. This will be echoed later in the play when Troilus, witnessing her infidelity with Diomede, insists with a crazed stubbornness, 'This is, and is not, Cressid!', discovering a 'bi-fold authority' at the heart of truth itself, a 'strange nature' that is, he says, both utterly divided and entirely indivisible (V.ii.137–52). Here is the tension between protagonist and witness, expressed as stark and helpless contradiction. But this tension has been partly undermined by the comment of the watching Thersites: 'Will 'a swagger himself out on's own eyes?' (V.ii.136). Surely he can *see* what she is, for he has *seen* the vileness of her betrayal. What better witness than an eye-witness? And the manner of the play largely locks us into this externality of perspective, even if it does so with a certain bitterness or regret. In what may have been a late decision, Shakespeare finishes the play with an epilogue by Pandarus in which we the spectators are addressed as complicit, his accomplices in the 'hold-door trade', the diseased brothel-work which is apparently all that love amounts to (V.x.51). Although this is grotesque enough for us to recognise it as distortion, and theatrical enough for us to recognise it as wilfully adopted, it is still the main perspective which the play offers us; we are given only fragile access to what the situational pressures bearing down on the lovers feel like from the inside.

Here, in this sinister knowingness, is a kind of context for understanding *Coriolanus*. For Coriolanus is strongly averse to being known; he repudiates what Hamlet desires of Horatio, any attempt to report him aright. He vehemently refuses to show his audience his scars, the outward marks of his essential valour. This is not only a matter of his antagonism to the common people, a patrician contempt for politicking.

It is equally strong when he rejects the accolade offered him by the noble Cominius after his heroic exploits at Corioli.

> Pray now, no more. My mother,
> Who has a charter to extol her blood,
> When she does praise me grieves me. I have done
> As you have done—that's what I can; induc'd
> As you have been—that's for my country. (I.ix.13–17)

He refuses to be recognised, to be distinguished; he refuses to accept that he *can* be recognised. When Cominius sweeps this aside and, with the whole army behind him, offers him public recognition of his heroism, 'in sign of what you are' (I.ix.26), his aversion goes beyond ordinary modesty into something strangely extreme:

> MARTIUS: No more, I say! for that I have not wash'd
> My nose that bled, or foil'd some debile wretch -
> Which, without note, here's many else have done -
> You shout me forth
> In acclamations hyperbolical,
> As if I lov'd my little should be dieted
> In praises sauc'd with lies.
> COMINIUS: Too modest are you,
> More cruel to your good report than grateful
> To us that give you truly. (I.ix.47–53)

Do they give him truly? Shakespeare has made it clear that Martius has indeed performed wonders on the field of battle. Cominius's 'good report' is not exaggerated or inaccurate. But for Martius, all report, all claim by others to tell his story, all audience feedback—which, according to Ulysses, *constituted* the hero—threatens the absoluteness of his self-identity, and is therefore to be repudiated.

The essential situation is given in the opening dialogue between the citizens:

> SECOND CITIZEN: Consider you what services he has done for his country?
> FIRST CITIZEN: Very well; and could be content to give him good report for't, but that he pays himself with being proud. (I.i.30–34)

What the citizens understand as Coriolanus' pride is his protection against dependency on 'report'. To accept such dependency is to experience that crisis which Troilus called 'bi-fold authority': this reappears in *Coriolanus* in explicitly political form, in the mixed constitution which allows a measure of power to the Roman people as well as to the patricians. Martius regards this as intolerable:

> It makes the consuls base; and my soul aches
> To know, when two authorities are up,
> Neither supreme, how soon confusion
> May enter 'twixt the gap of both, and take
> The one by th' other. (III.i.108–12)

Such 'double worship', as he calls it, can only lead to 'unstable slightness' and the blurring of all strong purposive action (III.i.142–48); it is better to meet the people's claims with force and ensure the victory of one side or the other. What the play shows with great clarity is how this political argument is continuous with Martius' deep aversion to others' claims to give him recognition. With some part of himself, he is relieved to be exiled from the city; now at last he can become the 'lonely dragon [...] fear'd and talk'd of more than seen' (IV.i.30–1). The warrior who told his applauding comrades that the blood covering his face prevented them from seeing whether he was blushing, takes pleasure in going muffled and incognito to his enemy Aufidius, unrecognised until he very deliberately names himself, in a kind of formal undoing of being named Coriolanus by others. The comical response of Aufidius's servants when they learn the identity of the stranger underlines how unknowable Martius is by those looking on.

> SECOND SERVANT: Nay, I knew by his face that there was something in him. He had, sir, a kind of face, methought—I cannot tell how to term it.
> FIRST SERVANT: He had so, looking as it were—Would I were hang'd but I thought there was more in him than I could think. (IV.v.154–59)

Menenius is the man who loves to tell his story, to bear witness to his greatness as 'the book of his good acts' (V.ii.15), but his stories of his hero are dismissed by the Volscian sentry as mere lies, and before the end of the play Coriolanus has repudiated Menenius too.

At times in this play, it seems that the terrific tension between protagonist and witness that drives so much Shakespearean tragedy can no longer be sustained. (*Coriolanus* is probably the last of the tragedies to be written.) In which case, rather than submit to the bottomless knowingness of *Troilus and Cressida*, Coriolanus will go the other way, maintaining a kind of inaccessibility, a privacy beyond the reach of any 'watchful state'. Although a figure of complex and subtle psychology, the verse does not allow us to be intimate with him, to identify in any sustained way with what he is feeling, as we can with Shakespeare's other protagonists. Significantly, the play is the least popular of all the great tragedies; it refuses to show us the wounds and scars that we are hungry to see. 'I banish you', says Martius to Rome—and some part of what is banished are the normal powers of the Shakespearean audience, for although we may be struck and fascinated by Coriolanus, we are never inward with the movements of his mind as we are with Hamlet or Othello or Macbeth. The crisis with his mother, when his claim to an absolute independence collapses, and strange tears rise within him, is marked by silence: his acknowledgement of human connection, though in one sense witnessed by the many who are on stage at this moment, finds no adequate reflection in anyone's words. Martius seeks for it in Aufidius, as if to push back against the derision of the onlooking gods:

> Now, good Aufidius,
> Were you in my stead, would you have heard
> A mother less? or granted less, Aufidius? (V.iii.191–93)

'I was mov'd withal' is Aufidius's dry reply, but we know that he is already calculating Martius's downfall. Martius then turns to the embassy, and assures them they will 'bear / A better witness back than words' to Rome (V.iii.204): that is, a peace treaty—but such a document can hardly express what has just happened within him, though it may be its consequence.

The peculiar pathos of Martius's estrangement is carried forward into the muted nature of the conclusion. The peace treaty with Rome has been signed, the city is saved and rejoices, and uniquely in the tragedies the death of the protagonist makes no difference to anything. Once more, now in Corioli as before in the market-place in Rome, Martius is easily provoked into antagonising those he might have placated. The hostile witness that Aufidius bears—calling him 'traitor' and 'boy of tears' (V.vi.84, 91)—allows no counterstatement of what it was that happened within Martius as he wept at the embassy. 'Boy of tears' classifies Martius as an only-too-intelligible case, a mummy's boy, in an insult which denies the strangeness of Martius's experience as he wept.

In response, Martius repudiates 'boy' with the re-assertion of himself as the hero who defeated the city, maker of orphans and widows, destroyer of families, *the enemy whom no city can make welcome.*

> Cut me to pieces, Volsces, men and lads,
> Stain all your edges on me. "Boy," false hound!
> If you have writ your annals true, 'tis there
> That, like an eagle in a dove-cote, I
> Flutter'd your Volscians in Corioles.
> Alone I did it. "Boy"! (V.vi.111–16)

Crucially, he acted not with others, not as the instrument of Rome, but as a singular individual. 'Alone I did it.' This, 'if you have writ your annals true', is the only story that can be told about him.

Heroes and megastars: seeing double

There is a modern play by Martin Crimp, *Attempts on her Life* (1997), which brilliantly reflects on the distance between the tragic figure and how they may be reported. The play consists of what Crimp calls '17 scenarios for the theatre'. Each scenario is a short piece, usually a dialogue or monologue, occasionally written for several speakers. No stage action is indicated; the pieces are written for anonymous voices, which Crimp specifies should 'reflect the composition of the world beyond the theatre'.[12] Each refers to a character, Anne, whom we never see or hear from. Each suggests something about her, or gives a fragmentary story; there are echoes and connections between pieces, but also a good deal of discontinuity. One recurrent suggestion is that she is involved in committing a terrorist outrage, in revolt against her society. Another suggestion is that she has repeatedly attempted and/ or committed suicide. Another is that she is a victim of the devastation inflicted in or upon some poor and undeveloped country. Another is that she is involved in pornography. Another puts her in the context of a sexual affair; another, that she is possessed by aliens. Her politics, where these appear, usually seem to be radically left-wing; but in at least one scenario her sympathies are with the extreme far right. Her name varies

---

12 Martin Crimp, *Attempts on Her Life* (London: Faber & Faber, 2007), preliminary unnumbered pages.

slightly: Annie and Anya as well as Ann(e), and sometimes she is not named at all, but simply referred to as 'she'.

The writing swings continually between suggesting reference to a real person and real events, and the discussion of a hypothetical personality or story, constructed as if for a film script or media campaign. In keeping with this second possibility, the voices are notably detached and shallow, continually running to stereotype and cliché. They stand in discomforting relation to the jagged evocations of real violence, trauma, and atrocity that repeatedly pierce this surface, only to be flattened into banality by the dominant idiom.

These scenarios tell stories about a tragedy—plural, inconsistent, and fragmentary stories. They take to an extreme the inadequacy of the attempts by some Greek choruses, and many Shakespearean onlookers, to comprehend the protagonist and the meaning of their fate. They give us, so to speak, the chorus without the protagonist—as if the obtuseness of society's means of understanding had rendered the protagonist invisible. In some ways the piece is a subversion of classic tragedy, pre-empting and emptying out what are traditionally understood as its attractions and consolations. The affirmation of the heroic becomes the construction of celebrity; the spectacle of violence is implicated in pornography; and the classic responses of sympathy and recognition are here merely the process by which the story of trauma 'strangely restores—I think it does—yes—our faith in ourselves', with palpable complacency.[13] Consumerist values are everywhere; the title 'attempts on her life' merges the violence done to Anne with her commodification in art—or in marketing.

> The camera *loves* you.
> The camera *loves* you.
> The camera *loves* you.
>
> We *need* to sympathise
> We *need* to empathise
> We *need* to advertise
> We *need* to realise
> We are the good guys
> We are the good guys

---

13 Ibid., p.22.

> We need to feel
> what we're seeing is real
> It isn't just acting
> it's far more exacting
> than acting
> We're talking reality
> We're talking humanity
> We're talking of a plan to be
> OVERWHELMED by the sheer totality
> and utterly believable three-dimensionality
> THREE-DIMENSIONALITY
> Of all the things that Anne can be
> ALL THE THINGS THAT ANNE CAN BE
>
> What's Hecuba to him or he to Hecuba?
> A megastar
> A MEGASTAR[14]

In this astringent parody of witness response, Crimp challenges the audience of tragedy as to their motives and their pleasures; or at the least he questions how much of the classic model can survive in the modern world.

Yet the work has two foci: not only these badly flawed witnesses, but also Anne's inaccessibility by any of these scenarios, an inaccessibility that preserves her possible reality.

> Some of the strange things she says to her Mum and Dad as a child: 'I feel like a screen.' [...] She says she's not a real character, not a real character like you get in a book or on TV, but a *lack* of character, an *absence* she calls it, doesn't she, of character.[15]

Perhaps Anne exists. Or perhaps, as composite terrorist, victim, and celebrity, she is nothing more than the construction of our needs and fantasies (perhaps there are no tragic heroes outside fictions). But in any case, at several moments the play sufficiently reminds us of the world of real suffering and real atrocity, even if that awareness turns to cliché in the moment of its articulation. As well as subverting tragedy, Crimp's work also connects with the authentic power of tragedy, the sense that the extremity of the pain it refers to can best be apprehended precisely

---

14 Ibid., p.25.
15 Ibid., pp.30–31.

in the failure of articulation, the gap between protagonist and chorus, the gap between the pain and the story told about it. Lavinia drew back; Cressida tried to leave; Coriolanus fell silent; Anne has evaded our gaze altogether. Yet there is no escape, while the play goes on. In one brilliantly self-referential scenario, we seem to hear two voices at an art gallery, discussing an exhibition or installation.

> — What we see here are various objects associated with the artist's attempts to kill herself over the past few months. [...] Isn't she saying, 'I don't want your help'? Isn't she saying, 'Your help oppresses me'? Isn't she saying the only way to avoid being a victim of the patriarchal structures of late twentieth-century capitalism is to *become her own victim*? Isn't that the true meaning of these attempts on her life?
>
> — Her own victim—that's fascinating.[16]

The paradox here is also that in which Coriolanus is caught: when everyone is looking at you and talking about you, shunning report becomes a kind of pride, trying to disappear becomes a fascinating spectacle.

If Crimp's voices sound glib and obtuse, we can also hear that obtuseness as strategic: a busy, premature processing which keeps at bay an understanding that would be difficult to bear. The imperfectness of witness discussed in this chapter can be understood not only as obtuseness but also as denial or defence. Dori Laub worked as a therapist with the survivors of trauma, in particular first- and second-generation survivors of the Holocaust. He listed a range of defences which the listener is liable to employ in order to 'maintain a state of safety', protecting himself from 'the intensity of the flood of affect that, through the testimony, comes to be directed toward him'. I quote three items from Laub's longer list:

> A sense of outrage and of anger, unwittingly directed against the victim [...] We are torn apart by the inadequacy of our ability to properly respond, and inadvertently wish for the illness to be the patient's responsibility and wrongdoing.
>
> A flood of awe and fear; we endow the survivor with a kind of sanctity, both to pay our tribute to him and to keep him at a distance, to avoid the intimacy entailed in knowing.

---

16 Ibid., pp.51, 55.

> Hyperemotionally which superficially looks like compassion and caring. The testifier is simply flooded, drowned and lost in the listener's defensive affectivity.[17]

There is, I need hardly say, a great distance between the real encounters that Laub is referring to and the much safer situation of the theatre spectator or reader. Nevertheless, these 'listening defences' suggest parallels with the ways that we, as audience and as readers, may respond to tragic drama, as well as with the responses of witness-figures within the plays. With regard to the 'wish for the illness to be the patient's responsibility and wrongdoing', the next chapter will discuss accounts of tragedy organised around the idea of a 'tragic flaw'. More relevant to the discussion at this point is the idea that 'a flood of awe and fear', endowing the suffering figure 'with a kind of sanctity', might be a strategy of avoidance rather than a mode of comprehension. This could be a description of many traditional readings of Shakespearean tragedy that have now come to seem problematic: yet something like 'awe and fear' seem inescapably necessary if we are not to be the kind of reductive witnesses who understand the action in all-too-familiar terms. So how might drama walk this tightrope, and find its way to a witnessing that affirms the specialness of the protagonist's experience without a defensive or self-serving glamourising or 'sanctifying' of their actions or their plight?

The voices in one of Crimp's scenarios salute Hecuba, and by implication Hamlet too, as a 'megastar', in an emphatic expression of that fascination with the protagonist that runs through all of them. This is the cheap language of celebrity, the 'acclamations hyperbolical' that Coriolanus despises. Yet we may recognise in the cry of 'megastar' the parody of a response to tragedy not easily dismissed: the account of the protagonist as *heroic*. The term is a tricky one, and potentially misleading. A tragic figure need not be admirable in any ordinary sense of the word. They may commit appalling acts, and strike us as themselves appalling. Or they may be reduced by suffering to the most wretched condition. But there is in their extremity a specialness that stands outside common practice and common understanding, and encountering this feels obscurely valuable or necessary or compelling. Such encounter is

---

17 Dori Laub, 'Bearing Witness, or the Vicissitudes of Listening', in *Testimony: Crises of Witnessing in Literature, Psychoanalysis and History* (New York and London: Routledge, 1992), pp.72–73.

fundamental to Greek tragedy, where a modern civic society gathered to watch actions from the archaic world of heroes. This seems to have been regarded as crucial to the good functioning of Athenian society, yet crucial because those heroes were so removed from their democratic audience. And yet not utterly removed: for those heroic figures often find themselves entangled in circumstances that are familiarly civic or domestic. Oedipus and Creon have citizens to deal with. Orestes travels from the world of Homer to the Athenian law-court. The great Heracles comes home from his mythic labours to a very domestic marriage and an anxious wife. Beneath what you might call these anachronisms or incongruities of plot lies the structural truth that it is civic Athens that is performing the heroic world to itself, as theatre. It seems to be crucial to a certain kind of tragic effect that the heroic and the familiar worlds are absolutely distinct—the heroic is for real—*and* that they are not, that they are subtly or catastrophically entangled with one another. In this area tragic theatre confers a kind of double vision, reflected in that 'double worship' that Coriolanus so detests as jeopardising the absoluteness of aristocratic rule, or in that way of seeing double which Troilus madly insists upon with regard to Cressida, or in the two very different fathers who call Hamlet their son. Shakespearean theatre has a much less secure anchorage in an heroic world than the Greek, and the viability of the heroic is just what is at stake in many of the passages discussed in this chapter. Shakespeare's lookers-on tend to dismiss exceptionality as delusion—Antony is 'a strumpet's fool', Macbeth is a 'dwarfish thief'—and not without plausibility; yet the plays register the burning anguish, the horror, generated by such dismissal. Very often, Shakespearean tragedy involves a convulsive reaction against the post-heroic world in which it finds itself, and against those witnesses who find the protagonist to belong ultimately and entirely to that world.

Fantasising the heroic: *The Wild Duck* and *The Master Builder*

That the viability of the heroic is at stake in Shakespeare is not difficult to see: his protagonists are generally high-status individuals, something which puts the question of their specialness directly into play. In modern drama that deals with the contemporary world, tragedy may seem to have passed altogether into the realm of common life; Arthur Miller's *Death of a Salesman* is sometimes cited as the paradigmatic case. Yet Miller's play still has at its heart Willy Loman's unquenchable need to see himself and his family as heroic beings, and his unbearable anguish when that need goes unsupported. The battling life of a successful travelling salesman is the screen onto which Willy projects the heroic; the great speech describing Dave Singleman's funeral, to which people came from all over the country, casts him as a Homeric hero, a modern-day Hector or Achilles, whose greatness was emphatically recognised and honoured by others. He was, in the desperately inadequate phrase that Willy uses to express his heart's desire, 'well liked'.[18] But no-one sees Willy and his sons as megastars, and in an external world that gives no support to his vision, Willy's growing inability to continue living in denial is for him an overwhelming threat and terror. The unbearable witness, the person whose presence he cannot endure for long, is his son Biff, who witnessed the shame of his father's hotel-room infidelity and carries the damage done by that moment through his own life of failure. This above all is the moment of being seen which Willy cannot bear steadily to hold in mind, or steadily to remember may be in Biff's mind.

The play, however, performs its own act of bearing witness. Miller's working title was *Inside His Head*, and the play stages Willy's inner world of fragmented memories and flashbacks as co-present with the external world; it grants them, at moments, *the same level of theatrical reality*. This does not affirm Willy as heroic, but it does call into question the hegemony of the reality principle, which would relegate Willy's inner life to the status of delusion or self-deception. The figures both of his shame and of the possibility of glory (his wildly successful and assured brother Ben) haunt the stage, as real to us as they are to him, and we recognise feelingly how accepting the terms of the external world might not an option.

Nevertheless, there is no witness figure *within* the play who can see those figures, or can tell a story of Willy that comprehends this inner life. His wife sees his fragility, and loves and respects him, but cannot enter into the intensity of his need; his son Biff urges him at the climax to throw the heroic story away, to accept the reality that they are a

---

18   Arthur Miller, *Death of a Salesman* (London: Penguin, 1961), pp.25, 38, 67.

'dime-a-dozen' family, that their story is a common one.[19] But this fails to enter into what is inside Willy's head, and marks him as peculiarly and irrevocably isolated. The desolation he inhabits is so extreme that the discovery that Biff loves him *in reality* comes as a bewildering, ultimately unbearable revelation.

Miller admired Ibsen, and *Death of a Salesman* owes a good deal to the concept of the 'life-lie' which Ibsen dramatises in *The Wild Duck*. This is the term given in that play to the individual's illusion of specialness, of possessing a meaningful destiny, which human frailty makes necessary. But whereas Willy gets no support from others for his belief that his and his sons' life is or ought to be heroic, Ibsen envisages a witness that affirms the tragic figure's exceptionality—and by so doing, brings their inner life more fully and dangerously into being. In *The Wild Duck*, Gregers Werle is accused by the disillusioned and pragmatic Dr Relling of living in 'a perpetual delirium of hero-worship. You've always got to have something outside yourself that you can idolize.'[20] Gregers constructs a scenario about Hjalmar Ekdal: Hjalmar's discovery that his life has been built upon a lie will set him free to embrace the truth with a new nobility of spirit. But when Gregers attempts to realise this scenario, nothing of the sort happens; Hjalmar is not the man that Gregers needs him to be, but resents the loss of his protective fiction, and responds with petty viciousness. The situation becomes toxic. Gregers, however, then tries out another story, that Hjalmar's daughter Hedvig can transform the situation by sacrificing the wild duck, her beloved pet. This will demonstrate the purity of her love and devotion to her father.

> If only your eyes could be opened to what really matters in life! If only you had the courage to make your sacrifice truly and joyfully, you'd see— he'd come back to you! But I still believe in you, Hedvig. I believe in you.[21]

But the result is disaster: Hedvig takes this notion of sacrifice in a much deeper sense, and kills herself.

Gregers' insistence on 'believing in' others, appointing them to heroic roles, is catastrophic. Ibsen also shows it to be pathological, rooted in the

---

19 Ibid., p.105.
20 Henrik Ibsen, 'The Wild Duck', in *Plays: One. Ghosts, The Wild Duck, The Master Builder*, trans. by Michael Meyer (London: Eyre Methuen, 1980), p.202.
21 Ibid., pp.203–204.

circumstances of Gregers' upbringing and the inheritance of guilt that he carries, which have left him with an overwhelming need to repudiate his father's cynical pragmatism. (*Hamlet* lurks in the background of the play.) His heroising impulse is treated, for the most part, with sardonic irony; for the most part, the unheroic banality of life is asserted as the reality principle that establishes the world of the play. Despite its shattering outcome, Ibsen asked that it should be played as tragicomedy.

However, there are some passages in the play which complicate that account; in these, the reality principle appears less than sovereign. The one I want to look at concerns the Ekdals' loft or attic. This is once or twice made dimly visible at the back of the stage, when the doors to it are opened, but we know throughout that it is there, and it is where Hedvig kills herself at the end. It is, we gather, a space of the imagination, containing old books, colouring pencils, stopped clocks, miscellaneous objects left by a sea captain called the Flying Dutchman.[22] It also somehow contains enough wildlife and greenery to constitute a miniature forest in which the grandfather Ekdal can go 'hunting', returning to his lost youth, in imitation of the real experiences of which life has since deprived him. Both he and Hjalmar go there to retreat from the pressure of any real responsibilities, as a comforting play area in which to pass the time. And it is where Hedvig keeps her wild duck. The loft comes up in a crucial conversation between her and Gregers. Remembering the time when the wild duck (now tame) was free, Gregers uses a highly poetic phrase.

> GREGERS: And she has been down to the bottom of the vasty deep.
>
> HEDVIG: (*glances quickly at him and represses a smile*). Why do you say 'the vasty deep'?
>
> GREGERS: What should I have said?
>
> HEDVIG: You could have said 'the sea bed', or just 'the bottom of the sea'.
>
> GREGERS: Oh, why can't I say 'the vasty deep'?
>
> HEDVIG: Yes, but it always sounds so odd to me when other people talk about 'the vasty deep'.

---

22 In the versions of the legend by Heine and Wagner, the ship's captain can only be redeemed from the curse by a woman's devotion—which involves, in Wagner, her suicide for his sake.

GREGERS: Why? Tell me.

HEDVIG: No, I won't. It's silly.

GREGERS: Not at all. Tell me now, why did you smile?

HEDVIG: It's because if I suddenly—without thinking—remember what's in there, I always think of it all as being 'the vasty deep'. But that's just silly.

GREGERS: No, you mustn't say that.

HEDVIG: Well, it's only a loft.

GREGERS: (*looks hard at her*). Are you sure?

HEDVIG: (*astonished*). That it's only a loft?

GREGERS: Yes. You are quite certain about that?

> *HEDVIG stares silently at him, open-mouthed.*[23]

Although she does not know it, Hedvig may be Gregers's half-sister; there is a sense of uncanny connection between them. Hedvig smiles because Gregers speaks out loud a phrase which she often has in her mind, a poetic phrase for an imaginative space, which figures the attic as a great expanse of unbounded sea, of unsounded depth. Hedvig has a rich imaginative life, she can see 'in a flash' the loft as something quite other than it appears, but she supposes there is a clear divide between that and the real, external world of 'other people'. Gregers has now crossed that divide, giving voice to her inner life. *It always sounds so odd to me when other people talk about 'the vasty deep'*. And he goes on to further challenge that divide, querying her common-sense statement that the loft is 'only a loft', or more precisely querying that she really means that when she says it. This strikes Hedvig very strongly. She does not, I take it, think that Gregers is having a psychotic attack. She is astonished because he has recognised something in her which she did not suppose could be recognised by another person, thereby making it newly or differently real. This is that area of the psyche in which our imaginative life constitutes, for us, reality—an area which the loft itself already loosely symbolises. The external reality-principle according to which the loft is only a loft is loosened; the symbolic world participates in reality, rather than being subject to it.

---

23   Ibid., pp.163–164.

To see others in this way is, we know, part of Gregers' pathology. He will use (and abuse) Hedvig as a symbolic figure, a figure of transformative power, in the redemption story that he is constructing.[24] But Ibsen makes us alive not only to Gregers' dubious motives but also to the energies which he releases. If the loft is not only a loft, if other people can validate what is in Hedvig's mind, if the symbolic has purchase on external reality, then the shabby actuality of the Edkal household might accommodate an act of sacrifice that possessed actual transformative power.

> GREGERS: Suppose you sacrificed for him the most precious of your possessions—the thing you love most dearly?
>
> HEDVIG: Do you think that would help?
>
> GREGERS: Try it, Hedvig.
>
> HEDVIG: (*quietly, her eyes aglow*). Yes, I will try it.[25]

The mode of *The Wild Duck* is almost entirely naturalistic—naturalism proclaiming, in Ibsen, the sovereignty of the familiar, external, social world. But its naturalism is haunted, albeit faintly, by the symbolic. This is most evidently so with regard to the Ekdals' loft. The doors to this space at the back of the playing area are only occasionally opened to us, and Ibsen's directions require, suggestively, that it extends back beyond what can be seen. How *can* it contain all that we are told it does, the wildlife and the forest, in however miniature a form? We are bound, I think, to entertain some idea of it as an alternative reality, a resource of the psyche, symbolically potent. When it becomes clear that Hedvig has killed herself in that space, the grandfather says: 'The forest has taken its revenge.'[26] An offence against the forest (illegal forestry work) is the source of the family's troubles, and the grandfather's resonant line invokes a cosmos like that of the *Oresteia*, in which larger powers work themselves out through human actions. In the theatre, the line generates uncertainty, perhaps anxiety, over how to hear such a story. We receive it largely, perhaps, as a piece of weak superstition, a painful attempt to fend off the wretchedness and pointlessness of the child's death by investing it in 'a flood of awe and fear', in Dori Laub's terms. Yet we may also feel something extraordinary in Hedvig's act, an act that no

---

24 Hedda's attempted use of Loevborg in *Hedda Gabler* is broadly parallel.
25 Ibsen, 'The Wild Duck', p.197.
26 Ibid., p.214.

other character in the play could have been capable of, which flows from her participation in that symbolic plane into which Gregers drew her when he gave her inner fantasy life external validation. Perhaps the net effect is of embarrassment or strain, whereby the inappropriateness of storying Hedvig's death as the product of larger forces, as if it existed on the plane of grand tragedy, has to be confessed in order that such an account may nevertheless be entertained.

Eight years later, Ibsen wrote *The Master Builder*. Like *The Wild Duck*, this play has a proactive witness-figure who tells a story designed to bring heroic action into being, thereby creating a tragedy. But in the later play this has a rather different effect, and I want to bring out the contrast as well as the parallel. At the centre of the play is the relationship between Hilde and Solness, the master builder of the title. Solness is the protagonist of the play, a man of great power in his profession, who has risen to the top by means of the misfortunes of others. But this is for him a fearful thing, since he believes or half-believes that his desires are able magically to produce real effects; as he puts it, there is 'troll' in him 'that calls to the powers outside'.[27] His pre-eminence is therefore deeply involved in guilt. When the play opens, Solness is fearful that his day as the master builder is nearly over, and that youth will 'come and bang on that door' to displace him.[28] As he utters that line, there is a banging on the door, and a young woman enters. The patness of this suggests that the action of the play may be responsive to Solness's mental state, although that very patness registers the strain this places on naturalism—for the effect in the theatre, if not uncanny, would be awkwardly melodramatic.

The young woman is Hilde Wangel, who was a girl ten years previously when Solness came to her village to build the church steeple and spectacularly climbed to the top to lay a garland upon it. She arrives now like a buried memory or fantasy, to tell Solness the story of what happened then.

> HILDE: It was so frightfully exciting and marvellous. I'd never imagined there could be a master builder anywhere in the world who could build such an enormously high tower! And then to see you standing there

---

27 Henrik Ibsen, 'The Master Builder', in *Plays: One. Ghosts, The Wild Duck, The Master Builder*, trans. by Michael Meyer (London: Eyre Methuen, 1980), p.292.
28 Ibid., p.260.

yourself, right up at the top! And you weren't at all giddy. That was the thing that—that made me feel giddy.

SOLNESS: What made you so sure I wasn't ——?

HILDE: Don't be silly! I knew it—in here. Otherwise, how could you have stood up there singing?

SOLNESS: (*stares at her, amazed*). Singing? Did I sing?

HILDE: You certainly did.

SOLNESS: (*shakes his head*). I've never sung a note in my life.

HILDE: Well, you sang then. It sounded like harps in the air.

SOLNESS: (*thoughtfully*). This is most extraordinary.

HILDE: (*looks at him silently for a moment, then says softly*). But it was afterwards that the real thing happened. […] You took me in your arms and kissed me, Mr Solness.

SOLNESS: (*gets up from his chair, his mouth open*). I did?

HILDE: Yes, you did. You took me in both your arms and bent me backwards and kissed me. Many, many times.[29]

A young woman passionately admiring an elderly man: the erotic charge already present at the start of this exchange confirms Hilde as the witness that the protagonist desires, the witness who tells the story of his greatness, and does so out of an intimate understanding. Hilde *knew* what Solness was feeling, 'in here'. As her story goes on, it becomes more questionable, yet also gets a degree of corroboration. For although Solness has never sung a note in his life, her claim gives him pause because what he actually did that day up at the top of the tower was to accuse and defy God—an extraordinary act indeed, which Hilde seems to be describing in her own way. His passionate kissing of her extends that sense of thrillingly audacious transgression into other terms. Solness has no memory of the kissing, and never positively agrees that it was so, but neither does he much dispute her story, and as the play goes on he behaves as if it were true. The play asks us not so much to choose between Hilde as fantasist and Solness as child abuser, as to see how Hilde's story has a performative effect, making real to Solness fears and desires that are already or now become aspects of his being.

---

29 Ibid., pp.266–267.

Hilde's story continues with the claim that after kissing her, Solness promised that after ten years he would present her with a kingdom. Now the ten years are up, and like a figure from fairy-tale she has come to reclaim that promise. What this seems to mean, we discover as the play goes on, is that he should assert himself once more as the heroic figure that he was and is to her. Since that day in the past when he defied God, Solness has never again climbed so high. He is now afraid of heights, a fearful and weary man, entangled in arrangements made to defend his pre-eminence against rivals, guilty about the cost of his success for others, and anxious whether the powers who wait upon him, as he half-believes, are for good or evil. What Hilde requires of him is that he rise above all such fears and scruples and act according to the magnificence of his true desire, under her influence and inspiration, and with her at his side. It is very much the same challenge that Lady Macbeth makes to her husband: 'Art thou afeard / To be the same in thine own act and valour / As thou art in desire?' (I.vii.39–41). What this would mean for Solness in practice is left unspecified; the demand seems barely compatible with the practical world, but is expressed in largely metaphorical terms. Leaving his wife to begin an affair with Hilde is loosely implied, but all is summed up in the idea that he will once more climb high, to the top of the steeple that he has just finished building. This is a feat that no-one else believes he could or should undertake, but at the end of the play, to everyone's amazement and Hilde's rapture, he achieves it—and then, giddy after all, falls to his death. Hilde's intervention in his life has effected both his triumph and his destruction.

That intervention consisted of a particular kind of witnessing. Hilde tells Solness his story—the story of a great man raised above the ordinary compromises of living in the world, whose desires and actions have special potency, able to transform or set aside the normal conditions of life. His anxiety that his secret desires have real effects—what Freud was to call 'the omnipotence of thoughts and wishes'[30]—is in a certain sense made good by her uncanny arrival. She recognises and speaks to his inner life as no-one else can, making it real to him, giving his secret fears and fantasies a place in the world. Gregers in *The Wild Duck* was a very

---

30 Sigmund Freud, 'The "Uncanny"', trans. by James Strachey, in *Art and Literature*, ed. by Albert Dickson, Penguin Freud Library, vol. XIV (London: Penguin, 1985), p.369.

different figure, but there is a structural parallel: the witness or story-maker, newly arrived, who has uncanny access to the protagonist's inner imaginative life, and through that act of recognition encourages that life to enter the action. 'I believe in you', Gregers says to Hedvig,[31] urging her to her great act, and Hilde likewise dangerously believes in Solness:

> SOLNESS: (*angrily*). You must believe in me unquestioningly.
>
> HILDE: I have believed in you for ten years. Unquestioningly.
>
> SOLNESS: You must go on believing in me.
>
> HILDE: Then let me see you stand up there, high and free!
>
> SOLNESS: (*heavily*). Oh, Hilde. One can't do things like that every day.
>
> HILDE: (*passionately*). But I want you to! I want you do! (*Pleadingly.*) Just once more, master builder! Do the impossible again![32]

These witnesses take a secret, symbolic, imaginative world across the boundary into expression, and thereby release great energies and great dangers.

This, I want to suggest, is akin to what the tragic drama itself is doing. But how it does this is various, and this is where the contrast between *The Wild Duck* and *The Master Builder* is helpful to notice. The later play is notably more hospitable to the reality of the symbolic. In *The Wild Duck* we are primarily alive to the destructiveness of what Gregers is doing, and to the large element of delusion and projection in his dealings with Hedvig. The reality of the external, social world is dominant; it is relatively faintly that we register the uncanniness of his connection with Hedvig, and imagine the possibility of an efficacious rite of sacrifice. In *The Master Builder*, the mode of the play is tilted more towards the symbolic. True, a 'realistic' reading is still available, and is kept in view throughout. By such a reading, Solness is delusional, on the verge of mental breakdown (his wife sees him that way, and has called in a doctor), and Hilde is a stalker who preys on his guilt and insecurity for her own warped gratification. But in dramatic tension with that reading is our sense of Hilde as an agent of revelation, whose rapport with Solness exists on a plane to which the play is willing to grant its own reality. The symbolic meaning which they find in the activity of

---

31 Ibsen, 'The Wild Duck', p.204.
32 Ibsen, 'The Master Builder', p.315.

building and climbing is one which the play is willing to support. When they rapturously speak of building together 'a castle in the air—built on a true foundation',[33] this strikes us as not (or not only) vacuous but as curiously self-aware in its endeavour to establish a reality other than the material. The overreaching folly of Solness's final climb, pragmatically regarded, is at least balanced by the symbolic reality of his achievement. Hilde's influence as proactive witness remains infinitely ambivalent.

Antony and Cleopatra

In conclusion, I want to turn to Shakespeare's *Antony and Cleopatra,* as a play much concerned with the dynamics of reporting and witnessing. It is flooded with messengers and other figures, minor and major, who carry report; a rapid survey yields some twenty-five instances. This is a play in which lives and actions are hugely subject to mediation and representation, as almost the primary means by which they are communicated and known. Antony and Cleopatra are assuredly 'megastars', figures who challenge ordinary measures of what is real or possible: but how substantially? The accounts given within the play stretch across the whole spectrum of possibility.

One large section of these are reports to Rome or by Romans of the goings-on in Egypt, and their tenor is often derogatory. I mentioned earlier the Roman soldiers at the start of the play who see Antony as 'a strumpet's fool' (I.i.13). Letters that come to Caesar from Alexandria speak of Antony's degraded, 'womanly' behaviour, 'th' abstract of all faults / That all men follow', drunk at noon, sporting 'with knaves that smells of sweat', giving away 'a kingdom for a mirth', neglecting his political responsibilities while tumbling on the bed of Ptolemy (I.iv.7–21). While these reports may suggest the limitations of the reporters, taken together they suggest that to see Antony and Cleopatra objectively, as they 'really' are, is to see them as figures of folly, decadence, and self-deception, subject to a degrading infatuation. Such reports partake of that tendency discussed during much of this chapter, according to which the witness, the one who sees, is a threatening figure who disallows some crucial aspect of the protagonist's experience. Their testimony

---

33   Ibid., p.316, repeating what was said earlier on p.308.

is something the protagonist must shun or deny if they are to protect themselves against disaster.

But the reports are many, and they are various. The stream of Roman reports indicting the lovers for their poor behaviour is immensely counterbalanced by Enobarbus' wonderful account of their first meeting at Cydnus. His interlocutors have already heard reports which, if they do not know whether entirely to believe, make them eager to hear more. 'There she appear'd indeed; or my reporter devis'd well for her', says Agrippa (II.ii.188–89). 'I will tell you', responds Enobarbus, and this shrewd and sceptical soldier unfolds an account that expresses rapture in the telling, and holds his listeners likewise rapt. Part of the magic of the speech is that it does not offer to describe Cleopatra at all, but speaks rather of her effect on all around her, including on Enobarbus himself, so that it becomes self-validating: her influence at Cydnus— on the elements, on Antony, on the people of the city—continues now, palpably, for as long as Enobarbus speaks. By the time we get to 'Age cannot wither her, nor custom stale / Her infinite variety' (II.ii.234–5), we know the experience of feeling that counter-rational claim to be true (which is not quite the same as knowing or believing that it is true).

Similarly contrasting accounts are given of Antony—emasculated, petty, and insecure, but also magnificent, generous in spirit, superlatively manly. 'Your emperor / Continues still a Jove', the Roman soldier tells Enobarbus, after Antony's messenger has brought Enobarbus's treasure after him (IV.vi.27–28). The continuing co-existence of these divergent reports tends to erode the possibility of any settled single account—like 'the swan's down feather, / That stands upon the swell at the full of tide, / And neither way inclines' (III.ii.48–50), or, more sourly, like how the 'vagabond flag upon the stream / Goes to and back, lackeying the varying tide, / To rot itself with motion' (I.iv.45–47).

If we try to get *behind* report to what is actually the case, we are likely to find support for both generous and derogatory accounts, to the point of contradiction or paradox, or else a void with regard to the intentionality or internal essence that might settle matters. Did Antony mean to leave Octavia even while he made his assurances to her? What did Cleopatra mean by her warm reception of Thidias, who came to win her from Antony, or by holding back half her treasure from Caesar's audit, as if hoping for a future after Antony's death? The play is carefully blank about such moments. This goes with a recurrent effect of *non sequitur*, as Antony flicks from conviction of his betrayal by Cleopatra to absolute trust in their love (and back again), or Cleopatra flicks from pettiness to majesty (and back again). Time, we may feel, does not run sequentially and coherently in the area of Egyptian love, but offers us rather a sublime inconsequentiality: so that even the loss of empire may seem of little consequence. Another part of this is the recurrent motif of finding that one regrets or deplores what one has desired or intended. Thus, Antony finds he now regrets the death of his troublesome wife Fulvia, just as he wept, it seems, over the death of Brutus; thus Caesar himself weeps, it seems, at the death of Antony which he has himself brought to pass. This grieving over the fulfilment of one's desire will be inverted insofar as Cleopatra succeeds in celebrating disaster as a triumph, making of desolation 'a better life' (V.ii.2). It is Cleopatra who stands closest to the epicentre of this mutability, both as the figure of whom we most wish to give divergent accounts, and as the figure most at home with 'infinite variety'. Hence, she can say this about the newly-married Antony:

> Let him forever go—let him not, Charmian—
> Though he be painted one way like a Gorgon,
> The other way's a Mars. (II.v.115–17)

Even here, and even to her, what Antony is depends on how he is painted. Cleopatra chooses the Mars over the Gorgon, but knows that both ways of viewing the painting are equally possible.

If such multiplicity robs report of its authority, it paradoxically enhances its significance. The protagonists' fluidity (Cleopatra) or more jagged oscillations (Antony) come to seem as much a function as a cause of the indeterminacy of report. It is no unusual thing for characters in Shakespeare to be sensitive to their reputation, but it is remarkable how readily the main characters in this play think of their actions as something to be witnessed, and as incomplete until they are witnessed. They play to an audience, actual or imagined. At the opening, when Antony affirms the nobleness of their love, he immediately adds

> in which I bind,
> On pain of punishment, the world to weet
> We stand up peerless. (I.i.38–40)

This imagining of or calling for witness is a recurrent reflex in how the major characters understand themselves. When Antony is trying to persuade Cleopatra to assent to his leaving, he puts it like this:

> Give true evidence to his love, which stands
> An honourable trial. (I.iii.74–75)

This casts her response to him as testimony at the trial that will determine what his love is. Cleopatra—the already legendary Cleopatra—is never alone on stage, and is always aware of eyes upon her, even or especially at moments of intense feeling. When she hears of Antony's marriage, this is her instant and utterly characteristic response: 'I am pale, Charmian' (II.v.58–59). Even Enobarbus hopes that by remaining loyal to Antony he will earn 'a place i' th' story' (III.xiii.46). Later, filled with remorse at his betrayal and preparing for death, he likewise calls for witness: 'O, bear me witness, night ... Be witness to me, O thou blessed moon ...' (IV.ix.5–7). Moon and night can testify to his remorse: but still, another kind of record is also to be kept. 'Let the world rank me in register / A master-leaver and a fugitive' (IV.ix.21–22). The effect is compounded by the fact that Enobarbus is all the while being observed by the sentries on watch, who hardly know what to make of what unfolds before them, but can see only that he is 'of note' (IV.ix.31).

This pervasive reference to witness gives it a large power in the play. Crucially, the lovers are not only the object of report by others, but themselves spend a good deal of time bearing witness to one another and to the quality of their love. It is hardly too much to say that their love consists in precisely this: the desire to have its specialness realised by the other person, alongside the anxiety that it may not be. 'If it be love indeed, tell me how much' (I.i.14): Cleopatra's opening challenge to Antony is the theme of the play. Their love is at its most exalted, intense, and erotic when recounted, when recalled or imagined at distance, when they are separated by absence or by death. Antony's most convincing and sustained expression of what Cleopatra is to him comes after he hears of her death; that he will find this to be a false report, or that moments ago he believed she had betrayed him, seems scarcely to matter. A different story is now to be told. Then, after his death indeed, it is Cleopatra's turn to bear witness:

CLEOPATRA: You laugh when boys or women tell their dreams;
    Is't not your trick?
DOLABELLA: I understand not, madam.
CLEOPATRA: I dreamt there was an Emperor Antony.
    O, such another sleep, that I might see
    But such another man!
DOLABELLA: If it might please ye -
CLEOPATRA: His face was as the heav'ns, and therein stuck
    A sun and moon, which kept their course, and lighted
    The little O, th' earth.
DOLABELLA: Most sovereign creature -
CLEOPATRA: His legs bestrid the ocean, his rear'd arm
    Crested the world, his voice was propertied
    As all the tuned spheres, and that to friends;
    But when he meant to quail and shake the orb,
    He was as rattling thunder. For his bounty,
    There was no winter in't; an autumn 'twas
    That grew the more by reaping. His delights
    Were dolphin-like, they show'd his back above
    The element they liv'd in. In his livery
    Walk'd crowns and crownets; realms and islands were
    As plates dropp'd from his pocket.
DOLABELLA: Cleopatra!
CLEOPATRA: Think you there was or might be such a man
    As this I dreamt of?
DOLABELLA: Gentle madam, no.
CLEOPATRA: You lie up to the hearing of the gods!
    But if there be, nor ever were one such,
    It's past the size of dreaming. Nature wants stuff
    To vie strange forms with fancy; yet t' imagine
    An Antony were nature's piece 'gainst fancy,
    Condemning shadows quite. (V.ii.74–100)

Cleopatra's report is openly hyperbolic. Even at his most impressive moments, the Antony we have seen could never have been as impressive as that. But this awareness is incorporated within the claim; Cleopatra positively solicits the contradicting voice of the reality-principle—'Gentle madam, no'—in order to override it, to stake her claim on the lived experience of fiction or 'dream'. As with Enobarbus's report of Cydnus, there is a real effect; the fact that she is inspired to such a vision of Antony is itself a kind of evidence. The speech has a real effect on

Dolabella too, for it turns him into the sympathiser who will betray Caesar's intentions to her.

> I do feel,
> By the rebound of yours, a grief that smites
> My very heart at root. (V.ii.103–05)

The lovers often speak about their love in hyperbolic terms, and the essential question of the play may seem to be what kind of credit we shall allow to, or withhold from, such hyperbole. But perhaps to speak of credit is misleading. I am trying to keep my distance from the sterile debate over whether either or both *really* grow into the magnificence that is at certain moments claimed for them, or whether their love *really* possesses that transcendent value which at certain moments they claim for it. Definitive answers on this point tend only to express the temperament of the witness. A certain doubleness of vision, sometimes expressed as oscillation, sometimes compacted into the single effect of hyperbole, runs throughout the play. Even at the end, hyperbole is always felt as such; when, in the sublime aria which is her final speech, Cleopatra looks forward to her reunion with Antony in an erotic afterlife (just as he had done with her), we know well enough that her 'immortal longings' are fantasy or 'dream', the imagining of a world rather than the world as it is. But our relation to such knowledge varies, and at this moment we are able to enter into the experiential reality of her high dream—undeterred by Dolabella's 'No', or the prosaic comedy of the Clown, who bawdily reports a woman who 'makes a very good report o' th' worm', of whose reliability he is sceptical (V.ii.255). For the play itself is supporting Cleopatra, through the soaring lyricism of the poetry that she speaks, as well as through the perfectly attuned responses of her women, who elsewhere strike an ironic or teasing note, but here seem like extensions of her being. We could say that the play itself bears witness: entering into the reality and power of Cleopatra's state of mind while also standing outside it, as a good witness must.[34]

---

34 For another example of a passage in which the play itself supports the high vision, there is the scene in which Antony holds his final 'gaudy night', with its several echoes of the Last Supper and of Christ's last days, immediately followed by a scene in which the God from whom he is descended forsakes him. It is not that we think of Antony as a Christ-figure, but the Biblical allusions, subliminal rather than pointed, support the strange grief of the servants at the feast, the awe of the

* * * * *

'Witnessing substitutes narrative for perception', wrote Derrida, and drew from that the inference that the witness is always blind. But a more generous view of narrative (such as that advanced by Paul Ricoeur) sees it as the key to interpretive understanding, albeit much invested in the organising structures of fiction; a large part of Ricoeur's project is to show how such imaginative structuring does not terminate in fiction but can alter and enlarge our understanding of life. In these final examples from Ibsen and from *Antony and Cleopatra*, I have been pointing to a new kind of witness: not the reductive onlooker who disallows the protagonist's specialness, but the rarer kind of witness who makes real the protagonist's inner life, bringing it into the world of expression and action through the story that they, as witness, tell. The witness-protagonist relation becomes a site of potentially transformative power. This is what Antony and Cleopatra do, at moments, for each other; what Gregers Werle does for Hedvig, what Hilde Wangel does for Solness; and what the drama itself does, in each case, to some degree. For theatre has always available to it a scepticism as to any sharp and hierarchical distinction between what is real and what is imagined; theatre has options other than the representation of the given external world.

The outcome for these figures, however, is their destruction; tragedy typically discovers the world to be inhospitable to the inner world of the mind, most usually through some determination of the plot. Solness falls from the tower; the lovers are no match for Caesar. This is not a theatre of unimpeded fantasy or positive delusion. But it is not only through catastrophe that the world's persisting presence is acknowledged, and I have tried to suggest how it can be acknowledged alongside, without detracting from, and sometimes in actual communication with, the symbolic vision which expresses a no less present and no less real inner mindscape. 'Gentle madam, no—You lie up to the hearing of the gods!' Or there is the wondrous metaphor with which Cleopatra dies:

> Dost thou not see my baby at my breast,
> That sucks the nurse asleep? (V.ii.309–10)

---

soldiers on watch: it is imaginable that something extraordinary is taking place. What Cleopatra will do with her 'dream' of Antony as demigod, the play itself does here.

This is metaphor, not hallucination—transformation as a visible process, not an invisible product, bridging the worlds with a kind of sublime playfulness: but in that way, yes, of course we see the baby. Witness is borne; the line enters into the reality of Cleopatra's experience while carrying that reality across into the external world—not least in the perfectly observed and utterly familiar detail of the nursing mother who is drowsily falling asleep.

The transformative story does not abolish, but alters our relation to, the criterion of truth. Earlier in the play, when Antony's marriage to Octavia is mooted, Agrippa says this about its desirable consequences: 'Truths would be tales, / Where now half tales be truths' (II.ii.133–34). In context, Agrippa means simply that Octavius and Antony will stop seizing on rumours as pretexts to fight. But perhaps we can hear a larger resonance in the phrasing, the intuition of some immensely desirable condition in which truth and tale, the pain and the story, would be one. If so, that intuition only serves to sharpen awareness of the gap that obtains meanwhile, where the imperfect witness of a 'half tale' is mostly all that can be had.

4. The Crime and Punishment Story

> Heaven the judicious sharp spectator is,
> That sits and marks still who doth act amiss.
> (Walter Raleigh, 'On the Life of Man')[1]

A good deal of tragedy concerns some crucial act, sometimes involved with some critical failure of understanding or mindset, which then leads to catastrophe. A good deal of thinking about tragedy highlights this sequence as key to understanding tragedy's significance and power. Catastrophe is shown to follow from that original mis-step as its consequence and its punishment; the mis-step is revealed as an offence against the laws of life, and in that sense a crime, whether or not knowingly committed as such. In this chapter I seek to think about that idea—of catastrophe as having its origin in crime—not so much as the subject-matter of tragedy but as a story that tragedy often tells and that is often told about it. The story is itself an interpretation, a representation, an attempt at bearing witness. I want to think about what makes this story so attractive, about the conditions for its persuasiveness, and also about the points where it breaks down or falls short. Where, at the level of the action, the punishment fails to fit the crime, to arrive as satisfyingly or as illuminatingly as might have been hoped, this reflects not only on the working of justice (whether human or cosmological), but also on a problem at the level of representation, in the way that the fundamental agony is narrated and understood.

This question of how things get represented is often dramatised within the tragedy. Take for example the end of *Hamlet*. With his dying words, Hamlet implores Horatio to tell his story, with all that that

---

[1] Sir Walter Raleigh, *Selected Writings*, ed. by Gerald Hammond (Manchester: Carcanet, 1984), p.55.

implies about the need to be witnessed, to be connected with the wider community, and to know that sense can be made of pain, terror, and disaster. We then hear about how Horatio proposes to meet that request, the kind of story he will tell to those still standing.

> So shall you hear
> Of carnal, bloody, and unnatural acts,
> Of accidental judgments, casual slaughters,
> Of deaths put on by cunning and forc'd cause,
> And in this upshot, purposes mistook
> Fall'n on the inventors' heads: all this can I
> Truly deliver. (V.ii.380–86)[2]

This effect of distancing, simplifying summary is one which often arrives at the end of a tragedy, as a signal of our release back into a more familiar world; our complex experience of *Hamlet* is here reduced, painfully but also reassuringly, to yet another blood-and-thunder tragedy. Horatio's account is not, however, merely generic, but loosely gathers up the specific events of the play. The carnal, bloody, and unnatural acts must include Claudius's original crime; the death of Polonius falls somewhere between an accidental judgment and a casual slaughter; purposes mistook are amply displayed in the final carnage. Interestingly, it is hard to find Hamlet's place in this narrative of bloody acts—as if it were easier to tell Hamlet's story by editing out his own participation in it. But what matters more is how the shape of the speech imposes a shape on the incidents themselves. Events which seem largely *casual* or arbitrary, merely chaotic, are 'in this upshot' resolved into a pattern of poetic justice, as purposes of death rebound upon their inventors. Rosencrantz and Guildenstern are hoist with their own petard, Laertes is killed by his own poisoned foil, Claudius is undone by his own too-clever plot. The story Horatio will tell emerges as the story of crime followed by punishment, and the structure of his speech suggests how the function of such a story is to dispel the sense of mere outrage and random violence, 'unnatural acts' and 'casual slaughters'. What emerges instead is the working of justice as a kind of mechanism that runs through events and gives them narrative shape.

---

2   Quotations from Shakespeare are taken from are taken from *The Riverside Shakespeare*, 2nd edn, ed. by G. Blakemore Evans, et al. (Boston and New York: Houghton Mifflin, 1997), unless otherwise stated.

How well this story fits the play, is a question. It has a certain cogency, in the way that Claudius supplies Hamlet with the means and occasion for his revenge; and in his escape from the death-warrant, Hamlet sensed the working of a divinity that shapes our ends. But it also feels like a great simplification, a needful rounding off, that answers as much to the need of the audience (both Horatio's and Shakespeare's) to hear such a story at the end of things, as to what we have seen to be the case. If we think of the crime as an origin (and the origin as a crime), then there is an obvious reassurance in imagining it as necessarily followed by punishment; atrocity is contained and dealt with, within the framework of a larger order. But perhaps we can peer further into the depths in which Shakespearean tragedy has its source. Suppose that origin is nothing so concrete as a crime, but a primal, inchoate distress, a vertiginous anguish and dismay, obscurely figured as the nameless 'something [...] rotten' which for Hamlet poisons life (I.iv.90), or the vortex that engulfs Brutus or Macbeth at the mere thought of murder, or the collapse into chaos that Othello suffers at the mere possibility of Desdemona's infidelity. To generate from that unbearable distress a story of crime and punishment would then be a kind of relief, an achievement. This is so whether the crime is located in another (Hamlet's strange exhilaration at hearing of his father's murder; Othello's terrible command to Iago to 'prove my love a whore' (III.iii.359); the savage retribution that Lear wishes upon his children) or committed by the one in anguish, as is the case with Macbeth. Having been exposed to the vortex represented by 'fair is foul' (I.i.11), some part of the audience *needs* Macbeth to kill and then to be undone and damned, needs the crime and punishment story to be set in motion and worked through.

This idea of a justice mechanism is invoked in and around tragedy a good deal. One of its clearest expressions in Shakespeare comes from Macbeth himself:

> But in these cases
> We still have judgment here, that we but teach
> Bloody instructions, which, being taught, return
> To plague th' inventor. This even-handed justice
> Commends th' ingredience of our poison'd chalice
> To our own lips. (I.vii.7–12)

What might have begun as a pragmatic anxiety—the risk of being found out and executed—becomes in Macbeth's inflamed imagination the automatic working of a terrifying infallible principle, whereby to strike against another is inevitably to strike against oneself. Similar are the fearful intuitions of the chorus in *Agamemnon* that blood will have blood, that the Furies are waiting, that 'the doer pays'.

> Yet someone hears in the air, a god,
> Apollo, Pan, or Zeus [...] and drives
> late to its mark
> the Fury upon the transgressors.³

> The spoiler is robbed; he killed, he has paid.
> The truth stands ever beside god's throne
> eternal: he who has wrought shall pay; that is law.⁴

They had it coming: it's that idea. The Greek term *dikē*, whose possible meanings range right across the fields of justice, revenge, retribution, penalty, and legal process, is much invoked and much contested in the *Oresteia*, but always with the idea of a dynamic force or principle larger than personal motive that is or should be working itself out in what takes place. Yet the very contestability of the term and its applications, in a play in which one speaker's notion of *dikē* is repeatedly set against another's, also tends to call it into question as a basis for authoritative judgment.⁵ In the first of the quotations given above, the chorus are groping, urgently but indistinctly, for some principle that will give form to their anxiety and horror. Some god hears, surely—even if it is hard to say which; some god acts, surely—even if strangely late in doing so.

In a revenge tragedy such as the *Oresteia* or *Hamlet*, the idea of crime followed by punishment is obviously at home. But it also comes into play in other tragic drama, with the idea that the tragic protagonist has gone too far, been too daring, grown too big, or become possessed by some immense and improper passion—and that this is a transgression

---

3   Aeschylus, *Oresteia*, trans. by Richmond Lattimore (Chicago: University of Chicago Press, 1953), p.36.
4   Ibid., p.86.
5   See Simon Goldhill, *Language, Sexuality, Narrative: The Oresteia* (Cambridge: Cambridge University Press, 1984), pp.208–283; or for a brief summary, see Goldhill, *Aeschylus: The Oresteia*, 2ⁿᵈ edn (Cambridge: Cambridge University Press, 2004), pp.30–33.

which disturbs the cosmos and against which the cosmos reacts. Such reaction is epitomised in the Furies, once aroused; in the *Eumenides* their great and terrible binding-spell reaches beyond the murderers of blood-kin to threaten all human presumption:

> Men's illusions in their pride under the sky melt
> down, and are diminished into the ground, gone
> before the onset of our black robes, pulsing
> of our vindictive feet against them.
> For with a long leap from high
> above, and dead drop of weight,
> I bring foot's force crashing down
> to cut the legs from under even
> the runner, and spill him to ruin. [...]
> All holds. For we are strong and skilled;
> we have authority; we hold
> memory of evil; we are stern
> nor can men's pleadings bend us.[6]

The Furies are ancient female deities, who come from further back and deeper down than the Olympians. They represent an enduring archaic reality which threatens all human 'pride', and humans ignore this reality at their peril. In the *Oresteia* as in other Greek tragedies, this is reinforced by the idea of an ancestral curse, some former transgression whose taint has been transmitted down the family line and is still active in the present. Elsewhere, we find the idea of an offence given to a deity in the past, which nominally explains the more truly bewildering destruction that follows. In the Judeo-Christian tradition this reappears as the idea of original sin.

What seems to be important in this story is the idea of a necessary process working itself out, through or beyond the contingencies of personal retribution or the discovery of the criminal. This sense of reflexive process is, for example, embedded in the dramatic irony of the Oedipus story as Sophocles tells it. What Oedipus says and does, returns upon him. When he declares at the start that his name is widely known, or says that he will avenge Laius as if he were his father, these moments of dramatic irony—which are everywhere in the play, as they are also in *Macbeth*—continually convey the larger narrative in which he

---

6   Aeschylus, *Oresteia*, pp.147–148.

is caught up. The hell machine, *La Machine Infernale*, was how Cocteau titled his own version of *Oedipus the King*, in a phrase which underlines this quality of mechanism. Where this point of view is adopted, what Oedipus does and what others do around him are no longer the free actions they appear to be, but all tend to the fulfilment of the oracle (in Cocteau, who tells the story forwards) or, in Sophocles, to the revelation of its fulfilment and the self-punishment of the criminal.

Despite its bleak implications, the crime and punishment story has a deep appeal to our imagination. This is well demonstrated by how incontestably innocent victims of atrocity—survivors of child abuse or rape or the Holocaust—tend to feel themselves culpable.[7] The story's potency is such that it can be generated from the mere fact of suffering or disaster alone. Job's comforters, so called, are fond of asserting it in response to Job's terrible afflictions and his bitter laments.

> Yea, the light of the wicked shall be put out, and the spark of his fire shall not shine. The light shall be dark in his tabernacle, and his candle shall be put out with him. The steps of his strength shall be straitened, and his own counsel shall cast him down. For he is cast into a net by his own feet, and he walketh upon a snare.[8]

If Job is not one of the wicked, he can therefore take comfort—but what is really being suggested, Job feels, is that it is precisely his suffering, his affliction, that proves him wicked.[9] Or if his personal criminality is hard to locate, then perhaps all men are wicked in the eyes of God:

> What is man, that he should be clean? and he which is born of a woman, that he should be righteous? Behold, he [God] putteth no trust in his saints; yea, the heavens are not clean in his sight. How much more abominable and filthy is man, which drinketh iniquity like water?[10]

Use every man after his deserts, quips Hamlet, and who shall escape whipping?

Job's comforters are concerned to assert God's justice, but the power of the crime and punishment story does not depend on theology. Simply

---

7   The drivers behind this can be profound. 'Only the ability to feel guilty makes us human, particularly if, objectively seen, one is not guilty.' Bruno Bettelheim, *Surviving and Other Essays* (London: Thames and Hudson, 1979), p.313.
8   *Book of Job* (King James Version) 18:5–8.
9   Ibid., 16:4.
10 Ibid., 15:14–16.

by sequencing events, story tends to posit causality. If a story is to be told about suffering, and there is no obvious or adequate oppressor in view, what could be more plausible than to understand suffering as punishment? As Clov tells himself in *Endgame*, with Beckett's usual economy, 'Clov, you must learn to suffer better than that if you want them to weary of punishing you'.[11] Why does Clov suppose that he is being punished? Because he suffers, and his suffering is otherwise unintelligible. For what does he suppose he is being punished? For suffering, since this means that he is obscurely culpable, and has not reached any point of expiation. The excruciating circle sketched here seems to me profoundly true of how extreme distress can be apprehended. The impulse—at its origin, a searching for relief—is to connect one's pain in some way with the regard of a consciousness outside the self, with 'them', who if they cannot be imagined as pitying can at least be imagined as punishing. Hamlet has comparable moments:

> Heaven hath pleas'd it so,
> To punish me with this, and this with me,
> That I must be their scourge and minister. (III.iv.173–75)

This is Hamlet's response to what might otherwise seem the grotesque mischance of his killing of Polonius. What was apparently an accident, a 'casual slaughter' becomes, in this telling, incorporated within a larger pattern. The reflexivity is there, neatly conveyed in the chiasmus me-this-this-me, accompanied by the idea of an infallible mechanism, which Hamlet calls Heaven's pleasure. Heaven's pleasure might be arbitrary or whimsical, but the lines strenuously banish this momentary insinuation by positing an intelligibility to events, a justness which exists just over the horizon of human perception. In these lines at least, Hamlet sees himself as involved in this process (he is working for 'them', he is 'their scourge and minister'), even though this means including himself among those to be punished.

Heaven's pleasure is, in *Hamlet*, notably murky and indistinct. I do not wish to argue that tragic drama, generally speaking, *endorses* the story of a crime-and-punishment mechanism which it frequently offers us. Rather, it brings it forward as one plausible story about human anguish

---

11   Samuel Beckett, *The Complete Dramatic Works* (London: Faber & Faber, 1990), p.132.

that has an immensely strong pull on the imagination, but presents it in ways that also expose it to question and to challenge. Insofar as it relies on some degree of viable belief in the will of Heaven, the activity of the gods, or the responsiveness of the cosmos, it is clearly vulnerable to more sceptical or secular tendencies of thought. We may think that 'Heaven's pleasure' is something that Hamlet *needs*, at this crisis, to invoke. Still more clearly, when Othello identifies his murderous intent with an elemental force of nature ('Like to the Pontic Sea ...', III.iii.453) or with 'Justice' personified (V.ii.17) or with deity ('This sorrow's heavenly, / It strikes where it doth love', V.ii.21–22), we are more conscious of the psychological need this serves than the intrinsic power of the claim. 'It is the cause, it is the cause', he intones over Desdemona's sleeping body, in words that mysteriously amplify judicial process ('cause' as case in law) into a sense of determining causality (V.ii.1). This enables Othello, like Hamlet, to see himself as the minister or medium of an overarching power. Just so, Clytemnestra claims in the *Oresteia* that it was not she who struck down Agamemnon but the ancient spirit of revenge, the *alastor*, which was working through her. It is a claim that the Chorus grudgingly half-accept, and in a drama where the Furies will appear on stage with other gods it has real force. Shakespearean tragedy, too, is a realm where non-human forces can be powerfully invoked. Even Othello's delusional soliloquy has an authentically dreadful aspect, insofar as we may indeed feel him to be a man *possessed*, albeit by a spirit yet darker than that of Justice; Iago, as is often noted, is at least metaphorically a devil. But we are also within touching distance of the comedic world of *Measure for Measure*, in which the appeal to the justice mechanism—'An Angelo for Claudio, death for death: / Haste still pays haste, and leisure answers leisure; / Like doth quit like, and *Measure* still *for Measure*' (V.i.409–11)[12]—is patently a matter of human and political fabrication.

A subtler version of the crime and punishment story, not so dependent on the gods and more sustainable in secular times, can be traced to Aristotle's *Poetics*. Aristotle argues that the figure who suffers in tragedy should be neither entirely good, since this would move us to outrage, nor entirely bad, since this would not arouse pity, but rather

---

12 Punctuation in the First Folio does not specify how many of these lines the Duke is claiming to hear cried out by 'the very mercy of the law'.

someone 'who passes to bad fortune not through vice or wickedness, but because of some *hamartia*.'[13] The root meaning of *hamartia* is missing the target; it may be translated as an error or mistake, perhaps due to ignorance or weakness. Deianeira committed *hamartia* when she sent the poisoned robe to Heracles thinking the poison was a love-potion; *hamartia* is incident to being human, pleads the Nurse to Hippolytus in extenuation of Phaedra's love.[14] What Aristotle is doing here is allowing as much misfortune into tragedy as he can while still resisting the claim that tragedy presents us with radical non-justice: this is part of his defence of tragedy against Plato. What the *hamartia* story likes is Oedipus, unwitting author of his own fate; what this story doesn't like and can scarcely cope with is Hecuba, multiply bereaved, stateless and homeless after the fall of Troy, enslaved and degraded and utterly wretched. It seems to be merely the chance and brutality of war that has brought her to her terrible depth of suffering in *Trojan Women*, a play in which the gods can change sides on a whim, and in which her fierce desire to see Helen identified and punished as the cause of catastrophe will never be realised.[15] Oedipus, by contrast, contributes to his own downfall. Yet Apollo was also involved, though you would never know this from Aristotle; he develops his theory as he does because he is uninterested in, or perhaps embarrassed by, the role of the gods. With a much weaker sense of the cosmos as actively implicated, Aristotle derives catastrophe more squarely from human action, human error. Tragic suffering follows intelligibly enough from that; our errors, as well as our crimes, are punished. Although the cosmos may no longer be involved, a story can still be told which makes the protagonist the author of his own pain.

This is one large step in the shift away from the gods and towards human psychology as that which explains and generates suffering. Aristotle is not there yet: *hamartia* seems to imply a single gravely

---

13 Aristotle, *Poetics*, 1453a. From *Ancient Literary Criticism: The Principal Texts in New Translations*, ed. by D. A. Russell and M. Winterbottom (Oxford: Oxford University Press, 1972), p.106.

14 *Women of Trachis*, line 1123; *Hippolytus*, line 615.

15 On *Hecuba*, the other surviving Hecuba play, see Martha Nussbaum's reading in *The Fragility of Goodness: Luck and Ethics in Greek Tragedy and Philosophy*, 2nd edn (Cambridge: Cambridge University Press, 2001). Nussbaum emphasises the element of (mere) contingency that turns Hecuba's pitiable and noble suffering after the death of one child into barbaric vindictiveness after the death of another.

consequential error, rather than an aspect of character. But it opens the door to thinking about the *propensity* for error as diagnostic of a character flaw or ingrained fault. Thus Hamlet reflects on how 'some vicious mole of nature', arising from birth, temperament, or habit, can bring even the best of men to be regarded as radically corrupt (I.iv.24). The twentieth-century metaphor of a 'tragic flaw' similarly made psychology do the work of what had once been theology. In schematic terms, it completed the movement from the sense that Apollo has entangled Oedipus, through the perception that Oedipus made a disastrous mistake in fleeing from Corinth and killing the man at the crossroads, all the way to the view that Oedipus makes that kind of mistake because that is the kind of man he is—because, let's say, he has an overweening confidence in his own powers. Catastrophe now makes sense because it follows intelligibly from the psychology of the protagonist. If the 'flaw' metaphor has exerted a compelling (often pernicious) influence, that is because it so perfectly conveys the necessity of the disaster—and so, in a certain sense, its rightness. The fault-line was there all the time, and when pressure is applied at the point of weakness, the thing of beauty shatters exactly as it had to. Something is revealed, something is fulfilled.

Although much recent thinking has moved away from the view that the psychology of character is the key to the protagonist's story, explaining and so at least formally justifying his downfall, it is worth dwelling for a little longer on why that view can be so tenaciously attractive. It gives the witness (like the critic) a story they can tell. It brings the relief of making the tragedy intelligible, while underlining the distinctiveness of the protagonist, thus holding him or her as safely different from ourselves. In the vacuum left by the absence of the gods, it sustains the idea of a justice mechanism: the protagonist suffers because of the kind of person that they are, and although their suffering may be cruelly excessive, it still speaks of a just reactiveness woven into the fabric of things. It establishes a form of guilt—and once this approach is set on foot, it is largely self-confirming, for any story-teller with a mind to do so can align character and motive with a given action, producing the perception of guilt. In Dostoevsky's *Brothers Karamazov* there is a climactic trial scene where the speech for the defence turns exactly on pointing this out.

> Injured moral and, still more, aesthetic feeling is sometime relentless. Of course, in the highly talented speech for the prosecution we have all heard a stern analysis of the prisoner's character and conduct [...] displaying profound psychological insight [combined with] what I might call an artistic urge, the need to create, as it were, a work of fiction. [...] I have purposely resorted to the aid of psychology, gentlemen of the jury, to show clearly that you can prove anything by it. It all depends on who makes use of it. Psychology induces even the most serious people to indulge in romancing.[16]

The prosecutor has been showing at exhaustive length that Dimitri Karamazov is just the kind of man who would have committed certain acts that implicate him in the murder; counsel for the defence counters that other aspects of Dimitri's behaviour show with equal plausibility a character that would not have committed those acts. One cogent story that reveals him as guilty is set against another that reveals him as innocent. (In the event, the verdict—which is in any case the wrong one—is influenced by external contingencies, leaving the judicial process absurdly distant from the truth. And although we discover the actual murderer, responsibility spreads indeterminately out from that individual towards others, to the point where it can be said in the novel that all are responsible for everything.) In the area of tragedy, explanation which rests on the psychology of the character can often be empty or circular, or else driven by what Dostoevsky's speaker calls the aesthetic urge to make a well-shaped story.

This can be disputed, of course; and in actual productions, much depends on the assumption the director makes about the primacy of character. Othello *can* be played as insecure (or narcissistic) from the start, Macbeth as ruthlessly ambitious and self-seeking, although in both cases with small warrant from the text. Although Othello is always capable of self-deception, when he asks at the end to be spoken of as 'not easily jealous, but being wrought, / Perplexed in th'extreme' (V.ii.345–46), this catches well enough the *strangeness* of what has happened to him. A man not easily jealous is overwhelmed by homicidal jealousy. Or in the case of Macbeth, a loyal subject kills his king in full awareness of the horror of the deed, and aware too that he is blasting his own

---

16 Fyodor Dostoevsky, *Brothers Karamazov*, trans. by David Magarshack (Harmondsworth: Penguin, 1958), pp. 857, 859.

happiness by doing so. Shakespeare's genius is to make these events credible without making them explicable; the concept of motive or character as explanatory becomes problematic, and tragedy enters at the point where that kind of psychological explanation falls short.

The crime and punishment story worked better when it brought in the cosmos or the gods, for a number of interrelated reasons. This version enables the sense that disaster is seen and can be comprehended, which is at the heart of all desire for witness. It makes dramatic negotiation possible: to externalise the desire for retribution in the Furies is no longer to be engulfed by it. 'Vengeance is mine, saith the Lord'.[17] It relieves the pressure on motive if the agent is to some degree possessed or compelled by an external force. It lifts some of the otherwise crippling weight that would come were disaster to be *only* of our own making. And it declares disaster intelligible, without necessarily making it intelligible to us or enforcing our identification with the process of condemnation. Heaven's pleasure may be mysterious or remote, or the gods may be fickle or arbitrary or opposed to one another, or the punishment may be so disproportionate to the crime as to leave space for human outcry; yet still the crime-and-punishment story obtains.

However, when a character in Shakespeare gives voice to this story, its cogency is laid open to question. Edgar gives the story in particularly pure form over the dying Edmund, as he invokes Gloucester's sin in begetting the bastard:

> EDGAR: The gods are just, and of our pleasant vices
>   Make instruments to plague us:
>   The dark and vicious place where thee he got
>   Cost him his eyes.
> EDMUND: Th' hast spoken right, 'tis true.
>   The wheel is come full circle, I am here. (V.iii.171–75)

Edmund had it coming; so did Gloucester. The gods are just, the wheel comes full circle, the cosmos automatically avenges itself on outrage done. Agency belongs not to human agents but to more mysterious,

---

17 'To me belongeth vengeance, and retribution, their foot shall slide in due time: for the day of their calamity is at hand.' (Deuteronomy 32:35). This is turned by Paul into a moral injunction: 'Dearly beloved, avenge not yourselves, but rather give place unto wrath: for it is written, Vengeance is mine; I will repay, saith the Lord.' (Romans 12:19).

4. The Crime and Punishment Story   105

impersonal forces: the gods, the place, the wheel. Dramas which employ analogous mechanisms—dramatic ironies, patterns of repetition, effects of 'poetic justice'—can then appear to be reflecting some principle of dynamic justice at work in life itself. Iago, for example, encourages Othello to place his killing of Desdemona within such a pattern.

> IAGO: Do it not with poison; strangle her in her bed; even the bed she hath contaminated.
> OTHELLO: Good, good, the justice of it pleases; very good. (IV.i.207–10)

The justice of it pleases. Edgar is similarly keen to establish that the gods are just, and in his overthrow of Edmund he discovers a principle that can equally make sense of the blinding of Gloucester. Although we may be appalled by what this drives him to say about his father, we recognise the urgency of his need. What both brothers are doing in this exchange is to find in the immediate act—Edgar's killing of his brother—the action of a higher or at least greater power. Edgar casts the killing as the culmination of a revenge tragedy, *Oresteia*-style: the father's sin in the remote past generated its own retribution, in a further crime which the son has now avenged. In fact, he has good reason of his own to kill Edmund, but he needs—or something needs—his personal motive to be gathered up into a larger force, a justice mechanism, and Edmund, surprisingly, agrees. This is not, of course, where the play will end; the wheel keeps turning past full circle, and no-one will say of Cordelia's death that the gods are just. But in this dramatic moment the drama supports this sense of a necessary outcome, a story properly completed. And yet it does so weakly, and the weakness also matters. The killing is framed by the formal ceremony of the duel, with trumpets and challenges and chivalric formulas, evoking the kind of medieval trial by combat in which God's judgement would become manifest; the action moves onto a more impersonal, ritualistic plane. But this is done through a stilted, quasi-archaic quality in the writing and staging that is awkwardly dissonant with what surrounds it. Even if we do not consciously reflect in the theatre that all this must somehow be Edgar's bizarre contrivance, some sense of contrivance attaches to the moment nevertheless, in uneasy tension with the sense that, yes, some larger process may here be working through to its necessary conclusion. The passage activates the crime and punishment story, as something we dread but also desire to hear told, but activates also a troubling awareness of that desire. What we don't want—from a story, at least—is 'casual slaughters'; better even the dark theology of Edgar than the non-theology of Gloucester, who finds that the gods 'kill us for their sport', randomly, casually, unintelligibly (IV.i.37). Yet *King Lear* contains both views, and by dramatising the characters' *need* for the crime and punishment story (which is also to some extent ours), calls it into question. It is true that Goneril and Regan die, finally, undone by their own actions, with their purposes 'fall'n upon the inventors' heads', yet these deaths come late and trivially. Lear had earlier called upon goddess Nature to strike Goneril with sterility, and for the gods to take his part and strike down the sinful, but those calls came increasingly out of need and helplessness rather than insight and power. Our sense of tragedy exists not in the fulfilment of the crime and punishment story but in its fragility, in the way that when and insofar as it does come, it falls short.

Any revenge tragedy falls somewhere on a spectrum. At one extreme, the avenger is felt as the instrument of a larger energy, surfing the wave of some more-than-human anger or retributive force. I have already cited Clytemnestra's breathtaking claim in the *Agamemnon*:

> Can you claim that I have done this?
> Speak of me never
> more as the wife of Agamemnon.
> In the shadow of this corpse's queen
> the old stark avenger
> of Atreus for his revel of hate
> struck down this man,
> last blood for the slaughtered children.[18]

This extraordinary claim is one which the chorus cannot entirely dismiss.

> What man shall testify
> your hands are clean of this murder?
> How? How? yet from his father's blood
> might swarm some fiend to guide you.[19]

---

18 Aeschylus, *Oresteia*, p.84.
19 Ibid.

We might also think of the central section of *The Libation Bearers*, the next play in the trilogy, where Orestes and Electra stand at Agamemnon's tomb, joining the Chorus in a tremendous incantatory lament which rises steadily into the determination to kill. The anger of the dead is being channelled here, drawn on to empower the living, reinforcing the explicit threats and instructions made by Apollo. But at the other end of this spectrum, the gods shaping the action may be revealed as plural and opposed to one another, as at the end of the *Oresteia*. Or the agent's sense of himself as the medium of a higher power may be altogether questionable, as when Othello casts himself as Justice personified. Or the gods may have simply gone missing, so that merely human action must fill their place if the crime-and-punishment story is to be fulfilled.

Consider Sophocles' *Electra*. It has no gods nor, remarkably, Furies, with little attention given to Orestes' killing of his mother, which is at the centre of the *Oresteia*. Instead of the trilogy's terrific, fearful sense of action leading inevitably to reaction, all the focus is on Electra and the damage done to her by her too-long wait for the arrival of Orestes. For her the Story has broken down, it has failed to complete itself, so that she is blocked and bound to the traumatising past. The chorus still hold, somewhat vaguely, to the hope of a divine patterning that will work itself out:

> Take courage, child, take courage—
> Zeus is still great in heaven.
> He watches over and controls all things. [...]
> The son of Agamemnon is not unmindful,
> Nor is he who rules as a god in Acheron.[20]

This associates Orestes with a divine force, in the manner of the *Oresteia*, and invokes the Justice Story as something written into the fabric of the cosmos. But Electra rejects this vision—for her it is now too late, the waiting has gone on too long, been too damaging; the thread of the story is broken:

> But most of my life has already left me
> Without hope, and I can endure no longer.
> I waste away, without children,
> Without a loving husband to shield me.[21]

---

20 Sophocles, *Electra*, trans. by Eric Dugdale (Cambridge: Cambridge University Press, 2008), p.19.
21 Ibid.

The image of her barrenness enforces the sense of a story broken off, truncated, ungenerative. The intensity and reiteration of her self-consuming laments suck the whole drama into itself like a black hole; although she is full of words, she cannot express her anguish, cannot deliver herself of her pain.

> But I, ever waiting for Orestes
> To come and put a stop to all this, die a wretched death.
> For by always saying he's about to act, he has destroyed
> The hopes I dare to entertain and those I don't.
> Friends, at times like this one cannot act with restraint
> Or show respect; when things are bad,
> One is forced to behave badly.[22]

When Orestes does come, he comes bearing the news of his own death, and this does something strange to the shape of the whole play. The great messenger-speech telling the death of the hero is, in this play uniquely, a fiction, a false climax; the timing of the whole play is out of joint. Electra's grief in response is the emotional climax of the drama, but it is a response to nothing. She resolves to take on herself, though a mere woman, the act of vengeance. 'The deed must be done by my hand alone; / I will certainly not leave it undone.'[23] But this is almost immediately taken away from her when Orestes reveals himself and takes over the action, effectively sidelining her. She is full of joy, and of a savage exultation, but there is something offbeat about this as a turning point; words continue to flow out of her like a torrent, so that both Orestes and the paedagogus repeatedly enjoin her to silence, just as Clytemnestra and the chorus had previously done. There is a strong sense of mistiming; the killings are swiftly done, and done inside the house with Electra on both occasions left outside. The killing of Aegisthus gets more attention than that of Clytemnestra. It is true that in Clytemnestra's cries the chorus hear the fulfilment of the cosmic story, as if they were part of the *Oresteia*:

> The curses do their work.
> Those who lie under ground are alive.
> Those who died long ago

---

22 Ibid., p.25.
23 Ibid., p.77.

Drain the blood of their killers—
The flow is now reversed.[24]

But sitting awkwardly with this is the sense of Orestes as a human, non-numinous, rather unimpressive and nondescript figure, who has committed an act which seems to have no reverberations in the cosmos. He says merely, 'All is well in the house, if Apollo prophesied well'[25]—that little 'if' being the only remaining mark of the tremendous ambivalence of the *Oresteia*.

I have suggested that these revenge tragedies fall at different places on a spectrum, where at one extreme the sense of a cosmic justice mechanism saturates everything, and at the other it is absent. But it should be added: they both fall *indeterminately*—that is, they activate an awareness of that whole spectrum of possibility, between a universe of efficient and unblinking punishment (which has its own kind of dread) and that terrible vortex of unsupported, dissociated, unregarded pain into which Electra is largely fallen. Each extreme is apprehended in its relation to the other, and tragic feeling arises, in both works, out of this double consciousness (the Story is powerfully invoked; the Story is not definitive) which they generate, albeit in different proportions.

The justice mechanism runs badly in *Electra*, the thin ghost of what Electra needs it to be. Shakespeare's early tragedy *Titus Andronicus* has a whole scene dedicated to announcing its entire collapse. The deranged Titus—his daughter raped and mutilated, his sons killed, himself spurned and mocked by the city he has given his life to defend—begins act 4 scene 3 by quoting a line from Ovid: *Terras Astraea reliquit*, the goddess of Justice has left the earth (IV.iii.4). He instructs his followers to dig down to the underworld to petition Pluto for justice, and to shoot arrows at the heavens bearing petitions to the various gods. The demand for justice is rendered grotesque and absurd, as Titus himself is surely if madly aware. Just before this scene, he learnt the identity of his daughter's attackers, and responded with another Latin quotation, this time from Senecan tragedy. '*Magni dominator poli, / Tam lentus audis scelera? tam lentus vides?*' (IV.i.81–82): Ruler of great heaven, are you so slow to hear

---

24 Ibid., p.103.
25 Ibid.

and see crimes?[26] To call a play like *Titus* Senecan might mean this: what Seneca offered Shakespeare was the vision of what happens to Greek revenge tragedy, the hurt which it exhibits, when altogether stripped of the crime and punishment story as embedded in the cosmos. For it can plausibly be said that the only larger-than-human force in Seneca's plays is *Natura*, red in tooth and claw, which (as Edmund knows) is not really a goddess at all.[27] When Seneca's protagonists call upon the gods or, more commonly, the elements to sympathise with and weaponise their passion, the dramatic emphasis falls much more on the urgency of their imploring and cursing, than on such response as they may (but often fail to) receive. In the final lines of Seneca's *Medea*, Jason sees her as bearing the message, wherever she goes, that there are no gods.

The grotesquely sensationalist mode of *Titus* reflects that state of affairs. With justice-as-goddess absent, what we have here are 'casual slaughters', Rome as 'a wilderness of tigers' (III.i.54). Without extra-human forces to drive the action and share the load, human nature buckles and distorts under the freight of vindictive feeling it must carry. The avenger runs mad, or becomes himself corrupt, or both. In *Titus*, the play's reiterated excesses of violence insistently demand some unimaginable response, both from the cosmos and from those who witness them, until they topple over into savage farce. The cosmic retribution story now appears only as parody. Tamora comes to Titus disguised as Revenge, come from the underworld to 'right his heinous wrongs':

> Knock at his study, where they say he keeps
> To ruminate strange plots of dire revenge;
> Tell him Revenge is come to join with him,
> And work confusion on his enemies. (V.ii.4–8)

Although he may be mad, he is not mad enough to be deceived by this; it is with sardonic irony that he greets Tamora as 'dread Fury' (V.ii.82). The Furies as real powers are dwindled into Tamora's ludicrous masquerade, and in consequence Titus sits in his study working on his plots of dire revenge like some writer of melodrama. The revenge he then

---

26 The quotation comes from Seneca's *Phaedra*, lines 671–672. Hippolytus is voicing his revulsion at Phaedra's desire.

27 For *Natura* in Senecan tragedy, see A. J. Boyle's discussion of *Phaedra* in *Tragic Seneca: An Essay in the Theatrical Tradition* (London: Routledge, 1997), pp.60–67, especially p.65.

achieves—feeding Tamora her rapist-sons cooked in a pie—is pitched in the register of black comedy, self-consciously parodic in its inheritance from the Tereus story in Ovid and the Thyestes play by Seneca, the two main routes by which Greek tragedy came to Shakespeare. Titus even cites one of these sources to the rapists before cutting their throats.

> For worse than Philomel you us'd my daughter,
> And worse than Progne I will be reveng'd. (V.ii.194–95)

The casting of Lavinia as a second Philomel had already been established earlier; here Titus returns to it once more, completing the parallel with macabre glee. Such conscious replaying of classical texts provides the best available substitute, but an evidently contrived one, for the reflexes of cosmic retribution which stamp their pattern on the *Oresteia*.

Parodic effects like these are frequent in the revenge tragedies of Shakespeare's period. In *The Revenger's Tragedy*, Vendice repeats Titus's Senecan question: why are the gods so slow to show their hand? He gets an immediate answer—but of the stagiest kind:

> Is there no thunder left, or is't kept up
> In stock for heavier vengeance? [*Thunder*] There it goes![28]

This is shamelessly clunky: divine intervention advertised as theatrical contrivance. After the bloodbath at the end, thunder is heard once more, and Vendice underlines even more clearly the theatricality of the effect:

> Mark, thunder!
> Dost know thy cue, thou big-voiced crier? [...]
> When thunder claps, heaven likes the tragedy.[29]

Vendice's name suggests that he might be an emblematic figure in an emblematic drama: vengeance personified, *the* Revenger. In such a drama, thunder that came right on cue would not be stagey, and such a figure might deliver that last line with serious weight. But as in much Jacobean drama, the older emblematic mode is shot through with, and destabilised by, the newer gesture towards naturalism: these are actual people in an actual court, and what happens is a matter of contingency or

---

28 Cyril Tourneur (attrib.), *The Revenger's Tragedy*, ed. by Lawrence J. Ross (London: Edward Arnold, 1982), p.91.
29 Ibid., p.115.

contrivance rather than cosmic patterning. The chief villain is poisoned by kissing a skull during an illicit assignation and, while dying, is forced to witness his wife cuckolding him; he is then stamped to death. This is not atrocity pure, but atrocity corrupted in its theatrical representation. As also towards the end of *Titus*, we have reached a point where we cannot take revenge tragedy seriously, find significance or satisfaction or closure in the casual slaughters which it displays. The assertion otherwise—that heaven is involved, that something momentous is taking place—can be given only in the mode of parody.

The Revenger's Tragedy appeared a few years after *Hamlet*, and if *Hamlet* is the kind of serious play which is being parodied, Shakespeare's play is itself much involved in parody. Hamlet parodies Laertes—the grieving revenger-in-earnest—in Ophelia's grave; he rewrites *The Murder of Gonzago* as a representation of the story told by the Ghost; and he is continually on the edge of sending up his own attempts to act and speak and feel as a grieving revenger should. In 1600, the play itself would have been recognised as a remake of an earlier *Hamlet* play (now lost); it clearly works with the stock materials of a familiar genre. Kyd's famously successful *Spanish Tragedy*, for example, also features a ghost calling for revenge, a grieving avenger who more than pretends to go mad, his female partner who kills herself for grief, and a crucially consequential play-within-a-play.

There is something self-lacerating about the parodic impulse in this context. *The Revenger's Tragedy* mocks itself, as Hamlet mocks himself, for its inadequate power of representation, its inability to bear good witness to the pain and rage and fear in which it has its origin. 'Remember me', demands the Ghost (I.v.91). Parody which self-consciously repeats the past in a weaker form has an evident relation to anxieties about the potentially endless cycle of revenge, in which the act of killing threatens to become absurd. But it also suggests a crisis of representation, a failure properly to 'remember', to bear good witness to that which generated the need for tragic expression in the first place.

One extraordinary scene in *The Spanish Tragedy* reflects acutely on this. This is sometimes referred to as 'the painter scene'; it appears among a set of additions to the old play in the edition of 1602. These added passages were probably written in the late 1590s, when Kyd was dead, and have been plausibly attributed either to Jonson or to

Shakespeare; the scene is included as Shakespeare's in the recent Oxford Shakespeare.[30] It introduces a new character, a painter whose son has been murdered. He comes to beg for justice from Hieronimo, who holds a judicial position at court. Hieronimo is the avenger of the play, whose son has likewise been murdered. At this point in the play, he is both playing mad and to some indeterminate degree deranged by grief. To the painter's appeal for justice, he replies that justice 'lives not in the world' but comes only from God, and the painter seemingly accepts that he must refer his cause to a higher power: 'O, then I see / That God must right me for my murdered son'.[31] But in an apparent swerve, Hieronimo then presses what is for him a related question: can the painter's art represent atrocity? He presents this question as a series of instructions for a painting that he wishes to commission. Can the painter make a painting that shows Hieronimo and his wife with their son when he was alive; and then the young man run through with swords, hanging from a tree; and the murderers, grim and sinister; and a violent noise or cry, that brings out Hieronimo in his night-dress, searching distractedly 'through alley and alley',

> the winds blowing, the bells tolling. the owls shrieking, the toads croaking, the minutes jarring, and the clock striking twelve. And then at last, sir, starting, behold a man hanging: and tottering, and tottering as you know the wind will wave a man, and I with a trice to cut him down. And looking upon him by the advantage of my torch, find it to be my son Horatio. There you may show a passion, there you may show a passion. Draw me like old Priam of Troy, crying 'The house is a-fire, the house is a-fire as the torch over my head!' Make me curse, make me rave, make me cry, make me mad, make me well again, make me curse hell, invocate heaven, and in the end leave me in a trance; and so forth.
>
> PAINTER: And is this the end?
>
> HIERONIMO: O no, there is no end: the end is death and madness! As I am never better than when I am mad, then methinks I am a brave fellow, then I do wonders: but reason abuseth me, and there's the torment, there's the

---

30 *The New Oxford Shakespeare: The Complete Works. Modern Critical Edition*, ed. by Gary Taylor, John Jowett, Terri Bourus, and Gabriel Egan (Oxford: Oxford University Press, 2016), pp.1682–1687.

31 Thomas Kyd, *The Spanish Tragedy*, ed. by J. R. Mulryne (London: A & C Black, 1989), p.132.

hell. At the last, sir, bring me to one of the murderers, were he as strong
as Hector, thus would I tear and drag him up and down.
He beats the painter in.[32]

Hieronimo seeks from the painter an adequate representation of the terrible events. But it is not credible that the painter will be able to give him what he wants. The sonic and kinetic details that he specifies, and above all the narrative movement that he demands, resist visual representation. Such resistance stands for the yet deeper difficulty of communicating trauma, having it understood or borne witness to by another—even, in this case, someone with comparable personal experience. There is a huge gap between the two figures on stage: the simple-minded painter, called upon to bear witness through his art, is baffled by the intensity of feeling with which Hieronimo madly re-plays the terrible scene, and baffled, too, by the mounting endlessness of his demands. If the painter could make the impossible painting that Hieronimo desires—if he had the technique needed to tell Hieronimo's story in the way that Hieronimo desires—then this might all end in the image of a kind of justice, with Hieronimo brought to one of the murderers and releasing his rage upon him, as Achilles did with Hector. Yet Homer's Achilles found no satisfaction in his repeated tearing and dragging of Hector's body, and Hieronimo's beating the innocent painter (as if for the failure of his art) confesses itself as a poor and impotent substitute for the genuinely releasing violence that he both craves and despairs of.

* * * * *

For the rest of this chapter, I look in more detail at three particular works: Racine's *Phèdre*, Kafka's *The Trial*, and Yaël Farber's *Molora*—an *Oresteia* rewritten for post-apartheid South Africa. I go to them partly because each is a remarkable work which deals iconically with a story of crime and punishment, in fascinating though very different ways. But I also try to draw a thread between them. The cosmos in *Phèdre*, like the world of *The Trial*, is an environment which unremittingly threatens hostile judgment: a perception which exactly reflects, and is largely given to us through, the protagonist's subjectivity. How the

---

32   Ibid., pp.134–135.

protagonist is seen is everything: yet no observer can be imagined who stands cleanly outside the circle of that subjectivity, who might tell the story from another point of view. The kind of agony that this entails is shown to be intimately related to the (im)possibility of witness, to the kind of story that can be told. All of which casts light on the salience of witnessing in *Molora*, through which the story set in motion by past crime can be rewritten. In this play the past is not all-determining, but susceptible of remaking, in tandem with the way in which the *Oresteia* in Farber's production is reimagined and remade. Narrative momentum is disrupted in all three works, though differently, paralysing the sense of unfolding chronological process on which the satisfactions of the crime and punishment story rely. The absence of such closure, though itself a source of anguish, creates in *Molora* a space in which a different kind of story can be envisaged.

Phèdre

In the preface to Racine's great tragedy *Phèdre*, Racine reassures his reader that 'the least faults are severely punished'.[33] In itself, this might be simply to say that the proprieties are observed, that the play does not question the working of a moral order. But Racine further states that Phèdre's 'crime is rather a punishment of the gods than a movement of her will'.[34] Crime and punishment are here collapsed into one: Phèdre's crime is her passion for her stepson and her passion is her punishment. This is exactly true to the play, where it is *her* torment, *her* self-loathing, that identifies her feelings as an abomination. We are not invited to think seriously about the evil of adulterous desire as such, or her momentary complicity in the slander of Hippolyte, which in Racine (unlike Euripides) is in any case also driven by her passion. The truly dreadful thing is the state of self-horror which Phèdre exhibits, unaltered, from beginning to end of the play.

This is repeatedly expressed as her pollution of the daylight. That image has particular force: Phèdre is the granddaughter of the Sun, whom she addresses in her opening lines and refers to with her last

---

33   Jean Racine, *Jean Racine: Five Plays*, trans. by Kenneth Muir (New York: Hill and Wang, 1960), p.177.
34   Ibid., p.175.

words. The sun or daylight is a potent presence throughout the play, as real a presence as the figures on stage, if not indeed more real than many of them. It sees all, and exposes all; it is in one sense the supreme witness, the mythological equivalent of the eye of God. But the gods in *Phèdre* are only present in a paradoxical sense; they are felt as impassive, removed, and inaccessible, in a manner that has been related to the 'hidden god' of Jansenist theology, with which Racine was deeply familiar.[35] In Euripides, Aphrodite's motive in seizing on Phaedra was clear, and in Seneca's version Venus's motive was again clear though different. But in Racine, it is impenetrable. Euripides' play opens with the appearance of Aphrodite in person, who declares her resentments and intentions; what then happens to Hippolytus is the punishment she wills, refracted through a subtle web of human motive and interaction. Such visible involvement by the god is inconceivable in Racine's play, and not only for reasons of seventeenth-century theatrical convention. The cosmos in *Phèdre* expresses no intention, nor—with Phèdre already burning with passion as the play opens—does it act upon or react to the human situation. Instead, what it is felt to do is to watch and to judge. The Sun looks down, everywhere, and in the most extraordinary speech of the play Phèdre reflects—with a terror the more terrible for being so steadily contemplated—that even in the darkness of death there can be no escape from the condemning gaze of her parentage, since her father, Minos, acts in the underworld as judge of the dead.

> Wretch! And I live!
> And I endure the sight of sacred Phoebus
> From whom I am derived. My ancestor
> Is sire and master of the gods; and heaven,
> Nay all the universe, is teeming now
> With my forbears. Where then can I hide?
> Flee to eternal night. What do I say?
> For there my father holds the fatal urn,
> Put by the Fates in his stern hands, 'tis said.

---

35 See Lucien Goldmann, *The Hidden God: A Study of Tragic Vision in the 'Pensées' of Pascal and the Tragedies of Racine* (London: Verso, 2016), especially pp.33–39, 317–318, 375–391. As will be apparent, I differ from Goldmann in one respect; I do not think Phèdre ever entertained the illusion that her passion was compatible with living in the world. On this, see Simon Critchley's reading, 'I Want to Die, I Hate my Life—Phaedra's Malaise', in *Rethinking Tragedy*, ed. by Rita Felski (Baltimore: Johns Hopkins University Press, 2008), pp.170–198.

> Minos in Hades judges the pale ghosts.
> Ah, how his shade will tremble when his eyes
> Behold his daughter there, confessing sins—
> Crimes yet unknown in Hell!³⁶

It follows that Phèdre's situation admits of no conceivable development or release. The crime and punishment story normally relies on extension over time, but is here collapsed into a single endless moment. Even death will not release Phèdre from the terrible scrutiny of judgment, but merely removes her contaminating presence from the daylight. Aristotle thought that a tragedy should show a complete action—that it should, simply put, tell a story from beginning to end. But although there is some plot activity around Hippolyte and Aricie and the question of succession, this strikes us as trivial; in *Phèdre* there is, essentially, no action. Racine repeats in a different way what he had already done in an earlier play, *Bérénice*, exhaustively exploring and confirming the anguish of the opening situation, establishing with a finality purely formal that there can be no resolution or even development. Whereas in Euripides the exposure of Phaedra's passion leads onward to the fatal exchanges between Theseus and Hippolytus, with a consequentiality grounded in a larger world, in Racine the death of Hippolyte simply returns us to the all-encompassing consciousness of Phèdre, whose dying speech dominates the final scene. The nullity of human action, the vanity of human will, the banality of worldly affairs, are conveyed in a vision that might be called Augustinian. But whereas in Augustine's *Confessions* all is set in the light of a conversion story, in which God's responding voice is heard and narrative completion becomes possible, Phèdre's confessions move nothing forward, but merely release what she feels as her depravity into the daylight.

What renders her confessions inoperative is the absence of any auditor who adequately responds to her words. There are three occasions in the play when Phèdre speaks her passion. When she reveals her love to the nurse, Oenone has just four lines of response, horrified but also perfunctory; she is far less of a presence than the nurse in either Euripides or Seneca. When Phèdre speaks of her passion for the final time, in the dying speech in which she discloses the facts to Theseus,

---
36   Racine, *Five Plays*, pp.214–215.

his response is similarly perfunctory; it is also obliterative. 'Oh! that the memory of her black deed / Could perish with her!'[37] He then closes the play by speaking of other things.

The other person to whom she attempts to speak her passion is Hippolyte. Here we see most acutely what it means for crime and punishment to be collapsed into one, rather than given as a narrative sequence. It falls to Phèdre herself to experience her affliction as simultaneously both. Her propositioning of Hippolyte is simultaneously an appeal to him to punish her, and to act as the heroic avenger of a monstrous crime.

> Venge-toi, punis-moi d'un odieux amour.
> Digne fils du héros qui t'a donné le jour,
> Délivre l'univers d'un monstre qui t'irrite.[38]

> Avenge yourself; punish an odious love,
> Son worthy of the hero who gave you the light,
> Free the universe of a monster who offends you.[39]

Theseus cleansed the land of monstrosity; let his son now follow him in removing another vexatious monster from the world. Phèdre begs to become that kind of story, a figure in a revenge narrative, and so to be released from her own consciousness. Her way of calling him Theseus's son—'qui t'a donné le jour'—underlines that the world of daylight, the world seen by the sun, properly belongs to him. In that world she is a monster, an abomination. And so, she opens or exposes her heart to him—'Voilà mon coeur'—only so that he may strike at it, to end her life and turn her into story. The desire to be penetrated is entirely one with the desire to be punished; the crime would be what it already is, the punishment. But the sword drops from his hand, or she takes it from him; he makes no move, and speaks no word at all in reply. When the Nurse hears someone else approaching she hurries Phèdre away. 'Évitez des témoins odieux', keep away from hateful witnesses.[40]

The inability of her auditors to bear witness to her inner life underlines what is dreadful in the silent, impassive witness of the Sun. The Sun does

---

37 Ibid., p.225.
38 Jean Racine, *Théâtre Complet*, 2 vols (Paris: Garnier-Flammarion, 1965) II, p.223.
39 Racine, *Five Plays*, p.198, slightly altered.
40 Racine, *Théâtre Complet* II, p.223.

not tell her story or point its direction, and for that reason its terrible pressure can be felt only as reflecting and confirming her own feelings of self-horror. Racine was writing at a time and in a culture where the classical gods had largely dwindled into literary decoration, or could be taken seriously only as allegories or figures of human faculties or feelings. To speak of Venus was a way of speaking about human sexual desire; the shift from the cosmological to the psychological was almost complete. Racine, however, reaches back beyond the modernity of his age to imagine a charged cosmos, containing powers that exist outside the circle of the mind.[41] Phèdre, like her Greek original, feels herself to be *possessed* by eros, an overwhelming desire for Hippolyte that never ceases to be alien to her.

> Ce n'est plus une ardeur dans mes veines cachée:
> C'est Vénus toute entière à sa proie attachée.[42]
>
>   it is no more
> A passion hidden in my veins, but now
> It's Venus fastened on her helpless prey.[43]

But Racine's Venus, as I have said, has no discernible intentionality or presence; she keeps her distance and her counsel, like the Sun. They exist for us only in Phèdre's appalled consciousness; no other character registers their pressure. Racine has thus placed Phèdre, with exquisite precision, at the interface between the cosmological and the psychological, at the point where each becomes an aspect of the other. The cosmos being both implacable and inert, it becomes realisable only as (from a psychological perspective) the projection of her self-loathing. Yet it is equally true to say that her self-loathing flows from her sense of how she is regarded,

---

[41] As well as the power of Venus and the gaze of the Sun, there is also the emergence of the monster from the sea which destroys Hippolyte, vividly described in the messenger-speech by Théramène. This representation of a supernatural force was immensely contentious in its day. But note that Hippolyte's death does *not*, in Racine, endorse the crime-and-punishment story. Such a story can be extracted from the Euripides version, where Hippolytus has offended Aphrodite by disparaging her, a disparagement then repeated by his rant against women, in a speech which appears to trigger Phaedra's move against him. In Racine, however, Hippolyte has impeccable manners and, being in love with Aricie, is sexually unobjectionable. The crime-and-punishment model comes to us only through Phèdre's subjectivity; it exists only in Phèdre's subjectivity.

[42] Racine, *Théâtre Complet* II, p.211.

[43] Racine, *Five Plays*, p.187.

from the kind of witness posited as adequate to the archaic intensity of her inner life. As she is possessed by a passion that is beyond the capacity of those around her to comprehend, it is the cosmos that becomes her witness, giving the only reflection of her affliction that is available to her. Her speeches make real a charged cosmos which the contemporary world (the world both of Hippolyte and of Louis XIV) knows nothing of—that cosmos from which she is authentically descended as, in Racine's darkly wonderful cadence, 'la fille de Minos et de Pasiphaé'.[44] But the cosmos being silent, it can only reflect her anguish back to her and upon her, both establishing her crime (polluting the daylight) and constituting her punishment. It is coterminous with the limits of her subjectivity, which there is nothing beyond. Everything is filled with—in both senses of the phrase at once—the consciousness of Phèdre.

The Trial

Subjectivity is also everything in Kafka's *The Trial*, to the point where it can hardly be recognised as such. Kafka's novel is the account of a man arrested, scrutinised, and eventually executed for some crime which is never revealed to him.

> Someone must have been telling lies about Joseph K., for without having done anything wrong he was arrested one fine morning.[45]

The book can be read as a parable of innocence oppressed, a dystopian prophecy of the evil of the totalitarian state, operating through the impenetrable procedures of a mindless bureaucracy. In this reading, everything that happens is felt to be driven by some obscure but inexorable force whose grounds are never apparent. The court is potentially everywhere; it comes to seem that everyone has or may have a connection with it. The book is haunted by a faint sense of religious allegory, with rumours of ever higher courts and higher advocates, evoking not only bureaucratic madness but also an ineffable sublime. If it is not God who accuses and condemns K., it is a bureaucracy so mysterious as to constitute a parodic version of the divine. With this

---

44 Racine, *Théâtre Complet* II, p.202.
45 Franz Kafka, *The Trial*, trans. by Willa Muir and Edwin Muir (Harmondsworth: Penguin, 1974), p.7.

mysterious, all-pervasive court, Kafka figures a kind of equivalent for those Greek gods and oracles who stand for an irresistible if frequently unintelligible fate, against which no effective agency is possible.

This dimension, which presents itself to the modern reader as essentially political, is one great part of the book's power. But it is shot through by a different quality of nightmare, the sense that K. is in some way colluding with or contributing to the forces that oppress him, so that the omnipresent processes of the court are not as purely external as they appear. 'Certainly, I am surprised, but I am by no means very surprised'[46] is K's comment on his arrest, and this idea—that the bizarre events of the narrative are half-expected or indistinctly foreknown—finds its echo in the way that so many of K's random encounters are with figures who already know of him and of his case. This is a mark of the court's omnipresence, to be sure, but that omnipresence is itself an expression of the way that the court and its influence are a reflection of K's own consciousness, for the narrative is told entirely from K's point of view. The narrative voice which tells us of the situation oppressing him is indistinguishable from K's experience of feeling oppressed, and this introduces a curiously self-fulfilling quality to the whole. His accusers, he is told, 'never go hunting for crime in the populace, but, as the Law decrees, are drawn towards the guilty'.[47] Or as K. puts the inverse of this thought, in a moment of bravado, 'it is only a trial if I recognize it as such'—which he immediately follows with 'But for the moment I do recognize it.'[48] Although the intimations of accusation are externally visited upon K., they are continually amplified by his responses, as though the whole narrative were responsive to an all-too-performative paranoia. Whatever he does seems to have the potential to worsen his case—whether he employs an advocate or dismisses him, whether he defies the Court or cooperates with it, and whenever he involves himself with women. He lives, so to speak, in the consciousness of perpetual potential *hamartia*, obsessively but ineffectually calculating and recalculating how he is doing in negotiating the minefield. 'Was it not also possible and even extremely probable that he was overlooking other

---

46   Ibid., p.7.
47   Ibid., p.12.
48   Ibid., p.49.

dangers as well, or blindly running into them?'[49] The attempt to prepare documents for his defence is itself felt as a punishment that presupposes the conviction of guilt. 'It looked like a kind of torture sanctioned by the Court, arising from his case and concomitant with it.'[50] Merely to declare his innocence—but of what unknown charge?—is received as hubris; 'don't make such an outcry about your feeling innocent, it spoils the not unfavourable impression you make in other respects.'[51] Even more self-defeating is to question the rightness of judicial process.

> 'But I am not guilty,' said K.; 'it's a misunderstanding. And if it comes to that, how can any man be called guilty. We are all simply men here, one as much as the other.' 'That is true,' said the priest, 'but that's how all guilty men talk.'[52]

In accordance with this, the narrative has at many moments a marked dream-quality. There are the sudden intrusions of erotic possibility, or the effect of K. finding his way by chance to the place appointed by his hearing, or the way that the scene of judicial whipping, which should take place elsewhere, mysteriously transfers itself to his place of work. Repeatedly, K's attention drifts from the matter at hand to fasten on some minor detail of his environment as if this held some latent significance, as is the way in dreams. This dream-quality underlines the impression that, in some elusive sense, K's plight is an aspect of his subjectivity, that he is obscurely in collusion with the forces oppressing him. At several moments, he takes no step to resist those forces despite apparent opportunities to do so—he fails to make a phone call to his friend the State Attorney, for example, or to seek information from the figure explicitly introduced to him as the Information-Giver. When his executioners are taking him to his place of execution, a policeman steps towards the group as if to intervene: K. hurries them all away from what might conceivably have been rescue. At the beginning it occurs to K. that those arresting him might have no authority to do so or even power to detain him: should he try just walking straight past them? But instead, 'he chose that certainty which the natural course of things would be

---

49 Ibid., p.153.
50 Ibid., p.148.
51 Ibid., p.19.
52 Ibid., p.232.

bound to bring'; 'If this was a comedy, he would insist on playing it to the end.'[53]

K. plays along with the necessary course of things, as he thinks of it. This feels like a rationalisation of his fearfulness, but also a relieving denial of the arbitrariness of events, that seeks for a Hamlet-like intuition of a something that shapes our ends. Such playing along with apparent necessity is exactly the subject of the parable which the prison-chaplain shares with K., which we gather constitutes the opening paragraph of the Law. In this parable, there is a man come from the country who wishes to gain access to the law. The door stands open, but an intimidating gatekeeper tells him that he may not yet enter: he is welcome to try (the gatekeeper seems to stand aside), but he should know that a series of ever more intimidating gatekeepers will await him inside. And so the man from the country waits by the gate, waits for some change in circumstances or in the gatekeeper's response, waits for many years until death comes for him and the door only then is closed, which he is told was made specially for him. One interpretation of this enigmatic tale is that the man could have walked straight in, that by assuming the gatekeeper would stop him he gave him the power to do so. This is only one interpretation, and the prison-chaplain explains at dizzying length that commentators differ and that many interpretations are possible. Nevertheless, he began by saying that K. was in error about the court, and that the parable addresses K's error.[54] Could that error be the assumption that the perception of necessity is well grounded? It is at the end of this discussion that the prison-chaplain makes what may be a crucial assertion: 'it is not necessary to accept everything [said by the gatekeeper] as true, one must only accept it as necessary'.[55] K. meets this with 'A melancholy conclusion. It turns lying into a universal principle'—or, in the original, *Die Lüge wird zur Weltordnung gemacht*, the lie is made into the order of the world. Kafka's narrative mimics exactly this principle: the world of *The Trial* is filled by the omnipresence of the fantastical court, and although we cannot say that this omnipresence is a lie, we are aware that it is sustained by K's consciousness, which

---

53   Ibid., pp.14, 11.
54   The German term used, *sich täuschen*—a familiar term meaning to be wrong or mistaken—is a reflexive verb, which can also imply self-deception.
55   Kafka, *The Trial*, p.243.

anxiously suspects itself to be uncertain, shifting, and fallible, but can access no criterion by which truth might be ascertained, no foothold in a world outside itself.

This effect is intensified by its resonance with the mode of Kafka's writing, so acutely uncertain of finding a readership, or (more radically) of *being readable*. A theatre piece, no matter how experimental, cannot but imply an audience. But the enigmatic quality of Kafka's fiction hopes against hope to find readers, to escape the condition of being a world unto itself. That such hope, inherent in the act of writing, was always on the edge of despair, is a matter of biography: *The Trial* was abandoned unfinished, like Kafka's other novels, with instruction that they be destroyed after his death. But this closeness to despair percolates the experience of the text itself, in K's anxiety that he will be badly judged because he has never been properly heard, has never established the kind of relation with another that would begin to clarify things by grounding his perceptions in a consciousness beyond themselves. Referring to Kafka's story 'A Hunger-Artist', David Constantine finds something of large implication for his whole project as a writer:

> The hunger artist is very anxious to have witnesses there in the cage with him, to see that he does not cheat. It is an image very close to Kafka's own anxiety that in moving away from mimetic and representational art into the greater autonomy of metaphor he is entering a zone where his criteria for success—which is to say, for truthfulness—are no longer obvious. His truth becomes less and less verifiable by anybody else.[56]

The absence of witness is central to this, for one of the things which true witness does is to create some space between one's immediate consciousness and the totality of the situation. K. is far from indifferent to those around him; a crucial aspect of his plight is his acute sensitivity to how he may be regarded. He is hyper-alert to the impression he may be making on others and whether he is losing or gaining ground in their esteem, speculating well beyond any sentiment which they express. His spurts of defiance or self-assertion go hand in hand with anxiety that he has given offence; his gestures of conciliation or propitiation express the fear that he is now a humiliated figure. These worrisome speculations

---

56 David Constantine, 'Kafka's writing and our reading', in *The Cambridge Companion to Kafka*, ed. by Julian Preece (Cambridge: Cambridge University Press, 2002), p.23.

turn almost all his encounters into encounters with the mysterious court that is judging him, a paranoia rationalised as the thought that the people he encounters must be employed by the court or have influential connections with it. For example, at the first hearing his attention is fixed less on the examining magistrate than on how the spectators in the room are responding to what he says: those in one half of the room seem to be for him, those in the other seem to be against, but then they intermingle, and meanwhile there is a row of greybeards who may be particularly significant and who remain completely impassive. In another corner, still others engage in erotic diversions and seem not to be attending to K. at all. As K. perceives them, their responses are plural, variable, and enigmatic; above all they are mirrors of the anxious speculations K. makes about them. This then leads to his discovery that beneath their outer clothing they all carry the insignia of the court, insignia which he failed to notice at first. Once more it is the restless activity of his consciousness that discovers the court to be everywhere, that *realises* the court as everywhere.

This mirroring quality means that the people K. encounters can never be felt as standing sufficiently outside him to be true witnesses. Without such witnesses, consciousness can find in the world only its own reflection.

All this is conveyed through Kafka's narrative voice, a remorseless form of free indirect narrative which renders the world of K's perception and reflections without demur or endorsement or supply of perspective of any kind. This impassive quality—felt especially in the deadpan rendering of what might easily have been registered as absurd or ridiculous—has some family resemblance to the terrible impassivity of the Sun in *Phèdre*. When the prison-chaplain has finished with the parable of the law, he walks with K. in silence, and K. wonders what is coming next, such as might clarify the priest's intention in speaking to him. But nothing is coming next. The priest walks in silence with K. for some time, through the steadily darkening and labyrinthine cathedral. K. asks about the exit, and the priest replies that K. is free to leave if he wishes. But this induces in K. a kind of panic; how, in the absence of intentionality, can there be an exit?

> 'I can't find my way out alone in this darkness,' said K. 'Turn left to the wall,' said the priest, 'then follow the wall without leaving it and you'll

come to a door.' The priest had already taken a step or two away from him, but K. cried out in a loud voice. 'Please wait a moment.' 'I am waiting,' said the priest. 'Don't you want anything more to do with me?' asked K. 'No,' said the priest. 'You were so friendly to me for a time,' said K., 'and explained so much to me, and now you let me go as if you cared nothing about me.' 'But you have to leave now,' said the priest. 'Well, yes,' said K., 'you must understand that.' 'First you must understand who I am,' said the priest. 'You are the prison chaplain,' said K., groping his way nearer to the priest again; his immediate return to the Bank was not so necessary as he had made out, he could quite well stay longer. 'That means I belong to the Court,' said the priest. 'So why should I want anything from you? The Court wants nothing from you. It receives you when you come and it releases you when you go.'[57]

That void of impassivity or indifference is terrible to K. His obsession with what impression he is making on others, together with his efforts to determine that impression though gestures of antagonism or conciliation, are attempts to fill that terrible void, attempts which largely return upon him as the echoes of his own anxiety. Beneath this is the dread that he may be judged—may already have been judged—*without ever being heard.*

The crime and punishment story thus emerges with particular clarity as related to the absence of witness. When the priest said to K., 'First you must understand who I am', could there have been some other response than K's repetition of what has already been told? Is there a possibility that 'You are the prison chaplain' misses? By knowing his interlocutor only as a functionary of the court, K's answer both re-affirms that the court is everywhere and blocks out the possibility of any more human relation. The idea that he is on trial acts to fill this void, to give the mind's anxiety and paranoia an apparently external object with the hope of a narrative shape. It is K. himself who insists that 'in the end, out of nothing at all, an enormous fabric of guilt will be conjured up.'[58] The sense of K's oblique complicity in the processes which enmesh him, along with the banality of his responses and the pettiness and ineffectuality of his enclosing self-concern, come to induce in the reader, and perhaps also in K. himself, a sense if not exactly of his guilt, then of his wrongness, of the radical inappropriateness of his responses to

---

57   Kafka, *The Trial*, p.244, slightly altered.
58   Ibid., p.165.

the obscurely challenging nature of his situation. Like some parody of a tragic hero, he veers between postures of bravado and feelings of the most abject humiliation, neither of which seem well founded. When his execution comes, we are not greatly surprised, and not greatly indignant, and neither is he. It is as if the gravitational pull of the Story is so great that it produces, alongside the manifest parable of injustice, a shadow-image of a justice more monstrous and disturbing than sheer injustice could be.

Yet the power of that shadow is also challenged. The impassive neutrality of the narrative voice sits on the edge of being readable as a deadpan black comedy that would be coming from somewhere outside the horror. The discontinuities of the narrative have the effect of weakening the chain of cause and effect which the Story requires. And the intimations that the world of the court is in some sense sustained by K's consciousness open the possibility that, if K. could only be seen from some *other* point of view—if there were, so to speak, a point of view—this might be transformative.

For this possibility, we are given one remarkable moment just before the end. One tiny moment of freedom and non-compliance enables K. to see, or to imagine, a figure who may come from entirely outside the Story:

> Then one of them opened his frock-coat and out of a sheath that hung from a belt girt round his waistcoat drew a long, thin, double-edged butcher's knife, held it up, and tested the cutting edges in the moonlight. Once more the odious ceremonial of courtesy began, the first handed the knife across K. to the second, who handed it across K. back again to the first. K. now perceived clearly that he was supposed to seize the knife himself, as it travelled from hand to hand above him, and plunge it into his own breast. But he did not do so, he merely turned his head, which was still free to move, and gazed around him. He could not completely rise to the occasion, he could not relieve the officials of all their tasks; the responsibility for this last failure of his lay with him who had not left him the remnant of strength necessary for the deed. His glance fell on the top story of the house adjoining the quarry. With a flicker as of a light going up, the casements of a window there suddenly flew open; a human figure, faint and insubstantial at that distance and that height, leaned abruptly far forward and stretched both arms still farther. Who was it? A friend? A good person? Someone who sympathized? Someone who wanted to help? Was it one person only? Or were they all there? Was help at hand? Were there some arguments in his favour that had been

> overlooked? Of course there must be. Logic is doubtless unshakeable, but it cannot withstand a man who wants to go on living. Where was the Judge whom he had never seen? Where was the High Court, to which he had never penetrated? He raised his hands and spread out all his fingers.[59]

K. sees or imagines a supportive witness, quite outside the apparatus of the trial—a figure who might be reaching out to him and might be able to enter into his feelings. This goes with a change in the narrative voice. The narrator normally registers K's subjectivity only as it is observed by K. himself, but in this series of urgent questions the narrator participates directly in the movements and emotions of his mind. The narrator's reaching out to K. mirrors the reaching-out gesture of the figure at the window, and this is further mirrored in the act of K's reaching up in a desire for, a belief in the possibility of, real connection. It is this imagined possibility of another's understanding and support that makes K., for perhaps the first time in the book, into a human being who convincingly wants to live. Such a being can overthrow even the unshakeable logic of the trial, we are told: this reads still as K's voice, yet can also be heard as the narrator's, speaking with the kind of unambiguous generality that Kafka never normally allows. Crucially, the sentence responds to and directly answers K's question; K's cry elicits a response. This moment of implied dialogue and support allows K. to challenge the entire process and authority of the trial. Where was the judge? Where was the high court?—as if questioning whether such entities even exist.

This challenge is not sustained; the crime and punishment story reasserts itself.

> But the hands of one of the gentlemen were already at K.'s throat, while the other thrust the knife into his heart and turned it there twice. With failing eyes K. could still see the two of them, cheek leaning against cheek, immediately before his face, watching the outcome. 'Like a dog!' he said: it was as if he meant the shame of it to outlive him.[60]

We might think of Othello, doing execution on himself as 'the circumcised dog'. Unlike Othello, K. does not set the seal on the crime-and-punishment story by his own self-punishing act, although he believes himself invited to do so. Something in him resists. Still, he would seem

---

59 Ibid., pp.250–251, slightly altered.
60 Ibid., p.251, slightly altered.

to accept that the story of his death is the story of his shame, and that it is as a culpably shameful figure that he must be regarded. This is, perhaps, to accede to the Story's all-determining power. Yet in those final words ('as if he meant', *als solle*), the narrator is neither impassive nor punitive, but reaches out to discern an intentionality behind K's words. This is to recognise or realise K., however uncertainly, as a person not wholly defined by the outcome of his trial. A person whose fate becomes, at that moment, tragic.

Molora: a post-apartheid *Oresteia*

Kafka's nightmarish telling of the crime and punishment story evokes it with great power, but the figure at the window momentarily suggests how a different kind of witnessing might undo the Story's logic-like grip on the mind. The transformative potential of witnessing is crucial to Yaël Farber's play *Molora*, first performed in South Africa in 2003, then revised and developed into the published version of 2008. The play re-imagines the *Oresteia* story as the testimonies of Klytemnestra and Elektra[61] at the post-apartheid Truth and Reconciliation Commission; Klytemnestra is white, Elektra black. Farber has elsewhere related the testimonial quality of her theatre work to the function of the Commission:

> The power of having a *listener*, was evident during the Truth And Reconciliation Commission. It was at least a platform for survivors to finally *speak* and have people *bear witness to their pain*. Without a listener who believes and empathises with you, you are dislocated from—yet deeply shaped by—your own story.[62]

Molora's staging reflects that parallel between theatre and the Commission. The playing area is flanked by two opposing tables with microphones at which the two women give testimony as to the past—testimonies which develop into a re-enacting of their conflict in the playing space between them. The *Oresteia* story is thus intertwined with that of contemporary South Africa; when Klytemnestra demands

---

61 I follow Farber's transliteration of the names to distinguish her figures from those in the original Greek plays.
62 Yaël Farber, *Theatre as Witness: Three Testimonial Plays from South Africa* (London: Oberon Books, 2008), p.24 (her emphasis).

to know where Elektra has sent the baby Orestes, for example, she subjects her to forms of torture that resemble familiar police methods of interrogation. This strong contemporary reference marks a great difference from *Phèdre* or *The Trial*: here there is manifest oppression, rooted in the actual crime of apartheid which the audience knows from the world outside the play, and the desire and rationale for justice—for condemnation and retribution—is all the keener. The source of the evil can be more plausibly located than was possible in the *Oresteia*. Yet *Molora* is not a contemporary play in Greek dress, but keeps a double focus: even while it adapts the Greek story to the legacy of apartheid, it invites us to see that legacy as illuminating the meaning of the Greek story, and to understand it by the light of that story. This double focus on past and present is conveyed through re-enactment: the central scenes of the play re-enact the *Oresteia* story even as they re-enact the conflict between Klytemnestra and Elektra. The question of whether it is possible to move on from the damage of history while still honouring its reality—the question of whether the Furies can plausibly be appeased—is present at the level of form as well as content.

For much of the play, events largely follow the Greek story (although Farber loosens its monolithic quality by incorporating lines from all three Greek versions). Klytemnestra kills Agamemnon, and claims to do so as an avenger: he not only sacrificed Iphigenia, but killed her first husband and child. She can therefore describe her deed as 'a Masterpiece of Justice', and repeat the defence made by Clytemnestra in Aeschylus: 'but I had an ally in this—for justice slew him, and not I alone'.[63] The baby Orestes is smuggled away to safety by Elektra, and when grown to manhood he returns, black-skinned like his sister; as in Aeschylus, the siblings set themselves to act as the instruments of vengeance.

> It falls softly—the spirit of revenge.
> The brooding Fury finally comes -
> leading a child inside the house
> to cleanse the stain of blood from long ago.[64]

---

63 Yaël Farber, *Molora: Based on the Oresteia by Aeschylus* (London: Oberon Books, 2008), pp.23, 36.
64 Farber, *Molora*, pp.46–47.

Elektra is speaking here at her testimony table, repeating the commentary of the Chorus in Aeschylus' *Libation Bearers*. Orestes duly begins by killing Ayesthus (Aegisthus), before brother and sister turn to address the 'greater deed' of matricide.

But now the determining Story begins to loosen and unravel, in ways that are all to do with Farber's Chorus. The Chorus is made up of seven women[65] from the Xhosa community, skilled in the arts of traditional singing and musical accompaniment; their music frames or accompanies the action. They sit on chairs at the back of the playing area, like a reflection or extension of the audience, also like the people who came to the hearings of the Truth and Reconciliation Commission, which were held in public. They provide commentary on the action in the manner of a Greek chorus, but at key moments they intervene in the action more significantly than any Greek chorus does or could. When Orestes kills Ayesthus, one of the women appears to him and rebukes him. She says, in Xhosa,

> My child! Why do you kill?
> A human being should never be murdered.
> Do you know that human blood will haunt you always?
> What you have done is terrible.
> Never kill again.[66]

Orestes is unsure whether she is real or a vision, the stage direction tells us, and this recalls the liminal status of the Furies who appear to Orestes, but not as yet to us, after he has killed his mother in the *Libation Bearers*. And the woman speaks, in part, like a Fury: 'human blood will haunt you always'. Yet utterly unlike the Furies is the concern for a possible future: 'Never kill again.' When Orestes goes with Elektra to kill Klytemnestra, it is the presence of the Chorus and their song that makes it impossible for him to do so.

> *ORESTES lifts the axe high over his head, but as he prepares to kill his mother, a WOMAN from the CHORUS starts to sing a haunting song. ORESTES tries to shake off the sound of it. […] He lifts the axe again, but the WOMEN rise*

---

65 In the directions to the 2008 text, there is also one man, whose role is to translate between English and Xhosa; Farber sometimes refers to him as part of the Chorus, but more often speaks of the Chorus as made up of women.
66 Farber, *Molora*, pp.69–70.

and move across the performance area. He tries several times to see the deed through—but cannot.[67]

Elektra is appalled at his reluctance, condemns him as womanly. She cannot 'forget her hatred', 'the Furies demand [the deed]'. She seizes the axe herself and runs at Klytemnestra; this time the women's intervention is direct.

> *The WOMEN of the CHORUS move swiftly as one. They grab ELEKTRA and overpower her.*
>
> *ELEKTRA screams in rage as they wrestle the axe from her hands. They restrain her and she finally breaks down and weeps for all the injustices done to her, her brother and her father. She slowly finds her breath. UMASENGWANA (Milking / Friction Drum) begins its deep, haunting sound. ELEKTRA emerges from the knot of WOMEN. She and ORESTES are focused on their mother—still cowering centre stage. They crawl toward her slowly. KLYTEMNESTRA— uncertain of what they will do to her—draws back in terror. As they reach their mother, they slowly stand together and extend their hands to help her up. Once on her feet, she is a broken woman. She backs away and leaves the performance platform, resuming her place at her Testimony Table.*
>
> *The WOMEN of the CHORUS explode into song, circling brother and sister.*[68]

Kafka's K. hoped that the person looking out at the window might be 'einer, der teilnahm'—someone who sympathised, but also, in the primary meaning of the German, someone who was taking part. The women in *Molora*, who sit as 'Witnesses to the testimonies',[69] take part in the most direct and dramatic way, and this proves transformative. As Klytemnestra had pleaded to an implacable Elektra, the given story may after all be rewritten, the atrocities of the past may not be all-determining:

> ELEKTRA: This night's end is already written.
> Our destiny must be played out!
>
> KLYTEMNESTRA: Nothing ... nothing is written.
> Do not choose to be me.[70]

If this rewriting of the ending depended merely on the physical restraining of Elektra, it would be meaningless. What makes the moment

---

67 Ibid., p.75.
68 Ibid., p.77.
69 Ibid., p.46.
70 Ibid., p.74.

so effective is the sense of *a transformative power in the act of witnessing*, as the women practise it.

There are three elements to this that can be specially underlined, all of which have implication beyond themselves. One is that the women have been participating in the whole of the action, especially through their singing and their music. Their singing accompanies the killing of Agamemnon; they acclaim the return of Orestes with a traditional song of initiation that urges him to do manly things and claim his inheritance; and as Elektra and Orestes invoke the resentment of the dead and unfold their project of retribution, the music of the Chorus everywhere strengthens the pulse of their action. The point is that they support and amplify *all* the emotions of the drama, the impulse to retribution no less than the desire for release from the bloody cycle of killing. Because of this, we do not feel their restraining of Elektra to be some thin liberal denial of atavistic forces, but to emerge out of an intimate, participatory understanding of those forces. The sense of their music as an ancient craft, and their wisdom as a traditional wisdom, helps here too.

As readers of Farber's play-text, we cannot hear that music. This is how Farber described it, and its effect on her, in an interview:

> It's called split or overtone singing. It's an extraordinary technique that they're trained in from a very early age. It turns the vocal cords into some kind of extraordinary musical instrument, that doesn't sound human but can only be from a human being, because it's so organic. The notes contrast with each other and create this vibration.
>
> It's an absolutely unearthly sound. While I was writing the show, I was eight months pregnant. It makes me think of what it must be like to hear the outside world from within the womb. The technique reduces sound to resonances and bass notes that create […] a calling, back to something ancestral, regardless of what culture you come from. It grounds the emotional storyline that the three actors carry. It sounds like earth if you could amplify what's going on beneath granite and rock and lava and water.
>
> When I heard it, I said, "This is the chorus. I don't need them to say a word. If they can just make that sound, I'll come home to whatever bitter truth you're trying to make me face. Just hold me in that sound, between

every horrifying and difficult scene to watch, and I will stay the course with you."[71]

Perhaps something of its quality or function may also be suggested by Toni Morrison's description of the sound made by the thirty singing women who come to Sethe's house at the climax of *Beloved*:

> The voices of women searched for the right combination, the key, the code, the sound that broke the back of words. Building voice upon voice until they found it, and when they did it was a wave of sound wide enough to sound deep water and knock the pods of chestnut trees. It broke over Sethe and she trembled like the baptized in its wash.[72]

The neighbourhood women have previously shunned Sethe, but their arrival now, and how they respond to what they see, is crucial. Like Farber's chorus, they will physically restrain Sethe from an act of violence that would perpetuate the atrocities of the past, and like Farber's chorus it is their collective presence, and the sound that they collectively make—something beyond or other than rational discourse—that makes possible a turning-point, a conceivable new beginning.[73]

What Sethe hears in the voices of the women is a fusion of the present with a memory from the past: 'for Sethe it was as though the Clearing had come to her with all its heat and simmering leaves, where the voices of women [...]'—and in the words that follow, quoted above, memory and the present moment interpenetrate one another. The second crucial element to the function of Farber's chorus is the dynamic relation between present and past that they activate. The protagonists in *Molora* are already doing more than merely testifying to the past when they re-enact it as theatre, unearthing what is buried, performing it in present time. But this by itself is only to make the past present, not necessarily to challenge its dominance. The Chorus of Women do more

---

71 Farber, Yaël, 'MoLoRa: The Independent Interview with Yael Farber', *Indy Week*, 17 March 2010, https://indyweek.com/culture/archives-culture/molora-independent-interview-yael-farber/
72 Toni Morrison, *Beloved* (London: Picador, 1988), p.261.
73 Sethe is of course overwhelmingly a victim. Yet the shadow of the crime-and-punishment story extends even to her, with the great feast given at her house being cast as an act of culpable hubris, and her subsequent act of killing her child placing her beyond the pale of the community's understanding or sympathy. It is this story of crime and punishment that the women set aside when they come to her house to exorcise the spirit that afflicts her.

than this, moving fluidly out of their position as present-time 'Witnesses of the testimonies' to influence what happens now, which becomes what happened then: past and present are both in play. Theirs is a witnessing that has a power to transform the past—that is, to transform its meaning for the present, to transform how we are able to regard it.

The third element I want to underline is the gender of the chorus: specifically, the traditionally female forms of nurture and protection that the Women give. More than once they encircle Elektra, forming a protective enclosure, shielding her from Klytemnestra or enabling her and her brother to play together like young animals. They act as midwives to enable Klytemnestra to give birth to the snake of her dream. It is a woman within the chorus who receives the baby Orestes from Elektra and takes the child to the other women, who *'gather around the "child", kissing and touching the bundle'*.[74] The same woman will later step forward to rebuke Orestes for killing Ayesthus and to warn him against further bloodshed; she addresses him as 'my child', for she has been as a mother to him.[75] And it is from within *'the knot of WOMEN'* that Elektra screams and cries when she is restrained from killing her mother; when she 'emerges' from that knot, crawling at first, there is more than a suggestion of a birth-event into a new life.[76]

At these moments, *Molora* intimates that there is a close analogy between this supportive, transformative witnessing and the kind of attention that a mother gives her child. This analogy will be explored more fully in the chapter that follows. In Farber's play, meanwhile, there is clearly a running contrast between the dangerous or destructive mothering of Klytemnestra and the good nurture offered by the Women— or, put differently, between the denial of birthright to the black children and the rich inheritance suggested by the traditional Xhosa practices.[77] We can also note that Farber makes the *Oresteia* story into one that is primarily about women (Orestes is the minor part, Agamemnon and Ayesthus are not presented by actors at all), and that the overcoming of a negative by a positive image of the female is a crucial part of its

---

74 Farber, *Molora*, p.29.
75 Ibid., p.69.
76 Ibid., p.77.
77 The Chorus's behaviour can be seen as expressing a communitarian ethics rooted in traditional southern African culture. See Philip Zapkin, '*Ubuntu* Theater: Building a Human World in Yael Farber's *Molora*', *PMLA* 136 (2021), 386–400.

meaning. This is likewise true of the *Oresteia*, where the Furies are transformed, or at least reconceptualised, as the Eumenides, or 'kindly ones': figures of terrible archaic female resentment and violence become figures of (mostly) benevolent nurture, whose presence in the city is a blessing. This largely happens because of how they are listened to. Athene's steady refusal to see the Furies as monstrous or disgusting, her steady countenancing of all the pain and rage that they bring, her steady vision of their integration within the forms of the city—it is how she regards them that is transformative. In the overall structure of the trilogy, too, the dominant images of destructive women with which we began—Clytemnestra most obviously, but also Helen as the chorus evoke her—have given way to the final section in which only female figures are present on stage, moving toward reconciliation and harmony. (This is so even if, as the price paid, there has been much displacement of female by male interests along the way.) In *Molora*, less ambiguously, the image of formidable female hatred given by both Klytemnestra and Elektra— formally opposed but also similar in their burning resentment—is displaced by the different female strength exhibited by the Chorus, until the destructiveness of both protagonists has drained away. This affirmative movement seems to depend on the ability to hold a positive image of the female figure and of broadly maternal function.

This is not to say that *Molora* quite asserts or achieves reconciliation. Something important is done when Elektra and Orestes help Klytemnestra to her feet, but they can hardly be described as reconciled. The stage direction that describes her as 'a broken woman' is sufficiently vindictive.[78] And although the praise-singer's final lines re-establish inter-generational harmony by invoking the ancestors, and the play ends with the assertion of new beginnings, this is accompanied by a more ambivalent symbol, inspired by the dust falling on the remains of the twin towers and the city of New York in the days after 9/11. '*A fine powdery substance gently floats down*' onto all on stage, while Klytemnestra comments, 'It falls softly the residue of revenge [...] / Like rain.'[79] 'Molora' is the Sesotho word for ash—what remains of bodies after burning, what remains after fire has burnt itself out, the residue of revenge. 'Like rain' recalls Clytemnestra's exultant image in

---
78   Farber, *Molora*, p.77.
79   Ibid., p.79. This line revises Elektra's earlier 'It falls softly—the spirit of revenge.'

Aeschylus, repeated in *Molora*, of Agamemnon's blood spattering her like the life-giving rain upon the land, but also transforms that image into something far gentler and more muted, even as ash itself marks that a transformation has taken place. Ash, unlike rain, brings no moisture; yet it can fertilise the soil. The falling ash marks that the time of revenge is over, yet also that the consequences of revenge affect everything. We are invited, I think, to see the image as healing, while being made aware that this depends on our choosing so to see it; we too are invited to take part. This accords with Farber's note on the staging of the play. *'Contact with the audience must be immediate and dynamic, with the audience complicit—experiencing the story as witnesses or participants in the room, rather than as voyeurs excluded from yet looking in on the world of the story.'*[80]

In *Molora*, the crime-and-punishment story is derailed with a completeness unusual in tragedy, although the *Oresteia* provides one powerful precedent. More often, the Story—once invoked—is played through to its outcome, but as a kind of feint, a sop to Cerberus: while it satisfies one part of the mind, space is created for a more complex apprehension to arise. Tragic feeling arises from our sense that the story of crime and punishment does not after all perfectly fit the case, even while we are compelled to acknowledge the strength of the forces that drive it. For we may be appalled by the damage done, the pain inflicted or self-inflicted, as the story plays itself through, demanding its own bloody sacrifices. Or in some versions, it may be performed with a parodic excess and exhilaration that constitutes its own form of undoing, announcing with a kind of hysteria its inability to represent the troubling matter in which it has its rise. In all these cases, we feel the story of crime and punishment to be a story, an attempt to give form and meaning to an anguish that is more inaccessible, more inchoate. Sometimes that attempt is dramatised, being visibly made by characters within the drama; sometimes it is enacted by the mode and vision of the drama itself. Real and indispensable though the categories of crime and just punishment assuredly are, tragedy refuses to terminate in such categories, in which the agent's responsibility could be satisfactorily ascertained by judicial process, and the split vote of the jury in the *Oresteia* would never come about. In tragedy, the crime and punishment

---

80   Ibid., p.19.

story is felt to be masking, expressing, and managing—often all of those at once—some more primal, yet more unbearable insecurity. That insecurity may be projected outward as a malevolent, persecutory world, or turned inward as the guilt that justifies such persecution, or converted into aggression against those cast as responsible for our distress. Any or all of those impulses will find support in the story of crime and punishment. It is one of the stories we resort to when no better witness of our pain can be found.

5. Giving Audience to Madness

> The mad are people who have never found, or never made, or never had, a sufficiently attentive audience. And this in itself might make us wonder what an audience is for. And remind us that the first audience is the family.[1]

This is an unpardonably long chapter, so it may be helpful to sketch the journey ahead. The chapter deals with how certain tragic dramas represent madness, states of mental disintegration or estrangement which are peculiarly challenging for those around them to relate to. The key issue is how the protagonist's inner life is felt to be supported or betrayed in the response of others. The phenomena of madness are understood as involved with an insufficiently supportive environment of onlooker and listener; to that environment they stand as both cause and consequence, as defence and also in some sense as riposte. My opening examples here are Beckett's *Not I* and Kane's *4.48 Psychosis*. Developing these thoughts into *Othello* and *Hamlet* brings in a new element: the mother-child relation as something which figures or informs the support or betrayal of the protagonist by the world, as the protagonist perceives it. This idea becomes central to the readings of *Macbeth* and *King Lear* which follow.

A second line of thought accompanies the first from the start, gathering strength as the chapter goes on. This explores the relation between witness figures within the play and the kind of witness offered by the play itself: the kind of attending which the theatre implies or creates. When it comes to apprehending states of delusion otherwise than as mere delusion, the space of theatre offers special possibilities. I bring this thought forward when looking at Pirandello's *Henry IV* and Ibsen's *Master Builder*, before exploring how *Macbeth* and *King Lear* grant experiential reality to the inflamed subjectivities of their protagonists.

---

1 Adam Phillips, *Missing Out: In Praise of the Unlived Life* (London: Penguin, 2013), p.174. From the appendix with Phillips' lecture, 'On Acting Madness'.

All roads in this chapter lead finally to *King Lear*. There I come in the end to think about grieving, and what it means to think of grieving as a form of fully accomplished witness. Grieving in *King Lear* is both overwhelmingly required and overwhelmingly difficult, certainly for many of the characters in the play: perhaps also for the audience in the theatre. Nevertheless, theatre makes a difference, and I try to suggest how at the end of *King Lear* the dimension of theatre affects the manner of our witness and the manner of our grief.

'Witness me. See me.' Beckett's *Not I* and Kane's *4.48 Psychosis*

'Tell my story', the dying Hamlet implores Horatio. I have tried to bring out the potency of this idea, the need of the person who has suffered catastrophe to find that catastrophe held and reflected in the mind of another. But before Hamlet makes this plea, he attempts to tell some part of his story himself, through the apology he makes to Laertes before their fencing-match. This apology must cover his killing of Polonius and his behaviour at Ophelia's funeral, both actions easily describable as deranged, and madness is indeed the term that Hamlet reaches for. However, he does so in a way which suggests the difficulty of his truly telling his story for himself.

> What I have done
> That might your nature, honour, and exception
> Roughly awake, I here proclaim was madness.
> Was't Hamlet wrong'd Laertes? Never Hamlet!
> If Hamlet from himself be ta'en away,
> And when he's not himself does wrong Laertes,
> Then Hamlet does it not, Hamlet denies it.
> Who does it then? His madness. If't be so,
> Hamlet is of the faction that is wronged,
> His madness is poor Hamlet's enemy. (V.ii.230–39)[2]

In this apology, which is really a confession that he is unable to apologise, Hamlet makes an awkwardly sharp distinction between mad and sane.

---

[2] Quotations from Shakespeare are taken from are taken from *The Riverside Shakespeare*, 2nd edn, ed. by G. Blakemore Evans, et al. (Boston and New York: Houghton Mifflin, 1997), unless otherwise stated.

By doing so, he cuts himself off from much of his behaviour in the play. He seems to have forgotten, or to be concealing, the fact that his 'antic disposition' was in some sense deliberately assumed. But in truth this was always a blurred area. In the original Hamlet story told by Saxo Grammaticus, there was some tactical purpose behind the revenger's pretending to be mad, but Shakespeare's Hamlet has no reason to do so: it brings suspicion upon him, rather than deflecting it. Playing mad is something that he wanted or needed to do; it seems to release some manic energy that both is and is not part of him, as well as shielding him from the imputations of an uncomprehending world. Was he straightforwardly 'not himself' when killing the figure behind the arras, or when outrageously disrupting Ophelia's funeral? If the account he gives Laertes seems discontinuous with his past behaviour, that itself underlines a different kind of truthfulness to the assertion of madness: not a temporary derangement of the now-restored true self, but a revelation of some more radical incoherence or self-division. 'What I have done' is replaced by an insistent hammering at the third person—'Never Hamlet!', 'Hamlet does it not, Hamlet denies it'—which conveys some radical slippage or fracture in the notion of Hamlet's identity. Telling my story includes, among its other strands of implication, the idea of telling the story that constitutes *me*, that gathers together the fragments which my self-experience presents, finding in them a continuous identity. For this, another person is needed, in whose view I become, or am found to be, a whole person with a coherent history. But Hamlet's attempt to stand as his own witness is hapless, splitting rather than unifying, still involved in the madness it repudiates.

Not I, declares Hamlet, as Mouth implicitly does in Beckett's play of that name. But whereas Hamlet claims to be standing on the further shore of madness, Mouth has no purchase on the raving she presents us with. She spews out fragments of memory and experience—jagged shards of what might be, but never become, her life-story—with a frenzied incoherence that has no first person to own it as her own, and vehemently denies that such a first person might come into being. 'Not knowing what ... what she was—... what? .. who? .. no! .. she! .. SHE!'[3] And the lips clench and the teeth set, as if to ensure that no terrible

---

3 Samuel Beckett, *The Complete Dramatic Works* (London: Faber & Faber, 1990), p.382.

word shall pass. Mouth is intermittently aware of 'something she had to tell ... could that be it? .. something that would tell ... how it was ... how she—... what? .. had been? .. yes ... something that would tell how it had been ... how she had lived', but before the end this something becomes 'nothing she could tell'.[4] Damage to identity is what Mouth unforgettably manifests but can never tell us about.

In the staging Beckett specifies all that is visible of Mouth is exactly that: illuminated lips, teeth, and tongue, like some strange life-form, with the rest of the face and body invisible in darkness, unknowable by us. The other figure in the play is described in Beckett's stage direction:

> AUDITOR, *downstage audience left, tall standing figure, sex undeterminable, enveloped from head to foot in loose black djellaba, with hood, fully faintly lit, standing on invisible podium about 4 feet high shown by attitude alone to be facing diagonally across stage intent on MOUTH, dead still throughout but for four brief movements where indicated.*[5]

This movement is specified as a 'simple sideways raising of arms from sides and their falling back, in a gesture of helpless compassion. It lessens with each recurrence till scarcely perceptible at third.' It is prompted by the first four of the five 'Not I' moments that most strongly mark Mouth's dissociated state, when Mouth insists on the pronoun 'she' in her 'vehement refusal to relinquish third person' (Beckett's note).[6] Since there are four of these movements, lessening to the 'scarcely perceptible' by the third, it follows that the final gesture of compassion is something less than scarcely perceptible. The fifth 'Not I' moment elicits nothing at all.

With Beckett's Auditor, the act of witnessing has been reduced to the faintest possible trace. The fear and pity powerfully expressed by the chorus in Greek tragedy, the sympathetic anguish and prospect of loyal testimony from Horatio, have faded to almost nothing. We can say that Mouth's tragedy is so incoherent, so damaged and fragmented in its expression, so trapped by its own need for denial, that no fuller response is possible than this 'falling back', this momentary gesture of a diminishing compassion that can effect nothing and lead nowhere.

---

4   Ibid., pp.381, 382.
5   Ibid., p.376.
6   Ibid., p.375.

(Perhaps all compassion in tragedy is 'helpless', but the urgency with which it is solicited surely hopes for more.) But we might also speculate that Mouth's incoherence—her raving madness—and Auditor's inadequacy are mutually constitutive. Mouth's raving makes her almost impossible to understand, but also: Mouth presents as raving because she is not being, and has not been, properly heard, properly attended to, with the kind of attention that would gather her fragmentary experience into that of a whole person.

Beckett's play would then be showing us, in negative, something of the need for, the function of, a good auditor, a good witness. These issues are intensified by the sense that the Auditor, who stands downstage, is both a version of and a challenge to the actual audience. Anyone who has been present at a performance of *Not I*—especially and most wonderfully if not previously familiar with the text—can testify to the urgent need the play induces *to make sense of what is going on here*. This would involve finding a way of relating to Mouth as a dramatic character, a person, rather than as a strange and alienating phenomenon. The extreme difficulty of doing this threatens us with merely duplicating the response of the Auditor, and at some level we feel that insofar as we do so we are failing Mouth as others may have failed her. (The peculiar interest often taken in the stress placed on the actor who plays Mouth is perhaps an attempt to address this anxiety—as if our concern for Billie Whitelaw or Lisa Dwan might make up for our stumbling concern for Mouth.) The Auditor is a site of potential compassion but also, darkly robed and hooded, an obscurely sinister figure, in whose proximity to indifference there is a kind of terror. Hence the felicity of the textual pun on an auditor as someone who scrutinises the accuracy of the accounts submitted, and who may withhold validation.

Elsewhere in Beckett's drama we come across other auditors, none of them paragons of sympathetic understanding, but whose presence seems obscurely crucial to the protagonist: they figure the possibility though largely also the denial of such understanding. In *Endgame*, Hamm's expansive egotism, his self-relishing as a tragic figure, goes hand in hand with the demand to have servant or parents available to listen to his self-dramatisations and his stories. In *Happy Days*, Winnie, buried in sand, draws some great comfort from the discovery that Willie is still in the vicinity and in earshot, however minimal his responses and support. These auditors enable a kind of coherent self-performance to continue; they preserve the main speaker from such solitude that even soliloquy would collapse in upon itself.

A particularly interesting variation is offered by *Krapp's Last Tape*. Each year, Krapp records his reflections on his life, preserving what he believes to be its fruits and significant moments for his own future listening. This might seem to provide guarantees against auditor-failure, for who could be a more sympathetic listener to one's story than oneself? But when Krapp now—elderly, something of an alcoholic, somewhat senile, perhaps somewhat deranged—listens to old recordings, we register the astringent discontinuity between what mattered to Krapp then and who he is now. Krapp is himself aware of this: 'Just been listening to that stupid bastard I took myself for thirty years ago, hard to believe I was ever as bad as that.'[7] The only evident continuity between them is an addiction to bananas. The boxes of tapes onstage represent the continuous story of a life's self-experience, but as Krapp flicks cursorily through them, impatiently fast-forwarding over passages that once meant a great deal to him, all we can witness is a story as fragmented and incoherent as that of Mouth in *Not I*.

Among these fragments, Krapp dwells only on one lyrical memory of sexual encounter, which he obsessively seeks out and replays. This is a moment when he and an unnamed woman were on the river together, on a punt on a sunny day.

> I asked her to look at me and after a few moments—after a few moments she did, but the eyes just slits, because of the glare. I bent over to get them in the shadow and they opened. Let me in. We drifted in among the flags and stuck. [...] I lay down across her with my face in her breasts and my hand on her. We lay there without moving. But under us all moved, and moved us, gently, up and down, and from side to side.[8]

The power and beauty of this memory lies not only in its sexual content, but in its image of suspension, the suspension of individual distinctness and ego, the self not as restless agent but as moved and held by a larger element. It is made possible when the woman looks at him: that is, when she responds to his request that she look at him, and her eyes truly open,

---

7   Ibid., p.222.
8   Ibid., p.223.

and they 'let him in'. Beckett's syntax—'Let me in' as a free-standing sentence—aligns the sense of an imperative need with the granting of what is desired: 'please let me in'/'her eyes let me in'. The pleading is magically identical with the granting, in keeping with the specialness of the moment. It is the experience of feeling fully held and witnessed by another, of being properly *seen*. When Krapp listens to this on the tape, he is himself suspended, lost in reverie, and only in that lostness re-connected with his past.

After that moment of precious suspension, the play and the tape run forward once more, reinstalling that sense of discontinuity which time brings, as the recorded voice continues. The older Krapp has no way of relating to or 'letting in' what those younger voices represent, despite traces of a hankering to do so, just perceptible in his keeping of the tapes and the strenuous but fleeting and easily baffled attention that he gives them.

* * * * *

The ghostly presence of the Auditor in Beckett's *Not I* dramatises the distance between Mouth's anguish and the possibility of that anguish being shared or understood by another. The staging posits some crucial relation between the frantic subjectivity of the monologue—delivered at manic speed, with the urgency of a trapped animal racing around the walls of its enclosure—and the inability of the Auditor to reach out to or make connection with Mouth. Her madness and her isolation are aspects of each other, and this raises the stakes for us as her actual auditors in the theatre. Can we do better? Can we recognise in the bizarre phenomenon presented to us the pain of an actual person, with at least the minimum coherence of being which that implies, and with some discernible if fragmentary life-story or life-situation? Or put another way, can we recognise *Not I* as a play, a play that represents and allows us to engage with another's experience, despite its experimental form and its power to bewilder and disorientate?

Comparable questions are raised by Sarah Kane's final play, *4.48 Psychosis*, in which the relation of madness to a possible auditor or audience is still more pressingly explored. The play-text scarcely looks like a theatre piece. It does not allot speech to distinct speakers, does not specify how many actors are involved, and offers almost no directions for staging. It consists of different sections written in strongly contrasting modes or tones, with abrupt shifts of idiom and register, having no obvious narrative line despite a good deal of internal patterning and echo. These sections present as the voices of a fragmented personality, with the whole work struggling to establish itself as an internal monologue but painfully failing, both formally and psychologically, to hold it together.

However, two recurring strands can be made out which contest the impression of a mind enclosed within itself. One consists of passages of impassioned second-person address, with a marked affective quality that is very different from the bleached, depressive, mock-neutral tone that largely obtains in the more purely internal passages. The second consists of passages set out as dialogue, with dashes indicating change of speaker, most of which read as conversations between a patient and a psychiatrist.

Let me begin with these passages of apparent dialogue. The voice of the patient is generally mocking, self-aware, antagonistic; the voice of the doctor is generally well-meaning, patient, professionally reassuring, and intermittently inept. Some of the patient's ripostes have a bleakly comedic energy, suggesting unexpected resources of irony and self-possession. But at the heart of the exchanges is a genuine debate, which might be said to go to the heart of tragedy. Is the sufferer ill and delusional, in a deplorable deficit condition with regard to normal rational functioning, or are they in a condition which the category of illness fails to capture?

> —Do you despise all unhappy people or is it me specifically?
> —I don't despise you. It's not your fault. You're ill.
> —I don't think so.
> —No?
> —No. I'm depressed. Depression is anger. It's what you did, who was there and who you're blaming.
> —And who are you blaming?
> —Myself.[9]

Similarly:

> —Why did you cut your arm?
> —Because it feels fucking great. Because it feels fucking amazing.

---

9   Sarah Kane, *Complete Plays* (London: Methuen, 2001), p.212.

—Can I look?
—You can look. But don't touch.
—(*Looks*) And you don't think you're ill?
—No.
—I do. It's not your fault. But you have to take responsibility for your own actions. Please don't do it again.[10]

This debate is crystallised in the question of the meaning of 4.48. 4.48am is the time when the patient regularly wakes, when what we may call her depression is at its most acute, when she expects to commit suicide.

> At 4.48
> when desperation visits
> I shall hang myself to the sound of my lover's breathing
> I do not want to die
>
> I have become so depressed by the fact of my mortality that I have decided to commit suicide
>
> I do not want to live[11]

This collapse of all desire, noted with alienated matter-of-factness, comes at the end of a sequence of self-denigrating statements, an accumulated conviction of utter worthlessness which cries out to be understood as dysfunctional, or at least as distorted by its overwhelming subjectivity. Yet in another passage set out as conversation with the doctor, the radical unhappiness of 4.48 is claimed as enlightenment, having a purchase on reality which is superior to that of normal daylight consciousness. It is now normal, well-adjusted consciousness which is seen as the delusional condition, one conferred by or conflated with the sorcery of medication.

> —At 4.48
> when sanity visits
> for one hour and twelve minutes I am in my right mind.
> When it has passed I shall be gone again,
> a fragmented puppet, a grotesque fool.
> Now I am here I can see myself
> but when I am charmed by vile delusions of happiness,
> the foul magic of this engine of sorcery,
> I cannot touch my essential self.

---

10 Ibid., pp.217–218.
11 Ibid., p.207.

> Why do you believe me then and not now?
>
> Remember the light and believe the light.
> Nothing matters more.
> Stop judging by appearances and make a right judgment.
>
> —It's all right. You will get better.
>
> —Your disbelief cures nothing.
>
> Look away from me.[12]

These exchanges express the opposition between the impulse to 'believe in' radical unhappiness, depression, and anger as the place of the 'essential self', and an external, clinical perspective that pathologises such life-threatening unhappiness as illness in need of cure.

The desperate absoluteness of that opposition is, however, repeatedly challenged. In the first place, it is complicated by the note of aggression with which it is sometimes expressed, an aggression which extends to the whole play's attitude to its hypothetical audience. 'Look away from me'—the essential motto of Coriolanus, and a repeated motif in Kane's play—addresses the audience even as it repudiates them; although overtly incompatible with the theatre as the place of seeing and witness, it maintains a residual theatricality, and is increasingly set against a contradictory demand: 'watch me', 'see me'. There are also other passages that envisage a relationship that could bridge the divide between inner world and other beings. We gather that one of the patient's doctors (presumably the one whose voice we hear) is perceived as unlike the others in having offered her a real connection, 'the only doctor who ever touched me voluntarily, who looked me in the eye'. 'I trusted you', 'I loved you', but in the end (or intermittently, for the sense of trajectory is problematic) this hope and trust are betrayed, in the patient's perception, by the doctor's refusal to relinquish a clinical stance. Like the others, the doctor still writes 'bare-faced fucking falsehoods that masquerade as medical notes',[13] and still maintains (though barely) the professional distinction between doctor and friend.

> —You've seen the worst of me.
>
> —Yes.

---

12 Ibid., pp.229–230.
13 Ibid., pp.209–210.

—I know nothing of you.

—No.

—But I like you.

—I like you.

(*Silence.*)

—You're my last hope.

(*A long silence.*)

—You don't need a friend you need a doctor.

(*A long silence.*)

—You are so wrong.[14]

This distinction has to be maintained, the doctor confesses, not only to enable clinical work to be done but for the doctor's own self-protection: 'I need my friends to be really together. (*Silence.*) I fucking hate this job and I need my friends to be sane.'[15] As throughout, the form of the piece leaves open whether the doctor is 'really' speaking, as a separate character on stage would speak, or whether these exchanges are as the sufferer recalls/intuits/fantasises them. In any production that respects the openness of Kane's script, we cannot tell whether the doctor's moments of crassness resolve out entirely into a critique of medical practice which pathologises distress, or are subjective projections of the sufferer's despair of being helped or properly heard, such that the doctor's voice is what the sufferer hears the doctor as meaning. Are we inside or outside the sufferer's mind? Reality as criterion is not reliably operative, and this kind of 'perspectival crisis' itself breaks down the boundary between internal experience and the external world. As one of Kane's best critics puts it, the audience are placed 'both within and outside of the spectacle, which itself both represents the experience of mental suffering and attempts to immerse the audience inside it.'[16]

In a different key from these sections of dialogue, but also contesting the absolute incommunicability of the self, are the passages that speak more directly and urgently of love. The love seems to be for a woman who is unresponsive or absent, perhaps dead, perhaps imagined. This love-object is sometimes spoken of in the third person, sometimes

---

14 Ibid., p.236.
15 Ibid., p.237.
16 Leah Sidi, *Sarah Kane's Theatre of Psychic Life: Theatre, Thought and Mental Suffering* (London: Methuen, 2023), pp.135, 137–138.

directly addressed, as if seeking to overcome—or simply to register—the acute isolation of the speaker.

> My love, my love, why have you forsaken me?
>
> She is the couching place where I never shall lie
> and there's no meaning to life in the light of my loss
>
> Built to be lonely
> to love the absent
>
> Find me
> Free me
>   from this
>   corrosive doubt
>   futile despair[17]

As with the moments that envisage a good relationship with the doctor, the impulse to connection imagines a healing or at least overcoming of the rending division between the speaker's inner life and her condition as regarded by others. This is enacted also in the form of the piece, where what threatens to be an entirely internal monologue, sealed within the mind, strives to achieve dramatic form, a form in which different voices encounter or engage with one another, and which is necessarily written with an audience in mind. Kane described the play as being about 'what happens in a person's mind when the barriers which distinguish between reality and different forms of imagination completely disappear […] you no longer know where you stop and the world starts'.[18] This description of the experiential reality of psychosis also speaks easily to the potentialities of theatre, its suspension of disbelief; the resonance between theatrical experience and psychotic experience makes space for a mode of understanding that is not objectifying or diagnostic.

As the work moves towards its deeply ambiguous close ('please open the curtains'), the tension between the need for connection and the failure of connection is expressed with great clarity. At 4.48, 'the happy hour', something becomes clear:

---

17 Kane, *Complete Plays*, p.219.
18 Quoted in Graham Saunders, *Love Me or Kill Me: Sarah Kane and the Theatre of Extremes* (Manchester: Manchester University Press, 2002), p.112.

```
         this vital need for which I would die
                                           to be loved
I'm dying for one who doesn't care
I'm dying for one who doesn't know
                                           you're breaking me
Speak
Speak
Speak
                                           ten yard ring of failure
                                           look away from me
My final stand
                                           No one speaks
Validate me
Witness me
See me
Love me
                                           my final submission
                                           my final defeat[19]
```

The antiphonal form of this passage (which will not quite survive until the end) is in itself a gesture beyond the isolation of the self towards the condition of drama, and although the passage moves towards death, it matters that this is now understood as a death 'for' something, for the sake of something rather than because of something, namely for the lack of an imaginable witnessing, an imaginable love. Allusions to the Passion ('why have you forsaken me?', 'It is done', 'look after your mum now')[20] also bring into play the bare possibility, at least, that this 'final defeat' may be not without meaning. The immediate anguish acquires a wider resonance. And if the final line—'please open the curtains', which is yet another imperative seeking a response—suggests an action in a hospital ward or at a deathbed, it also expresses a desire to let in the light, to make visible. Light breaking in, as into a dark or sealed chamber, has been an intensely ambivalent motif in the play: the epiphanic moment of 4.48, the light that must be 'remembered' and 'believed in', also appears at four separate moments as 'Hatch opens. / Stark light'[21]—an intrusion from outside that reveals matter for terror and despair. 'Please open

---

19   Kane, *Complete Plays*, p.242–243.
20   Ibid., pp.219, 242, 243.
21   Ibid., pp.225, 230, 239, 240.

the curtains' re-imagines this bleak event both as an exchange between persons and as the object of desire. Significantly, it grounds this desire in the situation of the theatre, as if only now discovering itself as theatre. At the end of a conventional play in the modern theatre, the curtains close between actors and audience, re-installing the boundary between illusion and reality, on one side of which the spectators safely find themselves. At the end of this unconventional play, the desire is for the opposite; the curtains of separation are to be opened, the subject wishes to see and be seen. Even supposing we could set aside the play's proximity to its author's death, *4.48 Psychosis* is an extraordinarily difficult work to engage with, but it *offers us* that difficulty as its core subject-matter, challenging us to receive it as—to collaborate in making it into—however barely and hazardously, theatre. 'Witness me. / See me.'

Othello, *Hamlet*, and maternal support

The distinguished psychologist Peter Fonagy has argued that 'the experience of having our subjectivity understood' is essential to the formation of what he calls 'epistemic trust'. From the experience of another person reliably mirroring my feelings back to me ('Look at me. This is what you are feeling'), there grows my larger 'willingness to consider new knowledge from another person as trustworthy, generalizable, and relevant to the self'. Without such experience, I am left in 'a state of interminable searching for validation of experience, coupled with the chronic lack of trust that we describe here as epistemic hypervigilance.'[22]

Trust and the lack of trust are at the centre of *Othello*, and Fonagy's account speaks acutely to Othello's jealousy: a term that implies a generalised anxious suspiciousness, beyond the specifically sexual. *Othello* in turn offers an opening into thinking about madness in other Shakespeare tragedies and its relation to being securely witnessed. Othello is generally described as jealous rather than mad, but madness is hardly too strong a term for the condition he falls into. When Iago sets him up to spy on his meeting with Cassio, he assures us that 'as

---

22   See Peter Fonagy and Elizabeth Allison, 'The Role of Mentalizing and Epistemic Trust in the Therapeutic Relationship', *Psychotherapy*, 51 (2014), 372–380.

he [Cassio] shall smile, Othello shall go mad' (IV.i.100). Othello's behaviour before the Venetian envoy strikes Lodovico as deranged: 'Are his wits safe? Is he not light of brain?' (IV.i.269). His conviction that Desdemona is unfaithful is based on almost no external evidence but is driven by insecurities and pressures from within. We watch him come apart before our eyes—'I think my wife be honest, and think she is not' (III.iii.384)—disintegrating at his lowest point into unbearable fragmentation.

> Lie with her! 'Zounds, that's fulsome! Handkerchief —confessions —handkerchief! To confess, and be hang'd for his labour—first, to be hang'd, and then to confess. I tremble at it. Nature would not invest herself in such shadowing passion without some instruction. It is not words that shakes me thus. Pish! Noses, ears, and lips. Is't possible? Confess? Handkerchief? O devil! (IV.1.36–43)

This is not wholly unlike the stream of semi-connected language that pours from Mouth in Beckett's *Not I*.

Like Mouth, Othello speaks these words in the presence of an unsupportive auditor, but Othello's auditor is the yet more disturbing figure of Iago, who has replaced Desdemona as Othello's confidant, his listener. I make the point in that way in order to emphasise—as Shakespeare does—that Desdemona's love is above all a matter of good listening, at least as Othello experiences it and reports it. In my second chapter, I spoke of how her response makes her a kind of ideal witness or audience for the tragic protagonist. Let me return here to that originating moment of Othello's great love and dwell more fully on what happened there for him.

Othello's life has been one of strange adventures, lived in the world of the battlefield without a break until the brief time he has spent in Venice. Desdemona's father invites him to the house, curious to hear his stories, and this interest taken in him is something which Othello already understands as love. 'Her father lov'd me; oft invited me; / Still question'd me the story of my life' (I.iii.128–29). But the daughter proves a still better audience:

> These things to hear
> Would Desdemona seriously incline;
> But still the house affairs would draw her thence,
> Which ever as she could with haste dispatch,

> She'ld come again, and with a greedy ear
> Devour up my discourse. Which I observing,
> Took once a pliant hour, and found good means
> To draw from her a prayer of earnest heart
> That I would all my pilgrimage dilate,
> Whereof by parcels she had something heard,
> But not intentively. I did consent,
> And often did beguile her of her tears,
> When I did speak of some distressful stroke
> That my youth suffer'd. My story being done,
> She gave me for my pains a world of sighs;
> She swore, in faith 'twas strange, 'twas passing strange;
> 'Twas pitiful, 'twas wondrous pitiful.
> She wish'd she had not heard it, yet she wish'd
> That heaven had made her such a man. She thank'd me,
> And bade me, if I had a friend that lov'd her,
> I should but teach him how to tell my story.
> And that would woo her. Upon this hint I spake:
> She lov'd me for the dangers I had pass'd,
> And I lov'd her that she did pity them.
> This only is the witchcraft I have used.
> Here comes the lady; let her witness it. (I.iii.145–70)

Othello's tale of wonders offers as its climax, its greatest wonder, how Desdemona listened to him. It is as if his experience has never really been present to him, never been charged with affective life, until this moment; as if her tears were what enabled him, in the line that follows, to feel for the first time his youth as 'distressful'. Othello's life has no story until he can tell it, and he can tell it properly only to a special kind of listener—one who is 'intentive':

> Whereof by parcels she had something heard,
> But not intentively.

Desdemona has already been devouring Othello's discourse with a greedy ear. 'Intentively' implies something more; it suggests that Desdemona is actively contributing something. She will no longer hear Othello's life 'by parcels', as a series of disconnected parts, but in a way that gathers it into a whole as the story of a person, a person that can be loved. It becomes, now, a 'pilgrimage', a meaningful journey with a sacred destination. If parts of his story sound rather like a fantastical traveller's tale, this is appropriate because what Desdemona is making real through her attention is an inner life where fact and fantasy are not distinct: that is, Othello's sufferings and adventures as they are present within his mind. The incantatory music of his language speaks of the potency of that inner life; it tells us that the mental realm he moves in has the exalted quality of romance. This makes it potentially vulnerable to the jagged edges of the world and to inimical ways of seeing the world— were it not supported by another. Desdemona gave Othello for his pains 'a world of sighs', and that phrase suggests not only a great many, but also that her reciprocating listening gave Othello a *world* in which his pains could find footing, could become real to him because they were recognised by her. Othello's dawning revelation that he and Desdemona *understand one another* is there in how they each pick up hints from the other's speech, as each draws the other out: he 'found good means / To draw from her' a request for his whole life-story, and she finds good means to draw from him a declaration of love. She has listened to him so well, so 'intentively', that intimate reciprocation and communication are wonderfully easy. Thus Othello *knows* with absolute confidence that Desdemona will, once again, support the story of himself that he tells, perfect witness that she is. 'Here comes the lady; let her witness it.'

As the action of the play will show, by committing himself to this love, Othello is greatly risking himself. Desdemona has drawn his inner life out into the world, an inner life of exalted feeling conveyed through his extraordinary lyricism of language, with the promise that in the world it can be supported, that her nature and her being will be its support. This, for him, is what it means to enter into marriage. His passion dares to exist, in that it has an object that reflects and reciprocates his feelings; the world, in Desdemona's person, can be trusted with his inner life. And this is so—but not quite so. When Desdemona comes before the senators, she indeed affirms, passionately, that her love is freely given. But she does not speak with Othello's voice; his note of lyrical exaltation is replaced by a tone not exactly worldly, but one which situates love's power within the given social world. When she says to her father, 'I do perceive here a divided duty' (I.iii.181), her perception of division recognises that there are, so to speak, two worlds, that the romance of their union must find its way within an unromantic world. Later in the scene she asserts to the Duke, 'I saw Othello's visage in his mind' (I.iii.252). This is to give the world of Othello's mind priority: she sees him in generous part through the lens of his own subjectivity, his inner life. But she does so while remaining steadily conscious of the degree of choice, or transformation, that that involves. The blackness of his skin is the play's insistent reminder that he and she are, for all their love, irreducibly separate beings, and in thus knowing herself to have set that difference aside she also acknowledges its reality. All of which is simply to say that the play allows Desdemona her separate existence, so that alongside her immense commitment to her love she may also sustain a warm friendship with Cassio, banter at the edge of bawdy with Iago, inhabit a different kind of intimacy with Emilia, and notice appreciatively that Ludovico is 'a proper man' (IV.iii.35). Her love, being freely given—not compelled, as by witchcraft—may conceivably be withdrawn. This is the risk that Othello runs (and of course that she also runs, though differently). But if love as Othello experiences it excludes the idea of separateness, then its betrayal is not so much a risk as a certainty.

Alongside his total assurance that all is well, Othello has moments when he glimpses how great the stakes are here.

> But that I love the gentle Desdemona,
> I would not my unhoused free condition
> Put into circumscription and confine
> For the sea's worth. (I.iii.25–28)

And again, in the last words of serenity that he utters, as Desdemona departs from him in Act 3:

> Perdition catch my soul
> But I do love thee! and when I love thee not,
> Chaos is come again. (III.iii.90–92)

Othello was made able to love, we recall, because he felt that Desdemona loved and pitied him: because his inner life was known and made real by her. To feel that assurance is simultaneously to become aware of the potentiality for chaos from which it provides rescue. When the assurance is withdrawn, the collapse that follows is total and extreme:

> But there, where I have garner'd up my heart,
> Where either I must live or bear no life;
> The fountain from the which my current runs
> Or else dries up: to be discarded thence! (IV.ii.57–60)

There could be no stronger expression of the self's dependence on another for its very existence as a coherent entity.

'The fountain from the which my current runs / Or else dries up: to be discarded thence!' Othello's dependency on Desdemona is as total as an infant's at the breast, and he imagines being discarded as an intolerable weaning. Which is also to imagine weaning—the necessary discovery of the separateness of others—as an intolerable discarding or betrayal. Nine months have passed since Othello came to Venice, a period of time suggesting the gestation of a new life about to come out into the world, along with a context of maternal nurture. The magical protection afforded by such nurture, and the catastrophe represented by its loss or drying up, appears again with Othello's handkerchief and the infinite calamity which he tells Desdemona attends her losing it—'such perdition / As nothing else could match' (III.iv.67–68). The handkerchief was given to him by his mother and has an intensely female ancestry. It was woven by an ancient sibyl out of the stuff of maidens' hearts, and given to Othello's mother by an Egyptian enchantress who was another specially talented witness, for she 'could almost read / The thoughts of people' (III.iv.57–58). While kept safely by Othello's mother, the handkerchief had the power to

> subdue my father
> Entirely to her love; but if she lost it,
> Or made a gift of it, my father's eye
> Should hold her loathed, and his spirits should hunt
> After new fancies. (III.iv.59–63)

Othello carries within him the belief there is something inherited from his mother which, while possessed, makes intimate relationships with others blissfully secure (although there is now incipient revolt in that word 'subdued', and in the return to the idea of love as magical enchantment that was so impressively rebutted in the senate scene). But the loss of that object turns intimacy into hatred and opens the gates to destabilising imaginations—'new fancies' meaning both other love-objects and ungrounded fantasies. In this scenario, the woman's actual behaviour is, remarkably, irrelevant; everything about the man's feelings towards her depends on the possession or the loss of the magical maternal inheritance.

What emerges here is a further model of good witnessing: the mother's relation to the child. Othello's rapturous speech of how he and Desdemona came to love is focused on how perfectly she attended and responded to him; there is no sense of his reciprocating curiosity about her own separate life. As the basis for a relationship between adults, this doesn't bode well; but it resonates with a child's properly and healthily narcissistic experience of maternal love.

The importance of the relation between the young child and the mother has been the particular concern of that strain in psychoanalytic thinking known as 'object relations theory'; among that group of thinkers, I want particularly to draw on the work of Donald Winnicott, and on Winnicott's emphasis on the mother's ability to 'hold' the child's feelings in the first months and years of life.[23] By 'holding', he means an exceptionally responsive attunement to the child's inner life: the mother is able to recognise and participate in the child's feelings, and to reflect those feelings back to the child in a confirming way. Through this, the child begins to sense that such feelings can indeed be 'held' in the mind, rather than being the tumultuous, unshaping engulfment which infantile passion otherwise is.

Most mothers are 'good enough' at providing this support, Winnicott believes, and his thinking is in some ways more sanguine than that of Freud, whose tendency to see inescapable conflict in the child's relation to their parents and the desiring individual's relation to the reality-principle has made him a more obvious support in discussions of tragedy. But Winnicott's emphasis on the value of being 'held' in the mind of another goes hand in hand with the understanding of how terrible is the alternative. Passion which is not 'held' in this way is unbearable in its intensity. Winnicott speaks at one point of its being like finding oneself within a den of wild beasts. The child is engulfed by conflicting feelings of love and hate, fear and rage, exposed to the terror of utter annihilation. There is an 'unthinkable or archaic anxiety'[24] generated by the child's intuition of their utter vulnerability; they have

---

23 I follow Winnicott in speaking of the primary carer as the mother, who most typically—though not always—has that role.
24 D. W. Winnicott, 'Ego Integration in Child Development', in *The Maturational Processes and the Facilitating Environment: Studies in the Theory of Emotional Development* (London: Karnac, 1990), p.61.

no way of managing the fact that their very existence is dependent upon the attention of external and therefore unreliable others, in an environment which (whatever its actual nature) their rage and fear make appallingly hostile. Moreover, the child's experience begins as sporadic and disconnected, 'in bits'; the child depends upon the mother to gather his bits together, to make possible a self-experience as a whole being.[25] But until and unless this happens, there is a radical incoherence of being which, being unsupported in its encounter with the world, is intolerable. Madness, in certain forms, manifests this incoherence; or, delusion can be a way of denying such incoherence by creating a world in which the emotions of the psyche seem to find an anchor. (Thus a monstrously unfaithful Desdemona gives Othello some object for his feelings—although disbelieving in her goodness is nearly as hard for him as believing in her infidelity is compelling: a further turn of the screw to his disintegration.)

In describing this condition of anxiety and disintegration, Winnicott is sometimes referring to the minority of situations where the 'holding' support in the early years was not good enough, situations more likely to lead to the psychiatrist's consulting room. But in other passages, he writes as if the radical vulnerability and danger negotiated in childhood were something that never leaves any of us, or that it can be triggered or duplicated by traumatic experience in later life which—in one way or another—cuts us off from the sense of being known or knowable by others. By this way of thinking, even the healthiest person has the potential to fall into that unthinkable archaic anxiety which, at some level, we all know about, or deny at our peril.

> No doubt the vast majority of people take feeling real for granted, but at what cost? To what extent are they denying a fact, namely, that there could be a danger for them of feeling unreal, of feeling possessed, of feeling that they are not themselves, of falling for ever, of having no orientation, of being detached from their bodies, of being annihilated, of being nothing, nowhere?[26]

---

25 D. W. Winnicott, 'Primitive Emotional Development', in *Collected Papers: Through Paediatrics to Psycho-Analysis* (London: Tavistock, 1958), pp.145–156.

26 D. W. Winnicott, *Home Is Where We Start From: Essays by a Psychoanalyst*, ed. by Clare Winnicott, Ray Shepherd, and Madeleine Davis (London: Penguin, 1990), p.35.

One of the simplest and commonest things said about tragedy is that it involves a fall out of security. Thinking about the value of being heard and 'held' provides a gloss on what that security consists in, and how it may be forfeited. In his Auschwitz memoir *If This is a Man*, Primo Levi wrote of a recurring dream or nightmare, in which he was able to tell of his camp experience after the fact, in a safe and friendly setting.

> It is an intense pleasure, physical, inexpressible, to be at home among friendly people and to have so many things to recount: but I cannot help noticing that my listeners do not follow me. In fact, they are completely indifferent: they speak confusedly of other things among themselves, as if I was not there. My sister looks at me, gets up and goes away without a word.
>
> A desolating grief is now born in me, like certain barely remembered pains of one's early infancy. It is pain in its pure state, not tempered by a sense of reality and by the intrusion of extraneous circumstances, a pain like that which makes children cry. [Levi discovers that this dream is shared by many of the inmates of the camp.] Why does it happen? Why is the pain of every day translated so constantly into our dreams, in the ever-repeated scene of the unlistened-to story?[27]

This electrifying passage speaks of the fear that although Levi's words may be heard, they will communicate nothing, that his listeners will fail to participate in his experience as he needs them to. The experience of living in the camp is so extreme, so strange and appalling, that it may be incommunicable or intolerable to those who hear of it. And their refusal or inability to enter into his experience affects Levi as threatening his very existence as a person ('as if I was not there'), generating a sense of falling terribly out of human communion. The nightmare is that there can be no bridge between the horror of Auschwitz and the world of ordinary social relations, no way of locating one in relation to the other. And remarkably, Levi associates the desolating grief 'born' in him with 'certain barely remembered pains of one's early infancy [...] a pain like that which makes children cry'. It is as if his situation had re-awakened those early feelings of pain in his mind. They are described as 'pain in its pure state', an internal condition which lacks any stabilising sense of external reality or intelligible cause.

---

27 Primo Levi, *If This is a Man / The Truce*, trans. by Stuart Woolf (London: Abacus, 1987), p.66.

How much am I claiming, if I claim that these considerations are relevant to tragedy and to Shakespearean tragedy in particular? I want to propose the mother-child relation as analogy for or perhaps as exemplary case of the need for witness, rather than as explanation. The need to be heard and understood remains recognisable and urgent throughout life, even if it is most influentially negotiated in early childhood. So I am not claiming that the intensities of tragedy must be related to childhood experience, only that the dramatist's conception requires that the protagonist enter into a naked intensity of feeling akin to that which the analyst posits in the young child. Nor am I claiming that the witness is always at some level a figure of the mother, nor that a tragic protagonist has a personal history behind what appears in the play which we can infer. Nothing here amounts to a method of interpretation, a key which unlocks matters otherwise hidden or mysterious, or discovers feelings in Hamlet or in Lear other than those which immediately appear.[28]

Where psychoanalytic insight seems helpful, however, is in understanding the intensity of the emotions generated in tragic drama when the support of witness collapses or goes missing—and why we do not find the extremity of the reaction simply eccentric or bizarre. That Othello should care *so* much that Desdemona could conceivably betray him—so much, that the foundations of his being crumble and give way; so much, that he destroys what he most loves—might seem, coolly regarded, the mark of a peculiarly dysfunctional personality. But it does not, in the dramatic moment, strike us as entirely strange. If we are appalled, we are also gripped: something *comes home to us* at these moments, in subliminal recognition of our own needs and vulnerabilities.[29] The power of tragedy

---

28   Interpretation is not the aim. Against the Freudian model, Winnicott came to believe that the task of the therapist was *not* one of interpretation, but rather the provision of an environment which tolerated confusion and uncertainty and the limit to what is communicable. In this wisdom there is something for the literary critic to share.

29   I do not mean to minimise the part played by Othello's racial difference. In *Tragedy and Postcolonial Literature* (Cambridge: Cambridge University Press, 2021), Ato Quayson traces how Iago, as master-manipulator of representations, draws on the contradictions of cosmopolitanism to induce in Othello an agony of incoherence that extends from his cultural environment to penetrate his self-experience. 'No one is immune from the inter-subjective inscriptions that the social world places upon the self, for the self is first and foremost the product of social relations' (p.81). This is part of Quayson's powerful larger argument about how the

reminds us that these are never definitively managed or entirely in the past. Even if we have been well listened to and 'held', and have built a self that engages successfully with the world, the potential for that primitive terror and rage and grief remains.

A passage comes to mind from Rilke's *Duino Elegies*, whose opening line proclaims that work's general relevance to these questions. 'Who, if I cried out, would hear me from among the orders of the angels?' If one of the great motifs of the *Elegies* is 'the absence of an echo [...] the despair at not being able to be heard',[30] that despair is, in the third elegy, set explicitly against the mother's presence to her child. There, the poet addresses the mother and speaks of her power to protect her child from what are, in the first place, night-terrors.

> over his new eyes you arched
> the friendly world and warded off the world that was alien.
> Ah, where are the years when you shielded him just by placing
> your slender form between him and the surging abyss?
> How much you hid from him then. The room that filled with suspicion
> at night: you made it harmless; and out of the refuge of your heart
> you mixed a more human space in with his night-space.
> And you set down the lamp, not in that darkness, but in
> your own nearer presence, and it glowed at him like a friend.
> There wasn't a creak that your smile could not explain,
> as though you had long known just when the floor would do that ...
> And he listened and was soothed. So powerful was your presence
> as you tenderly stood by the bed; his fate,
> tall and cloaked, retreated behind the wardrobe, and his restless
> future, delayed for a while, adapted to the folds of the curtain.
>
> And he himself, as he lay there, relieved, with the sweetness

---

unsupported position of the colonial or postcolonial subject—between (at least) two worlds and belonging securely to neither—brings a 'loss of hermeneutical coherence' (p.10) that makes them peculiarly vulnerable to tragedy. To give a narrative account of the self requires 'facing outward to an external point which elicits the self-accounting' (p.32); Quayson's attention to how self-experience is entangled in the modelling offered by the immediate environment, compromised or contaminated by historical contingencies as this may be, is the line along which his account broadly dovetails with my interest in the ruptured relation between self and witness, or child and mother.

30 Hannah Arendt and Günther Stern, 'Rilke's *Duino Elegies*', in Hannah Arendt, *Reflections on Literature and Culture*, ed. by Susannah Young-Ah Gottlieb (Redwood City, CA: Stanford University Press, 2007), p.1.

> of the gentle world you had made for him dissolving beneath
> his drowsy eyelids, into the foretaste of sleep—
> he *seemed* protected ... But inside: who could ward off,
> who could divert, the floods of origin inside him?[31]

In representing the world to the child as friendly rather than alien, indeed making the world such, the mother is also protecting the child from impulses within, or more precisely from that surge from the abyss which would flood the external world with 'more ancient terrors', overwhelming its separateness. The mother can protect the child from that, can make the external world safe, for as long as she stands tenderly by the bed and smiles. But she cannot permanently abolish what is within, 'the floods of origin', the sleeper's dream-world, his 'interior wilderness, / that primal forest', place of 'more ancient blood', which the following lines establish as the site of fascination and even desire, as well as terror.

> Loving,
> he waded down into more ancient blood, to ravines
> where Horror lay, still glutted with his fathers. And every
> Terror knew him, winked at him like an accomplice.
> Yes, Atrocity smiled ... Seldom
> had you smiled so tenderly, mother. How could he help
> loving what smiled at him.[32]

Rilke's celebration of the mother's power to nurture and protect goes hand in hand with acknowledgement of the reality of that which the child is protected from. The mother's smile competes with the smile of Atrocity, which likewise says to the child: we have an understanding (*war wie verständigt*), I know you, your feelings are known and shared by someone who stands (albeit equivocally) outside yourself. The fascination of atrocity, which is such a large element in tragedy, is identified in these lines as the dark double of the mother's nurturing presence, involved with it from the very start.

None of this is to insist that the protagonist's tragedy is rooted in their childhood or in their relations with the mother. Still, where a mothering

---

31 Rainer Maria Rilke, *The Selected Poetry of Rainer Maria Rilke*, trans. by Stephen Mitchell (London: Picador, 1987), pp.163–165.
32 Ibid., p.165.

figure coincides with the appealed-to listener, there may be a special charge of emotion. (It is interesting to discover that the source for Beckett's Auditor was a mother waiting for her child.)[33] When Hamlet harangues Gertrude in the closet scene for the vileness of her relationship with Claudius, the intensity of his reproaches has been understood as arising from his obsession with the sexual, and/or his competitive (Oedipal) rivalry with her partner, and/or a deep sense of contamination by the maternal body.[34] But we can add to this a simpler observation: he needs his pain to be properly heard. Gertrude's liaison with Claudius has been the manifest sign of her failure to enter into Hamlet's grief. From the beginning of the play, she has treated his distress as something less than infinite. She cannot or will not show that she feels what he feels. For her, life goes on, and what she probably regards as an accidental death has luckily favoured an adulterous preference. What is traumatic for her son is for her no such thing. And this disjunction between how the child feels and how the mother feels is unbearable for Hamlet.[35] Palpably, what we see in this scene is that Hamlet hates Gertrude as well as loves her, has no way of reconciling these emotions, but obscurely feels that

---

33 In Morocco in 1972, Beckett observed 'a solitary figure, completely covered in a djellaba, leaning against a wall. It seemed to him that the figure was in a position of intense listening'. This was, he then discovered, 'an Arab woman waiting there for her child who attended a nearby school.' Enoch Brater, quoted in James Knowlson, *Damned to Fame: The Life of Samuel Beckett* (London: Bloomsbury, 1996), p.589.

34 Janet Adelman's brilliant study, *Suffocating Mothers: Fantasies of Maternal Origin in Shakespeare's Plays* (New York: Routledge, 1992), tracks Shakespeare's recurrent imaging of the maternal body as stifling or contaminating. She persuasively argues that this male revulsion at one's inescapably female origin—epitomised in the Hamlet-Gertrude scene—is one of the great drivers of Shakespearean tragedy. The emphasis on the mother as oppressive that Adelman locates can be understood as rage at the failure of maternal 'holding', and in that respect speaks to my own approach; I am indebted to her study, even if I am more inclined to see the destructive mother as simply the dark side of the positive function I associate with witnessing. On the question of Shakespeare's 'complicity' in the feelings he dramatises she is particularly interesting, and I return to this later in relation to Cordelia.

35 Winnicott describes the effect on the child of an insufficiently responsive mother, who requires the child to adapt to *her* needs, in a way that is strikingly applicable to Hamlet. 'The feeling of real is absent and if there is not too much chaos the ultimate feeling is of futility. The inherent difficulties of life cannot be reached, let alone the satisfactions. If there is not chaos there appears a false self that hides the true self, that complies with demands, that reacts to stimuli, that rids itself of instinctual experiences by having them, but that is only playing for time.' D. W. Winnicott, 'Primary Maternal Preoccupation', in *Through Paediatrics to Psycho-Analysis* (London: Karnac, 1992), pp.304–305.

if he could get her to acknowledge his anguish in the right kind of way, there might be some prospect of moving forward. This implies, among other things, her registering but also surviving his hatred; 'I will speak daggers to her, but use none'[36] (III.ii.396). He may represent this as an attempt at her moral reform, but the urgency behind his assault on her speaks of a more primitive demand. Primo Levi's recurring nightmare was of 'the unlistened-to story'; he described his need to make those who were not there participate in his experience as a 'violent impulse', something as fundamental as the impulse to self-preservation. When Hamlet violently assaults Gertrude with his words, he is screaming at her *to hear what he is telling*, and so to enter into what he is feeling, despite his despair that she seems unable to do so. Or we might even say that he is seeking to communicate his trauma by traumatising her, if that is what it takes.

Madness is very much in play in this scene. Externally regarded, Hamlet's behaviour must appear as deranged: in a state of high excitement, he madly kills Polonius, hallucinates his dead father, and pours his disgust and horror over Gertrude with little cognisance of the separate person that she is. But Shakespeare also makes us intimate with Hamlet's mind. The Ghost may reflect Hamlet's subjectivity, his 'prophetic soul' (I.v.40), but it is also a theatrical reality, and the information it brings becomes established as a reality of the plot. For all that Hamlet behaves in a deranged way, we do not readily think of him as mad because, at one level, he knows the truth, and that knowledge is what is driving him here. Claudius and Shakespeare have between them supplied him with an actual crime which supports his prophetic soul, his inner world of hate and horror. Nevertheless, there remains a gap between the intensity of his emotions and what his listener is able to enter into. Gertrude finds it hard to understand what disturbs him so terribly; and many spectators and readers have felt that Claudius and Gertrude are not shown by Shakespeare to be as vile as Hamlet

---

36 This may seem like a weakened (or more civilised) revision of Orestes's killing of his mother, the substitution of metaphorical or verbal violence for the real thing. But survivability is an important principle in Winnicott's thinking. There is immense reassurance for the infant in the mother's ability to survive, undamaged, the rage and hate that the infant feels for her from time to time. I discuss this further in relation to Cordelia.

needs them to be. Hence the question of madness remains, if madness involves the insistent imposition upon others of an inner world which they cannot recognise. When Hamlet harangues Gertrude, not only projecting his feelings onto her but also demanding a response, he is seeking to find some purchase in the external world for what he feels. Specifically, he is seeking to find that his feelings can be 'held' in his mother's mind. Does he succeed? There is latitude for the director here. When Gertrude is brought to acknowledge the black spots in her own soul, this is a kind of corroboration of what Hamlet has in his mind, and brings him a degree of relief. The rage and horror abate, and the scene can be played in such a way that they achieve a tenuous understanding. Hamlet can now imagine, as a future possibility, some blessed reciprocation between them, when a good relation between child and parent will be restored:

> Once more good night,
> And when you are desirous to be blest,
> I'll blessing beg of you. (III.iv.170–72)

There is a huge ache of desire around those lines. But the scene can also be played to suggest that Hamlet has drawn Gertrude into his inner world—has to some degree drawn her into his estrangement. The good witness, like the good-enough mother, is someone who can *make connection* between the child's raging feelings and the external world—who enters into those feelings, yes, yet holds them as a separate being, without being overwhelmed by them. It is a function of that necessary separateness that the witness can show back to the sufferer what they feel, can find words to tell their story. But it is precisely the condition imposed by Hamlet that Gertrude should *not* tell his story, that she should not reveal to others that he is 'not in madness / But mad in craft' (III.iv.187–88). She duly reports to Claudius that Hamlet is 'mad as the sea and wind' (IV.i.7). But whether she intends this as a calculated deception, or whether this stands well enough for her as a summary of his behaviour in that scene; whether she speaks as an ally of his conscious intent, or as herself succumbing to the greater reality of his madness, is—like so much in *Hamlet*—hard to tell.

Playing and playing mad: Pirandello's *Henry IV*

In Hamlet's lines to Gertrude, he distinguishes between being 'in madness' and being 'mad in craft'. What is it to be 'mad in craft'? Hamlet would seem to say that he is only pretending to be mad or only playing mad, but playing mad when you have no reason to do so (which is Hamlet's case) doesn't seem entirely sane. In the play as a whole, it is clear enough that the 'antic disposition' which Hamlet puts on is no mere disguise but releases real energies from within him. Feelings of emptiness and cynicism, of misogyny and of disgust with both himself and the world, are projected outward with an equivocal degree of commitment, a relishing of their hyperbolic performance that allows Hamlet to mean them and not quite to mean them, leaving space for their possible eventual disavowal. His character is something that, for much of the play, Hamlet performs or plays, holding open the notion of a coherent identity that sits somewhere between the character(s) that he plays (manic, melancholic, philosophical, satirical …) and the source of that playing. Only as the end approaches and the time for performing closes down does Hamlet seek to leave behind his madness, and the performing of identity gives way to the need for a narrative identity, a story which someone else could tell. In the meantime, being 'mad in craft' occupies a middle space between madness and sanity, suggesting some crafty negotiation of intentionality, some sense that madness is where Hamlet wants to be, at least for a time. This chimes with the fascination that madness often has in tragic drama, the pull that it exerts on its audience as a space to which we likewise are drawn. The madness of Lear or of Ophelia or of Agave in Euripides' *Bacchae*—all figures who are deeply 'in madness', without any shadow of pretending—does not strike us only as the terrible affliction which it would do in life, but also, though obscurely, as transmitting an energy-source, presenting as a release from or protest against constraint, perhaps even as an enhanced mode of being or perception. Insofar as tragic theatre challenges the sovereignty of rationality, the mad figure may strike us not as eccentric but as close to the heart of things.

To think about this, let me return to the model offered by the object relations school of psychoanalysis, and to the thought of Winnicott in particular. Whereas some strains of Freudian thought have a strongly developmental cast, figuring dysfunction as stuckness or regression and maximal adjustment to the environment as the optimal goal, object relations theory is more reluctant to suppose that we can leave infant emotional conditions behind, but thinks rather 'in terms of states of mind and not of stages of development'.[37] The child's fears, fantasies, and needs persist through life, and the inner or imaginative life in which they persist has a claim on reality as strong as that of the external world.[38] Yes, they can be managed, first by the presence and then by the internalisation of a nurturing figure, and they can be brought into self-awareness and co-existence with more truly other-oriented relationships, but they cannot be outgrown. Instead, they persist in the adult psyche as needing to find expression and acknowledgement, to be heard and 'held', with slippage into alienation or crisis as the permanently threatening alternative.

> It is sometimes assumed that in health the individual is always integrated, as well as living in his own body, and able to feel that the world is real. There is, however, much sanity that has a symptomatic quality, being charged with fear or denial of madness, fear or denial of the innate capacity of every human being to become unintegrated, depersonalized, and to feel that the world is unreal.[39]

To this, Winnicott added a striking footnote:

> Through artistic expression we can hope to keep in touch with our primitive selves whence the most intense feelings arise and even fearfully acute sensations derive, and we are poor indeed if we are only sane.[40]

Tragic drama is an obvious candidate for such a form of artistic expression. To be affected as tragic drama affects us is not to be 'only sane': in the case of Shakespearean tragedy, we enter into modes of experience which manifest to observers as 'madness', but which we are made to know too intimately to categorise in that distancing way.

---

37 Margot Waddell, *Inside Lives: Psychoanalysis and the Growth of the Personality* (London: Karnac, 2002), p.196.
38 Winnicott: 'It is important for us that we find clinically *no sharp line* between health and the schizoid state or even between health and full-blown schizophrenia.' *Playing and Reality* (London: Penguin, 1974), p.77.
39 Winnicott, 'Primitive Emotional Development', in *Collected Papers: Through Paediatrics to Psycho-Analysis* (London: Tavistock, 1958), p.150.
40 Ibid., p.150.

In the account of the psyche that Winnicott gives, the developmental goal is not simply to yield as much of our inner (child's) life to the external (adult) world as we can bear to. More unequivocally than Freud, Winnicott finds danger in what he calls 'compliance'; the inner world is no less real than the external and should not be sacrificed to it. Instead, ways must be found for the two to dance together. The good-enough mother is found both to belong to the child's inner world and to be a separate, external being, allowing mediation between the worlds. Such mediating power is then extended to other sites, in particular Winnicott's 'transitional object'—the comfort blanket or beloved toy that is the magical carrier of the child's passionate life while still being sufficiently part of an external world to bring the sense of being supported from outside. Later, this flowers into other forms of playing, which come to include those forms of art which acknowledge a dual obligation to the nature of the world and the life of the mind. To grasp the whole of Winnicott's thought, it is important to see how this capacity for play or transitional space is thought of *both* as a means to an end (adaptation to the world, acknowledgement of others as others, responsibility, political life) *and* as an end in itself, the site of properly creative living, the place of 'feeling real'. Space for creativity is key to this. From the baby's illusion that he creates the presence that answers his need, flowers the 'hope that there is a live relationship between inner reality and external reality, between innate primary creativity and the world at large which is shared by all'.[41] That live relationship is, according to the argument of this book, what the good witness might provide—including that witness offered by tragic drama. But in the absence of such witness or such a play-space, the insistence that the world be as the mind creates it readily presents itself as madness.

One begins to see how playing mad, or being 'mad in craft', might preserve a crucially valuable space for Hamlet which strict sanity would deprive him of. And as an extension of that, how a theatre which to some degree plays along with such an impulse might open such a space for the audience.

To put some more flesh on these thoughts, I would like to turn to Pirandello's *Henry IV*, first performed in 1922, which offers a particularly

---

41   D. W. Winnicott, *The Child, the Family, and the Outside World* (London: Penguin, 1964), p.90.

clear example of a tragic protagonist who plays mad. The play is set in the world of contemporary Italy, but the curtain rises on what is apparently the throne-room of the medieval German Emperor Henry IV. This historical world corresponds, we gradually discover, to the inner life of the protagonist (whom we must call Henry since Pirandello gives him no name of his own, leaving us with only that of the role he plays). We thus have two time-worlds superimposed on one another, and the drama turns on the relationship between these two worlds, and the possibility of establishing a connection between them.

The back-story, gradually revealed to us, is that twenty years previously the protagonist was taking part in an historical pageant or masquerade, in which he had chosen the role of Henry IV. Thrown from his horse, he suffered a blow to the head, after which he believed that he was in truth the medieval ruler. His nephew then created for him a setting in which to accommodate that delusion, complete with people employed to pose as his servants and associates in this historical costume-drama. However, as the play progresses, Henry claims that some eight years ago his delusion cleared, and he became aware of his situation. Nevertheless, he chose to continue living and acting as the Emperor within this artificial setting, rather than return to life in the twentieth century. Recovering his sanity (or something like sanity), his response was to play mad, living in a manner that might be regarded as equally if differently deranged.

The immediate occasion of the drama is the arrival of figures from Henry's circle, accompanied by a psychiatrist. They have heard rumours that Henry has moments of near-lucidity and have decided to intervene. Their plan is to shock him into recovery by engineering a confrontation between the past or fantasy world and the present. The most important of these figures is the Marchesa Matilda, to whom Henry was intensely attracted at the time of his accident, and who seems to have partially reciprocated that attraction; however, she settled in the end for laughing at him for his intensity, though not without conflicting feelings. This is how she recounts the situation to the doctor:

> One of the many misfortunes that happen to us ladies, my dear Doctor, is to find ourselves now and again before two eyes that look at us with a contained and intense promise of everlasting devotion! (*sentimento duraturo*) [*She breaks out in high-pitched laughter.*] There is nothing more

5. Giving Audience to Madness   171

> ridiculous. If men could only see themselves with that everlasting devoted look of theirs. I have always laughed about it —then more than ever! But I must confess: I can do so now after twenty and more years. When I laughed at him this way, it was also out of fear, because one, perhaps, could have believed in a promise like that from those eyes. But it would have been very dangerous.[42]

The pressure-point here is the word 'everlasting': something that could keep its identity through the fluctuations of time. Such devotion (intensely subjective, dependent on the lover not seeing himself from outside) seemed to the Marchesa incompatible with the ways of the modern world and thus 'ridiculous'. (Iago mocked at the notion of love as high romance.) But she now acknowledges that with her mockery went a fear that a connection might after all be possible—a connection between them as lovers which would also be a connection between two different worlds, and therefore (as tragedy often shows such connections to be) 'very dangerous'.

For her role in the masquerade, the Marchesa chose her historical namesake the Marchesa Matilda of Tuscany, and it was this that triggered the protagonist's choice of 'the great and tragic Emperor' who was Matilda's medieval contemporary. In various ways, the historical figure of Henry IV is shown to be a fitting carrier of the protagonist's inner life and the contradictions of that life. Most obviously, he is a figure of great power—serving the fantasy of omnipotence. It is merely another manifestation of that imperial power when, in his recovered condition, Henry relishes his domination of those required to collude in his fantasy. But Henry IV is also a deeply insecure figure, mistrustful and suspicious, prone to fits of rage and anxiety. This is linked to the loss of connection with his mother; he tells how at the age of six the bishops 'tore me away from my mother, and against her they used me', and we hear also of the 'obscene rumour' spread by his enemies about his mother's sexual behaviour.[43] Since the loss of his mother, his life has been full of enemies plotting against him, and although this is true enough of the power-politics of the eleventh century, it also perfectly expresses the mindscape of paranoia. Henry's great historical adversary was Pope Gregory VII,

---

42   Luigi Pirandello, *Henry IV*, in *Six Characters in Search of an Author and Other Plays*, trans. by Mark Musa (London: Penguin, 1995), pp.86–87.
43   Ibid., p.97.

and we hear in the play of his great terror of the Pope's supernatural, magical powers, such as his ability to call up the dead. ('A persecution complex!', the psychiatrist patly exclaims.)[44] At the height of their conflict, the Pope excommunicated Henry, undermining his power-base, and in what became a famous act Henry travelled to Italy to seek Gregory's absolution, and is said to have waited outside the castle of Canossa for three days as a penitent—barefoot in the snow—until granted an audience with the Pope. In the play Henry wears this penitential sackcloth over his regal robes, and declares that 'my life is all made of humiliations', although Pirandello's exacting stage direction requires—'in contrast to' such humble repentance—'a fixed look of suffering which is frightening to behold'.[45] His chosen historical role thus gives external form to the conflicted fantasy-life of the psyche: powerful yet insecure, enraged yet fearful, humbled by constraint yet resentful of humiliation.

The castle of Canossa belonged to Matilda of Tuscany, powerful supporter of the Pope and therefore, in history, Henry's frequent and vigorous enemy. However, the story goes that at Canossa she pleaded for Henry to the Pope, and that she was instrumental in their all three taking communion together. When the contemporary Marchesa chose the role of Matilda for the masquerade, she recalls that the protagonist chose the character of Henry so that 'from then on he would be at my feet like Henry IV at Canossa'.[46] So for Henry, Matilda is both the enemy who seeks to resist and destroy him, and the conceivably sympathetic figure whose support might enable him to enter into communion once more, releasing him from his alienated and wretched condition. Here too the historical story gives form to powerfully conflicting feelings, and in some degree holds them together.

All this indicates why it might suit the protagonist first to choose the role of Henry IV, and then to become Henry IV as a fantastical way of projecting a painfully conflicted inner life. But something else needs to be added. We never feel that the figure we see is purely delusional; the discovery that he has recovered from his injury merely confirms our sense that he is *playing* Henry IV, acutely aware of the theatricality of his performance and so simultaneously detached from it. He swings

---

44   Ibid., p.92.
45   Ibid., pp.96–97.
46   Ibid., p.86.

between magniloquent over-emphasis and a cursory running through of his part that verges on dropping out of role altogether. He verges too on glancing at his own memories and situation and at the situation of those who have come to visit him, behind their historical costume. For example, he points out to the Marchesa the over-obvious hair dye which signals that he is playing a Henry much younger than he is, while noting her own use of cosmetics as exactly similar:

> God forbid that I should show disgust or surprise! Foolish aspiration! Nobody wants to recognize that certain dark and fatal power that assigns limits to the will.[47]

That dark and fatal power is the course of time which turns hair grey, or more generally stands for the pressure of external reality. Fantasy offers to create a space in which that power is suspended, a space which stretches across the spectrum between delusional and playful. Henry seeks to override the dark power in the playing out of his fantasy life, but he knows here that he is (merely) playing at youth.

This consciousness of role-playing seems to be his defining characteristic, stemming from before his freakish accident. Here is Belcredi, the Marchesa's admirer/lover, struggling to explain to the psychiatrist the way in which he was always eccentric, and the peculiar way in which he projected his eccentricity:

> I don't mean to say that he was faking his eccentricity; quite the contrary, he was often genuinely eccentric. But, Doctor, I could swear that he was acutely aware of himself in acting out his eccentricity. And I think this must have been the case even in his most spontaneous actions. Furthermore, I am certain he must have suffered because of it. Sometimes he would go into the funniest kinds of angry fits with himself! [...] And why? As far as I could tell, because that instant lucidity that comes from acting a part suddenly excluded him from any kind of intimacy with his own feelings, which seemed to him to be not exactly false—because they were sincere—but rather like something he had immediately to give the value of—what can I say?—of an act of intelligence, to make up for the lack of that sincere and cordial warmth that he felt was missing. And so he would improvise, exaggerate, let himself go—that's it—in order to forget his troubles and to see himself no longer.[48]

---

47 Ibid., p.98.
48 Ibid., p.88.

This sounds very much like one reading of Hamlet's 'antic disposition'. It also expresses a point of view that is central to the play. From this point of view, personal identity or 'character'—as we normally lay claim to it for ourselves and encounter it in others—is masquerade; it pretends to a definiteness and fixity (*sentimento duraturo*) that the passage of time is continually undoing. For people to behave as if their selves possess such solid reality makes them ridiculous, reveals them as 'clowns'—the derisive term Henry uses for those around him. To occupy this point of view is to take an ironic attitude, to see life as theatre, characters (including one's own) as *dramatis personae*, the masks used in the play.

Within the theatre, this attitude almost inevitably sounds like insight. But it is also, as Belcredi perceives, a position of suffering which leaves Henry permanently alienated, excluded from intimacy with himself or with others. Here is Henry to the psychiatrist, who is wearing the costume-disguise of a medieval monk:

> None of us lie or pretend! There's little doubt about it: in good faith we have fixed ourselves, all of us, in a fine concept of our own selves. Nevertheless, Monsignor, while you hold tight, clinging with both hands to your holy cassock, there slips away, down your sleeves, like a snake shedding its skin, something you are not aware of: life, Monsignor! And it's a surprise when you see it materialize there all of a sudden in front of you, escaping from you. Spite and anger against yourself, or remorse, also remorse.[49]

And here is Henry later, now revealing his true state of consciousness to his alarmed mock-attendants, on why crazy people—those who make manifest the incoherence and vulnerability of the self—are frightening to others:

> You feel that it can also turn into terror, this fear of yours—something that makes you feel the ground beneath your feet disappear and takes away the air you breathe. It must be that way, gentlemen. Do you know what it means to find yourself standing in front of a crazy person? To find yourself face to face with a person who shakes the foundations of everything you have built up in and around you, the logic of all your constructions! [...] Mutable! Changing! You say, 'This cannot be!' and for them everything can be. [...] Because how terrible it is, terrible if you do not hold on very tight to what seems true to you today and to what will

---

49   Ibid., p.99.

seem true to you tomorrow, even if it is the opposite of what seemed true to you yesterday! How awful it is to have to flounder, the way I have, in the thought of this terrible thing which drives one truly mad: that if you are next to someone and looking into his eyes—the way I looked one day into a certain person's eyes—then you can imagine what it is like to be a beggar in front of a door through which you shall never be able to enter. The one who does enter will never be you with your own interior world and the way you see it and touch it, but rather someone unknown to you, like that other one who in his own impenetrable world sees you and touches you ...[50]

Although we cling to fixities, and most especially the fiction of our solid identity or self, life is on the move, changeable and changing—*volubile!*—and to know this is to feel the self as a masquerade, a theatrical role. Mental illness, being 'crazy', is both a terrifying demonstration of this vulnerability and, perhaps, a creative response to it: living as Henry does, with that conscious projection of self as a role, allows him to continue as someone in spite of the slippages and discontinuities of time, and to hold his incoherence in the act of performance. But this is also a position of suffering. Henry's speech finishes with a powerful image of privation, that of the beggar in front of a door that is closed to him. To go through that door would be to become someone else, someone unknown and unrecognisable, so that the beggar's pleading could never be granted. It is impossible to imagine, at this moment, how the needs of the inner life could be met by conditions outside the self, so radical is the divide between them. That look from Henry's eyes, which speaks of a *'sentimento duraturo'*, becomes laughable—does it? must it?—in a world of slippage and change, in which trauma and disaster rupture continuity, in which Henry's loving sister dies, and in which youth becomes old. Why did Henry not return to the world when his delusion cleared? Because, he says, 'I understood that not only my hair but all the rest of me as well must have turned grey, and everything collapsed, everything was over, and I realized that I had arrived hungry as a bear to a banquet that was already over.'[51] The landslip in time created by trauma opens up, again, an image of radical privation, of

---

50   Ibid., p.122, translation slightly altered.
51   Ibid., p.132.

need that cannot be met. Henry understands this with great clarity, but his understanding only heightens his suffering and his rage.

The look into the eyes is what passes between Henry and the Marchesa, and it is from her, if from anywhere, that relief might come, and a passage between his inner life and the external world might be opened. For in his mind she belongs to both worlds. As Matilda of Tuscany, she is Henry's great enemy who may nevertheless support him at his moment of crisis; as herself, she is the woman whom he loved with that dangerous look, who mockingly rebuffed him, but who was, at the moment of the masquerade, minded 'to show him that my heart was no longer as hostile towards him as he might have imagined'.[52] At the end of Act One, she presents herself to him not as Matilda of Tuscany but in a maternal role, in the guise of Henry IV's mother-in-law, whose daughter accompanied him on his journey to the Pope. Henry addresses her along with the doctor, who is also in medieval dress, but the essence of his plea is to her. He points fearfully to the modern portrait of himself in the masquerade costume of Henry IV as a work of magic in which his enemy the magician-Pope has imprisoned him; this, he says, is his 'true condemnation'. Could she effect his release from confinement within this fixed and loveless role?

> Now I am a penitent and I shall remain so; I swear to you that I shall remain so until he [the Pope] receives me. But then the both of you, once the excommunication has been revoked, must beg the Pope on my behalf to do this which he has power to do: to release me from that, there [*points again to the portrait*], and allow me to live wholly this poor life of mine from which I am excluded. One cannot be twenty-six years of age for ever, Lady! And this I ask you also for your daughter's sake: that I may be able to love her as she deserves to be loved, so well disposed as I am now, full of tenderness as I am now, made so by her pity. There you have it. This. I am in your hands.[53]

This is a mad speech which pleads to be rightly understood, rightly heard. Henry cannot, by himself, re-enter life. But at this moment he can imagine, through the figure of the historical fiction, how Matilda's supportive understanding might enable him to do so. It matters that she is such a richly composite figure for him at this moment. As Henry

---

52 Ibid., p.113.
53 Ibid., p.102.

IV's mother-in-law, she is a maternal figure, restoring the mother from whom he was torn away by his enemies when young. As Matilda of Tuscany, she is the enemy who became his friend at his moment of greatest need. She is also herself—it's clear from the preceding dialogue that Henry has recognised her—the woman whose acceptance of his love might have given (might still give) his inner life a foothold in the world. And she is also the daughter of whom he speaks. Historically, this refers to Henry's wife, who pleaded with him in the snow at Canossa for admission to the Pope; and in the play, Matilda's actual daughter looks uncannily identical to the portrait of her younger mother. The daughter's pity of which Henry speaks confuses, and thereby holds together, then and now: the historical support he was given at Canossa, the reciprocation of his love which Matilda may have shown him twenty years ago, the compassionate understanding of his pain which she may show him at this moment. The function of this pity is that it will enable him to emerge from his 'excommunicated' state and, specifically, once more to love. (We might think here again of Othello's love, brought into being by Desdemona's pity, itself brought into being by how she listened to his story.)

All this depends, however, on the speech being rightly heard, its complicated sub-text understood. Pirandello's theatre audience are placed in roughly the position of the Marchesa: can we understand the implications of Henry's speech, can we recognise the human reality beneath the play's dazzlingly clever conceit, thereby releasing him from his fixed role? In the study this may be clear, but in the theatre, and especially at a first encounter, it is asking a lot of the audience, and the real possibility that we may fail—and thereby fail Henry, fail to take him back into human communion—is part of the drama.

As for the Marchesa, she has listened well, and is profoundly affected. The first act ends with the stage direction: 'The Marchesa is so deeply moved, she drops suddenly into a chair, almost fainting'.[54] In the second act she is contemplating, not entirely consciously or voluntarily, 'a certain intention stronger than herself'[55] (stage direction), and she insists, against the others, that Henry recognised her.

---

54 Ibid., p.102.
55 Ibid., p.103.

MATILDA: And then his words seemed to me to be full, so full of regret for my youth and for his own—and for the horrible thing that happened to him, and has held him there, in that masquerade from which he is unable to release himself and from which he wants so much to free himself.

BELCREDI: Of course! So that he can start his love affair with your daughter. Or with you, as you believe, now that he has been made tender by your pity.

MATILDA: Of which there is much, I beg you to believe!

BELCREDI: Clearly so, Marchesa! So much so that even a miracle-worker would most probably attribute it to a miracle.[56]

When, as Henry IV's mother-in-law, she comes to take her leave of the king, he takes her to one side and asks her, with charged insistence, whether she wishes him to love her daughter.

HENRY IV: Well, then, is it your wish?

MATILDA: What?

HENRY IV: That I return to loving your daughter. [*He looks at her and quickly adds in a mysterious tone of warning mixed with alarm:*] Do not be a friend, do not be a friend of the Marchesa of Tuscany!

MATILDA: And yet, I tell you again, that she has not begged, she has not implored any less than we have to obtain your pardon.

HENRY IV: [*quickly, softly, trembling*] Don't tell me that! Don't tell me about it! For God's sake, my Lady, do you not see the effect it has on me?

MATILDA: [*looks at him, then very softly, as if in confidence*] Do you still love her?

HENRY IV: [*bewildered*] Still? How can you say still? You know then, perhaps? No one knows! And no one must know!

MATILDA: But perhaps she, yes, she knows, if she has begged so on your behalf.[57]

As if this comes closer than he can bear, at this point Henry switches into animosity that cuts off any further rapport.

But the rapport is clearly there. Establishing it depends on the inbetween, indeterminate status of the dialogue, which flickers between referring to Henry's historical fantasy-world and to his actual feelings

---

56   Ibid., pp.106–107.
57   Ibid., p.116.

for the Marchesa. When he endeavours to explain himself at the end, the Marchesa is noted to be 'enchanted' by all that he says, 'fascinated by this "conscious" insanity'.[58] Conscious insanity: that is to say, we do not feel that Henry is simply faking his madness, detached from his performance, in control of the double meanings. He may know that he is not living in the eleventh century, and that his visitors are in costume or disguise, but this does not mean that the eleventh century is not real to him. The doctor likens this capacity of mind to that of a child, in a way that anticipates Winnicott: Henry can 'recognise disguise as such [...] and at the same time believe in it, the way children do, for whom it amounts to a mixture of play and reality'—although such play-capacity is rendered 'extremely complicated' in his case, the doctor adds, by his entanglement with a fixed image.[59] The possibility of his re-entering the world does not imply his leaving his inner fantasy-life behind, but of finding some way of connecting or accommodating both together.

This bears on why the plan for his cure ends in disaster: it supposes a simple binary opposition between delusion and actuality, such that Henry could be carried across from one state to the other. The portraits of Matilda of Tuscany and Henry IV are replaced by living people identically posed and costumed, who are to step out of their frames and 'come to life': the shock of witnessing this will release Henry likewise to step out into real life—that is the doctor's plan. But Henry first collapses in terror, and then is enraged by his visitors' presumption: for the masquerade permeates real life no less than it characterises the throne-room, and his performance as Henry IV, even if undeluded, was still not the game or joke which they take it to be. 'You are not crazy', Belcredi insists, and Henry responds by seizing a weapon and running him through. 'Am I not crazy? Here, take that!'[60] After this there can be no way back: the protagonist will be, in the final words of the play, locked into his condition 'for ever'. And the most piercing of the cries that goes up at the end, Pirandello specifies, is that of the Marchesa.[61]

---

58 Ibid., p.134.
59 Ibid., p.104.
60 Ibid., p.135.
61 I find it impossible not to reflect on the biographical context. Pirandello had recently committed his wife Antonietta to an asylum, after many years of managing or trying to manage her terrorising, delusional, and sometimes violent behaviour, which at one point had driven their daughter to attempt suicide. (In

The general thought I want to introduce here has to do with the contrast between the outcome within the play and our experience of the play. The doctor forces a confrontation between Henry's inner life and the reality of the external world; he acts in this respect as an agent of that 'dark and fatal power that assigns limits to the will', enforcing a sharp dichotomy between sanity and madness, to catastrophic effect. The play, however, significantly supports or colludes with Henry's fantasy life, creating an in-between space, as we have seen—felt particularly in those charged dialogues with the Marchesa and in the affinity between 'conscious insanity' and conscious theatricality. The play might be said to mimic the action of Henry's nephew in supplying a play-world which answers to his inner life. Without supposing ourselves for long to be in the eleventh century, we are reminded of how easily theatre accommodates such supposing, and certainly the figures from real-world contemporary Italy seem less real, less interesting, than the consciousness of Henry as he lives at the border between the two worlds. Henry plays mad, but the play plays along with him, up to a point, and this theatrical hospitality to his madness is crucial to the tragic effect.

The general principle appears in a helpfully clear, almost schematic form in Ibsen's *Master Builder*, a play already discussed in an earlier chapter. Solness, the master builder, believes that his mere wishes have the power to produce real effects—believes it enough, at least, to be

---

all such cases one must wonder about the husband's contribution to the wife's madness, but Antonietta seems to have had a disturbing upbringing with a tyrannically jealous father; her mother is said to have died in childbirth because the father refused to allow a doctor to be present.) *Henry IV* is a play that urgently tries to bring us into affinity with what it also recognises as a bizarrely disturbed condition of mind—to find a way of honouring that condition without glamourising it. Asked by a journalist whether his wife's illness had allowed him 'to study the world of the mad, their psychology and their logic', Pirandello replied: 'Whoever suffers and lives the torment of a person he loves is unable to study it because that would mean assuming the indifference of a spectator. But to see life being transposed in the mind of my poor companion enabled me later to convey the psychology of the alienated in my creative writing. Not the logic. The lunatic constructs without logic. Logic is form and form is in contrast with life. Life is formless and illogical. So I think the mad are closer to life. There is nothing fixed and determined in us. We have within ourselves every possibility, and suddenly, unexpectedly, the thief or the lunatic can jump out of any one of us.' Gaspare Giudice, *Pirandello: A Biography*, trans. by Alastair Hamilton (London: Oxford University Press, 1975), p.119. For Pirandello's relationship with Antonietta and for her illness, see pp.57–66, 82–87, 98–101.

terrified, obsessed, and fascinated by the idea. Surely the man is on the verge of psychosis, of madness? So his wife fears, and a doctor stands ready to make that diagnosis. Yet when (as he recounts it) Solness imagined his wife's house burning down, it burnt down in fact; when he imagines youth knocking at the door, the youthful Hilde knocks at the door. She enters the play for all the world as if she were the incarnation of his unconscious fantasies, come to free him of his fear and his guilt by showing him that those fantasies can, after all, discover an object that exists in the world. Which is to say that the drama itself, to some large degree, colludes with or supports the 'madness' of Solness. Its naturalism barely contains passages written in a more expressionist mode. When Hilde and Solness frame their exchanges in increasingly symbolic terms, speaking of the trolls that may attend on them, or of the castles in the air that they will build, these words strike us neither as deranged nor as merely figurative, but as having power and meaning. We are more inclined to see Hilde as an uncanny figure than a neurotic stalker seeking to impose her fantasies on the world (although both perspectives remain available). Uncanniness, as Freud understood it, is generated when the world appears to validate an illusory mode of perception or projection that properly belongs only to a young child, whose deference to the reality-principle is still weak. This fits well enough with Solness's sense of 'the omnipotence of thoughts' (Freud),[62] and with our sense of Hilde as the paradoxically real creation of his mind. Theatre has a comparable power to create a real object for feelings that previously had none, and Ibsen draws on this power. Solness's inner world is, to some large extent, made real upon the stage; if this is madness, it is a madness with which the play sympathises and which it supports.

And yet: this is true *only* to some large extent. To call Hilde uncanny is to register what the feeling of uncanniness always tells us: that *something is wrong here*. We never enter so entirely into the expressionist mode of the play as to lose our hold on mundane reality. If Hilde encourages Solness's fantasy life, this is not without a certain mockery. Her feyness co-exists oddly with a kind of hearty downrightness. And her infatuation with Solness, or with her heroic idea of him, is complicated by her real

---

62 Sigmund Freud, 'On the Introduction of Narcissism', in *The Penguin Freud Reader*, ed. by Adam Phillips (London: Penguin, 2006), p.360.

concern for his suffering wife. The wife has made herself into a martyr to duty, and is easy to dislike or dismiss, but Ibsen shows us what lies behind her rigidity: an inconsolable maternal grief for her dead children, infected, as she supposes, by the fever in her mother's milk that was contracted as a result of the fire. Somewhere deep beneath the action lies this immense maternal grief, grief at the failure of maternal support, grief at the horribly broken relation between mother and child. 'Those two little boys—are not so easy to forget.'[63] It is an unvoiced lament, expressed neither by the grimly stoical wife nor with any fulness by the play itself, but whose weight nevertheless pulls down hard against the febrile restlessness of Solness's mind. When at the end Solness suspends his vertigo for long enough to climb to the top of the tower, 'doing the impossible', our sense of symbolic triumph is poised against our perception of an act of folly, as his heavy body then falls to the ground. This is a balancing act which Solness himself cannot sustain.

Macbeth

Imperfect speaking and the inner world

'Nothing is / But what is not.' The uncanny quality that I have been discussing in *Henry IV* and *The Master Builder* could well be glossed by Macbeth's response to meeting the witches (I.iii.141–42). It is a state of mind that arises at the juncture between madness and sanity, in the mixture of excitement and disturbance that comes when the buried life of the mind appears to generate or be reflected by phenomena that are out in the world. For these phenomena bring dangerous witness to what would otherwise remain unrealised.

At the start of *Macbeth*, we are given a contrast between two different kinds of witnessing. In the second scene, Macbeth is introduced to us through two strong acts of reporting, as first the bloody sergeant and then Ross bear witness to his extraordinary prowess in the battle. He is acclaimed as 'noble Macbeth', 'Bellona's bridegroom' (I.ii.67, 54), an irresistible force guaranteeing victory, a man who 'well [...] deserves'

---

63 Henrik Ibsen, *The Master Builder*, in Plays: One. Ghosts, The Wild Duck, The Master Builder, trans. by Michael Meyer (London: Eyre Methuen, 1980), p.285.

the heroic 'name' given to him by others (I.ii.16). This great prowess entails great violence, yes, and we may feel some tension when the warrior who 'unseam'd' the rebel leader 'from the nave to th'chops' is saluted as a 'worthy gentleman' (I.ii.22–24)—a phrase which stretches hard to accommodate such elemental violence within the cause and form of civilisation. That all this blood should be cleansing, like Christ's at Golgotha, is a strenuous idea:

> Except they meant to bathe in reeking wounds,
> Or memorize another Golgotha,
> I cannot tell— (I.ii.39–41)

The troubling physicality of that image of bathing in reeking wounds—in blood that cleanses, a conceivable image of the function of tragedy itself—carries some strain, and for a moment the story breaks down; the wounded soldier can speak no more. But the narrative is immediately taken up again and made good, as Ross enters to 'speak things strange' and bring the story to a triumphant conclusion. Macbeth's near-magical victory over all opposition is grounded by the certainty and sufficiency with which his prowess is recognised by the community. The story is complete, entire, admitting no question. We are given the good witnesses who securely establish the hero. Hamlet, at the end of his play, implored Horatio to heal his 'wounded name', to establish his commendable identity through the story he tells. What Hamlet asked for at the end, Macbeth begins with.

But in the next scene, Macbeth encounters reporters of a very different kind. The witches too give him his titles, present and future, telling his story forwards; but they are equivocal beings in every sense, and they tell that story in a fragmented, incomplete, enigmatic way. They are what Macbeth calls them, 'imperfect speakers' (I.ii.70). Their speaking exists at the uncertain border between what is really out there and speakable of, and a fantasy world which it would be madness to confuse with reality.

> Were such things here as we do speak about?
> Or have we eaten on the insane root
> That takes the reason prisoner? (I.iii.83–85)

When he then hears this fragmentary story of himself partly confirmed, as the king's emissaries bring him the title of Cawdor, there arises in

Macbeth an extraordinary state of mind. The encounter with the witches, so swiftly reinforced by the news about Cawdor, suggests to him that there might be some footing in the external world, some speakable form, for half-thoughts and half-desires that in themselves are 'but fantastical'.

> This supernatural soliciting
> Cannot be ill; cannot be good. If ill,
> Why hath it given me earnest of success,
> Commencing in a truth? I am Thane of Cawdor.
> If good, why do I yield to that suggestion
> Whose horrid image doth unfix my hair
> And make my seated heart knock at my ribs,
> Against the use of nature? Present fears
> Are less than horrible imaginings:
> My thought, whose murther yet is but fantastical,
> Shakes so my single state of man that function
> Is smother'd in surmise, and nothing is
> But what is not. (I.iii.130–42)

In verse of astonishing power, we feel Macbeth's shuddering, bottomless fall into a condition which the word 'terror' only weakly indicates. The weird women's prophecies, now partly confirmed, have opened him to an idea or a desire which comes in some sense from within, but which he can scarcely be said to have had until this moment. The terror stems from its content: imagining himself as murderer. But it stems also from the nature of the witness that is involved. The women have brought into life some secret or latent part of Macbeth's being. But what kind of life? They both do and do not belong to the external world. They are out there, on the heath, speaking to Banquo as well, and they are right about Macbeth's promotion to Cawdor. But they also melt away 'as breath into the wind' (I.iii.82). They are more than projections of the mind, yet the anchorage they offer the mind in the world, the corroboration that they bring, is profoundly equivocal. 'Were such things here as we do speak about?', asks Banquo (I.ii.83). Their anchorage in reality is as 'imperfect' as the story that they tell. And this is where the terror lies: Macbeth's buried fantasy has been half-exposed, half-recognised and half-realised by external witness, but yet is not securely supported. 'Nothing is / But what is not.' The engulfing reality of what is 'but fantastical' erodes the solidity of the external here-and-now: whatever fearful thing might be actually present is less, far less, than 'horrible imaginings'.

We might note in passing that Macbeth's speech repeats, in verse of much greater intensity, the speech of Brutus in *Julius Caesar* as he contemplates the murder of Caesar.

> Since Cassius first did whet me against Caesar,
> I have not slept.
> Between the acting of a dreadful thing
> And the first motion, all the interim is
> Like a phantasma or a hideous dream:
> The Genius and the mortal instruments
> Are then in council; and the state of man,
> Like to a little kingdom, suffers then
> The nature of an insurrection. (II.i.61–69)

Cassius's words worked on Brutus like the weird women's words on Macbeth, and Brutus, like Macbeth, was transported into that phantasmal, interim condition evoked by the experience of prolonged sleeplessness, in which the inner life of fantasy runs loose in search of some footing in the world. *Julius Caesar* was the first in the great sequence of Shakespeare's tragedies, and it is arguable that this sense of *phantasma*, of radical confusion between inner and outer worlds, or between the realms of desire and action, was the impetus for much that followed.

The anxiety generated by this liminal condition is such that Macbeth will do anything to get beyond it. It is sometimes said that Macbeth is the tragedy of ambition (the crime and punishment story), but Macbeth never sounds greatly ambitious, nor much looks forward to ruling as King. It could almost be said that he kills Duncan in order to give substance to the image of his fear, to find for it an object in the world, to turn it into a conceivable story that can then be put behind him. If we must speak of motive at all, it makes more sense to see him as driven by fear, by the need to put an end to the unbearable anxiety which this imperfect speaking has induced. Lady Macbeth asks the tremendous question: 'Art thou afeard / To be the same in thine own act and valour / As thou art in desire?' (I.vii.39–41). Kingship, as a symbolic idea, is that state against which her question would have no leverage, a state in which desire seamlessly becomes act. *Le roi le veut*, the king's will is law. But meanwhile—and Macbeth is much concerned with the meanwhile—there is nothing but radical fear, radical insecurity, in their appallingly slow convergence.

The weird women activate what is 'fantastical' within Macbeth, but they then offer his fantasy-life only a shadowy support. The fuller support comes from his wife, perfectly attuned to her husband's barely spoken 'imaginings', and able to reflect them back to him with the assurance that they do indeed belong in the world. In the first two acts of the play, the Macbeths know each other more intimately than any other couple in Shakespeare. It is this intimate understanding which allows Lady Macbeth to recognise and affirm those 'black and deep desires' which, by himself, Macbeth can hardly bear to look steadily at (I.iv.51). She understands his conflicted condition, too—up to a point—well enough:

> Yet do I fear thy nature,
> It is too full o'th'milk of human kindness
> To catch the nearest way. Thou wouldst be great;
> Art not without ambition, but without
> The illness should attend it. What thou wouldst highly,
> That wouldst thou holily; wouldst not play false,
> And yet wouldst wrongly win. [...] Hie thee hither,
> That I may pour my spirits in thine ear ... (I.v.16–26)

That extraordinary image of the milk of human kindness conveys the nurturing aspect of her relationship with him. If Macbeth is her warrior-husband and sexual partner, he is also at some level an unweaned child. There is great insight in her intuiting that their relationship reaches down to this primal level, but also great blindness. For what she proposes is a harsh weaning. She finds something derisory in Macbeth's conflicted state, in the persistence of infant tenderness into adult life. To displace that milk, she will pour her spirits into him—an unmaternal feeding, not unlike that which she offers to the spirits that tend on mortal thoughts:

> Come to my woman's breasts,
> And take my milk for gall. (I.v.47–48)

Three times in this first part of the play Lady Macbeth refers to mother's milk,[64] and always with this dual implication of herself as capable of giving but also of withholding or failing in that primal intimate support.

> I have given suck, and know
> How tender 'tis to love the babe that milks me;
> I would, while it was smiling in my face,
> Have pluck'd my nipple from his boneless gums,
> And dash'd the brains out, had I so sworn as you
> Have done to this. (I.vii.54–59)

It is a specifically maternal power that Macbeth recognises in her when she enables his resolution to commit the murder: 'Bring forth men-children only!' (I.vii.72) The play's obsession with children—their murder, their survival and continuance—circles round the question of whether a child's sensibility is compatible with living an adult's life. Her repeated appeals to Macbeth to be 'a man' are primarily to his masculinity, but they also, I think, involve the demand that in being an adult male he no longer be a child, not be 'the baby of a girl', in the phrase that Macbeth half-uses about himself in his terror before Banquo's ghost (III.iv.105). Hence, although she understands that Macbeth is fearful, she cannot enter into the terrible intensity of that fear, in the way that a good enough mother enters into her child's fear. She cannot 'hold' it for him and with him. At the moment of crisis in the murder scene, she understands that his terror is that of a child, but does not (or dares not) understand how much that means:

> MACBETH: I'll go no more.
>   I am afraid to think what I have done;
>   Look on't again I dare not.
> LADY MACBETH: Infirm of purpose!
>   Give me the daggers. The sleeping and the dead
>   Are but as pictures; 'tis the eye of childhood
>   That fears a painted devil. (II.ii.47–52)

---

64 The milk of Macbeth's traumatic weaning surfaces again near the end of the play in 'whey-face', his brutally contemptuous term for the serving-boy who is pale with terror. Cowards like children are full of milk where there should instead be blood.

The one moment in which her resolution falters is when she remembers herself as child—that is, acknowledges that you never entirely cease to be the child that you were. 'Had he not resembled / My father as he slept, I had done't' (II.ii.12–13). But otherwise, in the name of adult rationality, she repudiates the child's susceptibility to being engulfed by their inner life—a susceptibility which adult consciousness must bracket off as *mere* fantasy, the mere *painting* of a devil.

In the banquet scene, this splitting apart gets its full dramatic realisation. Macbeth's participation in social reality is shattered by the intrusion of Banquo's ghost, a reality which is real only to him, while his wife tries but fails to mediate between the two worlds. The only 'story' she can imagine that would support his behaviour is again cast in dismissive terms, as belonging merely to the domestic world of women:

> O, these flaws and starts
> (Imposters to true fear) would well become
> A woman's story at a winter's fire,
> Authoriz'd by her grandam. (III.ii.62–65)

Richard II had imagined such a scene of female story-telling as a site of real value; in *The Winter's Tale*, the child's story of sprites and goblins is acknowledged as 'powerful' by the women and, in effect, by the play. But for Lady Macbeth here such women's stories, which mother-figures might 'authorise', are things to be outgrown, discarded with contempt, irrelevant to the business of real life. She is not only unable to see the ghost, but more importantly unable to grant the reality of her husband's terror. As if in response to what she cannot give him, Macbeth will decide to return to the weird sisters, those other female tellers of stories, in the search for some narrative that will bring relief to his present terrors. But they will prove once again to be only 'imperfect speakers'.

The relationship between the Macbeths was already shown to be breaking down in the wonderful scene between them before Banquo's murder. Lady Macbeth begins by reaching out to her husband, although fearful that she can no longer reach him:

> How now, my lord, why do you keep alone,
> Of sorriest fancies your companions making,
> Using those thoughts which should indeed have died
> With them they think on? (III.ii.8–11)

Not the least tragic aspect of the play is her desolation at the growing understanding that she is losing him to the world of 'fancies'; his mental anguish has a hold on him that she cannot cajole or bully or reason him out of. He no longer sleeps, or more precisely, his sleep is only nightmare, given over to 'these terrible dreams / That shake us nightly' (III.ii.18–19): the border between nightmare and waking consciousness has all but disappeared. 'O full of scorpions is my mind, dear wife!'; one barely feels that he means this as metaphor (III.ii.36). He is on the verge of, if not already given over to, madness; his consuming terror of Banquo and Fleance, of how the unfinished story might yet turn out, is evident paranoia, a projection of the dark world of his mind. Yet in this play, and when we hear this verse, we cannot think this dark world of threat unreal: we know it is in some sense out there, as the witches are.

>   MACBETH: Then be thou jocund; ere the bat hath flown
>   His cloister'd flight, ere to black Hecat's summons
>   The shard-borne beetle with his drowsy hums
>   Hath rung night's yawning peal, there shall be done
>   A deed of dreadful note.
>   LADY MACBETH: What's to be done?
>   MACBETH: Be innocent of the knowledge, dearest chuck,
>   Till thou behold the deed. Come, seeling night,
>   Scarf up the tender eye of pitiful day,
>   And with thy bloody and invisible hand
>   Cancel and tear to pieces that great bond
>   Which keeps me pale! (III.ii.40–45)

Macbeth withholds full knowledge of his intentions from her, as he had never done before. A gap is widening between them, as his mind spirals within its vortex. Yet he is also trying thereby to protect her. There is momentary tenderness as well as horror, brilliantly conveyed in feeling the tenderness of the eye which the night stitches shut, with a sensitivity that both belies and underlies the flinch from 'beholding the deed'. For all the vertiginous force of his incantatory lines, Macbeth is simultaneously attempting to give comfort to his dear wife. 'Be thou jocund', 'dearest chuck'—these expressions of intimacy and affection co-exist extraordinarily with the dreadful thing that he intends and the dreadful place that his mind is now in. But that is the point: he addresses her, still, as someone who might be able to share and hold this experience with him; it is through their relationship that all this blood and horror may yet be connected back to a good world which holds their good marriage. For Macbeth, their relationship holds, in Winnicott's terms, the 'hope that there is a live relationship between inner reality and external reality, between innate primary creativity and the world at large which is shared by all'.[65] That relationship is, however, breaking up before our eyes; she speaks less and less in this scene, dismayed or overwhelmed by the intensity of his feelings, feelings that take him ever further from her. Once so extraordinarily close, they are now breaking apart, as a direct consequence of how well she knew and understood his mind. Hence the scene's immense irony, inseparable from its immense and terrible pathos.

After the banquet scene, which confirms the widening abyss between them, they are never again together. In the sleepwalking scene in the final act, she has taken over his sleep-disrupting nightmares, and the two figures who witness this, the waiting-gentlewoman and the doctor, cannot engage with her, as if a glass wall had descended between her mind and the world of others. Like Beckett's silent Auditor, although they stand in the place of witnesses, they cannot properly tell of what they have heard and seen. 'I think, but dare not speak' (V.i.79). Only the doctor's extraordinary exclamation, 'God, God forgive us all!' (V.i.75), suggests a moment of recognition, of imaginable kinship.

Finally, when Macbeth hears of the death of his wife, the person who came closest to entering into what he feels, the collapse of narrative possibility is rendered complete. The philosopher Paul Ricoeur has written that 'time becomes human time to the extent that it is organised after the manner of a narrative.'[66] Macbeth's great speech of desolation despairs of any narrative arc to life ('Tomorrow and tomorrow and tomorrow ...', V.v.19) and with it all notion that a life is something about which a meaningful story could be told.

> Life's but a walking shadow, a poor player,
> That struts and frets his hour upon the stage,
> And then is heard no more. It is a tale

---

65 D. W. Winnicott, 'Further Thoughts on Babies as Persons', in *The Child, the Family, and the Outside World* (London: Penguin, 1964), p.90.
66 Paul Ricoeur, *Time and Narrative*, trans. by Kathleen McLaughlin and David Pellauer (Chicago: University of Chicago Press, 1984) I, p.3.

Told by an idiot, full of sound and fury,
Signifying nothing. (V.v.24–28)

One of the blessings of having a tellable story is the possibility of closure. A tellable story confirms that a life, or a given portion of a life, has shape and direction, and however disturbing its events may have been, there is the possibility of standing outside them and the hope that distress is not perpetual, boundless, subjectively as eternal as damnation. Macbeth's speech makes this connection in its negative form: it is impossible to tell a story, and likewise impossible to get to an end. This is what the death of his wife means, what it terribly brings home.

She should have died hereafter.
There would have been a time for such a word. (V.v.17–18)

Macbeth's response to the news of her death—conveyed in the first place by a great wordless 'cry of women'—is that there is no time now, in the heat of battle, to mourn his wife; to hold her funeral, say, and in particular to find the language which her death demands. Hereafter would have yielded such a time. And then he hears what he is saying, and reflects with infinite bitterness that the time for such a word *never* arrives, that life is an endless series of anticipations and regrets in which the work of mourning can never take place, and the story of pain can never be told.

Mourning and ending

In *Mourning Becomes the Law*, Gillian Rose distinguishes between what she calls 'inaugurated mourning' and a mourning which is 'aberrated' or 'incomplete', an endless melancholia which she links to the failure or renunciation of representation. Her thought is that successful representation, making 'the suffering of immediate experience visible and speakable',[67] overcomes estrangement from the world of others, opening the possibility of a return to that world. In the context of bereavement, this means acknowledging

---

67 Gillian Rose, *Mourning Becomes the Law: Philosophy and Representation* (Cambridge: Cambridge University Press, 1996), p.36.

the law that decrees the absence of the other, the necessity of relinquishing the dead one, returning from devastating inner grief to the law of the everyday and of relationships, old and new, with those who live.[68]

'Relinquishing' and 'returning' should not be heard as unduly upbeat, for Rose is speaking more of a particular way of embracing grief than of passing beyond it. Acknowledging the law that decrees the absence—or separateness—of the beloved other is also to acknowledge the pain the law inflicts.[69] Yet without such acknowledgement, 'there can be no work, no exploring of the legacy of ambivalence, working through the contradictory emotions aroused by bereavement',[70] and the mind remains trapped, as Macbeth is, within the past's endless recurrence, with a future that never arrives.

A simple example of achieved mourning comes at the end of *Macbeth*, when Siward is brought news of his son's death in the battle:

> SIWARD: Then he is dead?
> Ross: Ay, and brought off the field. Your cause of sorrow
>   Must not be measur'd by his worth, for then
>   It hath no end.
> SIWARD: Had he his hurts before?
> Ross: Ay, on the front.
> SIWARD: Why then, God's soldier be he!

---

68 Ibid., p.70.
69 One way of showing this is through the difference between Rose's distinction between good and bad modes of mourning and that made by Freud in 'Mourning and Melancholia'. In that essay, Freud sees continuing attachment to someone who has died as a kind of misapprehension of reality, which a healthy mourning process properly effaces. Since the loved person now lives only in the mind, attachment to them is to nothing, to a mirage. The readmission of the world replaces grief, in a kind of zero-sum game. But Rose's conception, unhappy with such firm oppositions, speaks more helpfully to the mourning which much great tragedy bequeaths us, acknowledging rather the necessity of grief, which now accompanies the readmission of the world. What lives only in the mind may still be vital to us. What is ended is not grief but grief's unbearable aspect and its usurpation of the world. This means that it can be communicated, spoken, or otherwise tolerably represented, that it can be received and taken in—not that it is displaced or diminished. 'Keep your mind in hell, and despair not' is the epigraph to *Love's Work*, Rose's personal memoir written alongside *Mourning Becomes the Law* as she approached her own death; the two works stand in several respects as commentaries upon one another.
70 Rose, *Mourning Becomes the Law*, p.70.

>Had I as many sons as I have hairs,
>I would not wish them to a fairer death.
>And so his knell is knoll'd.
>MALCOLM: He's worth more sorrow,
>And that I'll spend for him.
>SIWARD: He's worth no more;
>They say he parted well, and paid his score,
>And so God be with him! (V.ix.9–19)

The nature and meaning of Young Siward's death are perfectly visible, fully represented by the public meaning of 'his hurts before' (i.e. he was facing his enemy, not running away). This fact successfully tells the story of how he died, and so the possibility that grief for him might have 'no end', although acknowledged, is passed through and decisively set aside—not least because the 'cause of sorrow' is shared and shareable by others. We don't doubt that his funeral rites—here compressed into the knell that is knolled—will provide fitting closure.

Young Siward's exemplary death is a very clean case, and one would hesitate to call it tragic; it sits in the play to demonstrate what, post-Macbeth, has become possible. Siward's grief is not engulfing; it does not dim the lights on the world. Much closer to the tragic is the grief of Macduff, where an all-but-unspeakable event elicits an unspeakable anguish.[71] In such situations the task of proper representation is very much harder, for all the reasons this book has tried to suggest. If, in Gillian Rose's terms, representation of our suffering reconciles us to the world, it is likewise true that successful representation requires an audience, and the task of finding a good witness to estrangement or extreme anguish is immensely problematic. In tragedies of madness, it is acutely possible that the inner life of passion will find 'no end' in the words of others or in external form—just as 'there is no end' to what Hieronimo required of the impossible painting that would represent his grief, in the scene from *The Spanish Tragedy* discussed in chapter four. Macbeth's 'Tomorrow and tomorrow and tomorrow' epitomises that endless pursuit of an unreachable finality that has been his throughout:

---

71 Shakespeare does not show us where or whether Macduff's grief will have an end. But it is noticeable that he is willing, if Macbeth yields, to take him alive. This feels like something other than insatiable vengefulness.

> If it were done, when 'tis done … (I.vii.1)

or

> Then comes my fit again. I had else been perfect … (III.iv.20)

or

> What, will the line stretch out to th' crack of doom? (IV.i.117)

'She should have died hereafter' crystallises this endless deferral, this endless failure of representation, in the funeral that Lady Macbeth will never have, because the time for the right, the conclusive word will never arrive.[72] I say 'conclusive', but a more capacious term might be 'releasing'. It is natural in relation to a death to think in terms of release as closure—the funeral rite, the funeral eulogy—and natural also for a mind in torment like Macbeth's to cast hope no further than the cessation of present anguish. But the function of a good funeral is to make possible a return to life in the world; Macbeth's anguish is boundless because the world does not exist for him beyond what his mind has made of it. (What his actions have made his actual environment into—the Scotland of howls and cries—is the secondary effect of this: though not, of course, secondary for others.) Thus we can say that the end of which Macbeth despairs would be his discovery of a world separate from him in which he can live, and the timely word of which he despairs would be the word which would represent and recognise his anguish, coming from that separate world, from another's voice. It would bring an end to madness.

The movement which Macbeth cannot make is staged by the play itself. There is a strong contrast between Macbeth's traumatised experience of endless recurrence, in which the past is never 'done' and so can never be told, and the extraordinary momentum of *Macbeth* the play, which moves so rapidly and inevitably towards conclusion. Its clarity of narrative line is felt as a movement from Macbeth's inner life out to the external world. In the first two acts, and above all in the scenes around the murder of Duncan, we are drawn intimately into Macbeth's

---

72   One might think here also of the 'maimed rite' of Ophelia's funeral—maimed twice over, first by the restriction of ceremony for a suspected suicide, and then by Hamlet's melodramatic intervention, ranting at Laertes for his failure properly to mourn Ophelia, a failure of mourning in which he evidently shares.

state of mind, which fills and colours the whole of the dramatic reality. This is achieved through the extraordinary intensity of the verse, and through the way the cosmos itself responds to his being—in, for example, the host of unnatural phenomena that take place on the night of the murder. If these express the reaction of the cosmos to atrocity, they also make manifest his own self-horror. Like the ghost of Banquo, they are in a certain sense the creations of his mind granted theatrical reality, and in them the play bears witness to the overwhelming reality of his mental state.[73] But this changes, as the world of the play gradually separates itself from the world of his mind, and we come increasingly to see him as a figure within a world that is larger than his tormented consciousness. This shift is apparent in the treatment of the three main killings. Duncan's murder matters in the play primarily for its effect on Macbeth, as an event in his consciousness; the killing is not made present to us but exists above all as the intensification of Macbeth's terror, the blood on his hands and in his mind. (Its apprehension was from the outset 'fantastical', a psychic reality more horrible than any actuality could be.) Somewhat similarly, it is not the reality of Banquo's death that unmans Macbeth, but the equivocal reality of Banquo's ghost, another horrible imagining where what should remain within, like blood, is made appallingly visible. Yet there is also a shift; we get to see Banquo's murder, and this scene of Macbeth's reaction is not private to the Macbeths but happens in the social world of the dinner-guests. By the time we come to the murder of Macduff's family, this killing matters entirely in and for itself, as an event in the world, brutal rather than nightmarish. It may rise up into Lady Macbeth's nightmares ('The Thane of Fife had a wife; where is she now?', V.i.42–43) but we observe these, with the Doctor, from the outside. In parallel with this shift,

---

73   Consider the contrasting case of Othello, immediately after he has killed Desdemona:
   O insupportable! O heavy hour!
   Methinks it should be now a huge eclipse
   Of sun and moon, and that th' affrighted globe
   Should yawn at alteration. (V.ii.98–101)
   It should, but it doesn't; there is no eclipse, no earthquake, no support from the environment for Othello's consequently 'insupportable' sense of what he has done, no recognition by the cosmos of the tremendous nature of his deed. There is a ghastly logic to this; he has killed the woman who once embodied his sense that he was truly known and recognised, who made good the living connection between his primal self and the external world. The collapse into bottomless dread that he now experiences is extreme.

what were symbolic or supernatural realities—in the play's collusion with Macbeth's self-horror and paranoia—become naturalised: so the forest itself rising against Macbeth, as in nightmare, becomes a device of military camouflage. Our intense absorption in Macbeth's subjectivity drains gradually away: we exhale, we find ourselves able to take stock, to watch from a greater and safer distance.

One moment in this transition is marked with particular clarity: the porter scene. The knocking on the gate at the end of the murder scene is the realisation of Macbeth's self-horror. It is the world conforming and answering to his fear, the cosmos as an extension of his mind. It triggers his deranged-but-psychically-compelling belief that the blood can never be washed from his hands, but will instead stain all the waters of the ocean. But the knocking is also the sound of the external world breaking in, and as it persists into the following scene it changes its character, for it comes to be incorporated into the porter's comic routine.

> Here's a knocking indeed! If a man were porter of Hell Gate, he should have old turning the key. Knock, knock, knock! Who's there, i' th' name of Belzebub? Here's a farmer, that hang'd himself on th' expectation of plenty. Come in time! Have napkins enow about you, here you'll sweat for't. Knock, knock! Who's there, in th' other devil's name? Faith, here's an equivocator, that could swear in both the scales against either scale, who committed treason enough for God's sake, yet could not equivocate to heaven. O, come in, equivocator. (II.iii.1–11)

Macbeth feels himself to be a damned soul; the porter's figuring of himself as porter of hell-gate has its grim point. But the tonality of the speech is this-worldly. It is outward-turning, delivered at least half to the audience; it is familiar and contemporary in its reference; its sardonic humour roots the idea of damnation in the life of the commonplace, the only-too-familiar. The porter, we immediately know, cannot be touched by tragedy, but leads a separate existence in a world that its destructiveness will not reach, and reminds us that such a world exists. (The gravediggers in *Hamlet* have a similar effect.) When he speaks of transgression and damnation, from his appropriately transitional place at the gate between inside and outside, he makes Winnicott's 'live relationship' between the vortex of Macbeth's subjectivity and 'the world at large which is shared by all'.[74] He does so precisely by *playing at being* the porter of hell, by a fiction-making which reminds us of what the drama itself is doing. This will lead, still, to horror; we are terribly aware of what the visitors are about to find. But the movement of the second half of the play, the readmission of the world, has begun.

This is not a matter of simply displacing the fantastical by the real, madness by sanity. We have entered too deeply into Macbeth's inner life for that. When, in the final speech of the play, Malcolm refers to 'this dead butcher and his fiend-like queen' (V.ix.35), we are startled and I think saddened to discover that such a summary is, in its way, perfectly accurate. For it is wholly inadequate to our experience of Macbeth and Lady Macbeth—our participation in their experience—earlier in the play. It fails to tell their story. The play offers us a kind of grief or mourning, not so much for their deaths, nor even for the progressive dehumanisation of Macbeth, as for the impossibility of 'holding' Macbeth's inner life to the end. As the play re-establishes the reality of the external world, we mourn the necessity of giving up the electrifying intensities of its early scenes, with a mourning the lonelier for being unshared by any character on stage. To mourn this necessity is not to valorise Macbeth's actions or motives, but to have felt the fascination of his inner life as a vital reality without which the Scottish state—and the play—are obscurely the poorer. Such mourning is a way of bearing witness, of making that live connection between inner life and external world which the Macbeths cannot sustain, a failure which manifests in them as madness.

King Lear

Lear as child

In discussing *King Lear*, and in particular the madness of Lear, I want to begin where the play begins, by thinking about Lear's need. What it is that he is asking for when he requires his children to express their love for him? He is readily satisfied by the hyperbolic assurances of Goneril and Regan. These are, however, merely the appetisers to the great feast

---

74 Winnicott, *The Child, the Family, and the Outside World*, p.90; quoted earlier.

he eagerly expects when Cordelia will speak, his favourite, the daughter he loves the most, the daughter who—as he knows and expects—loves him the most. It is by getting what he wants here that Lear will feel able to give away his kingdom, as if Cordelia's love guaranteed him against any real loss in his giving up of power. When what he is asking for is denied (by Cordelia here; by Goneril and Regan later), this generates a convulsion of denial and rage which will take him into madness.

Lear's response to the frustration of his desire is infantile. From that obvious point, it is only a small further step to say that his original demand for love is likewise infantile. But 'infantile' is a pejorative term, carrying the view that infant sensibility shall not survive into adult life in any significant way; it is also a dismissive term, confident that such behaviour can or should be put in its place. If we think entirely of Lear's childishness in that way (which is Goneril's and Regan's way), I believe we lose the drama from the outset. That Lear begins as egotistical, foolish, and tyrannical is not in doubt: but Shakespeare asks us also to enter into the depth of Lear's need, for which the situation of a young child provides, at the least, a helpful analogy.

Let us return to the thinking about child development touched on earlier. In the first stages of life, the child's vulnerability and dependency are terrifyingly total. The unbearable anxiety which this would cause if fully registered is held at bay by the subjective sense of omnipotence: that is, the sense that the world, insofar as it gets registered at all as an external environment, conforms itself reliably to the child's inner life. This—the omnipotence of '*His Majesty the Baby*', in Freud's phrase[75]—is crucial to the basic security needed for the development of a self unappalled by the conditions of existence. What Winnicott emphasised was how this sense of omnipotence is made possible through the supportive presence of another person. If the baby's desires are not to engulf him in anxiety, dread, and rage, they have to be immediately met, as if by magic. The first intimations of hunger generate food, as the good mother meets the baby's desire in the moment of its formation. And the infant's other passions are similarly met by being acknowledged, recognised, and 'held', unconditionally, as if the mother's loving awareness were infinite and beyond any possibility of fluctuation or shortfall.

---

75 Freud, 'On the Introduction of Narcissism', p.376.

Of course, there must come development beyond this. The mother is not to support the child forever in this magical condition of mind, which in an adult would be delusion or psychosis. This development, in Winnicott's view, happens of itself. The nurturing mother is not magical, but belongs to the real world, and will sometimes be slow to understand and slow to provide. The good mother will be, in Winnicott's famous phrase, 'good enough', not perfect, not flawlessly the magical function of the child's desire. This imperfection, this capacity for occasional but mendable failure, is functional; she gradually but inevitably brings with her the intuition of a world beyond the child's psyche, separate from it and potentially resistant to it. But the weaning from omnipotence needs to be gradual. It is only if these intimations of a separate external world are accompanied by much reassuring support, much counterbalancing sense of pliancy, that the child can begin to acknowledge the existence of a world where his writ does not always run. Only in this way can the abdication from omnipotence tolerably take place.

The most obvious figure of omnipotence in Shakespeare is the King—whose word is law, whose utterance is performative, who operates within a court of supporters and flatterers. In practice, Shakespeare's kings do not enjoy unlimited power, but exist in a world of opponents and constraints. But some, at least, feel entitled to such a power, are resentful of limitation; they know that this is what kingship means or ought to mean. *Richard II* is Shakespeare's first great study of the grief involved in the loss of the dream of omnipotence. Richard denies to the last possible moment the pressure of external realities. If others abandon him, then angels and even stones will fight for him against the rebels. Our perception of this as delusion, the last stand of a narcissist, is mightily complicated by the Elizabethan idea of the sanctity of kingship, as well as by the soaring lyricism of his verse. Something immense does seem to be at stake. When political reality finally forces itself upon him, his sense of privation and annihilation is total. His fall as he experiences it is not into some humbler human state, with all its ordinary and familiar limitations, but radical: if he is not King, then he is nothing at all.

> I have no name, no title,
> No, not that name was given me at the font,
> But 'tis usurp'd. Alack the heavy day,
> That I have worn so many winters out

And know not now what name to call myself! (IV.i.255–59)

BOLINGBROKE: Are you contented to resign the crown?
RICHARD: Ay, no, no ay; for I must nothing be. (IV.i.200–01)

That word 'nothing' comes back in Richard's dungeon soliloquy:

Then am I king'd again, and by and by
Think that I am unking'd by Bullingbrook,
And straight am nothing. But what e'er I be,
Nor I, nor any man that but man is,
With nothing shall be pleas'd, till he be eas'd
With being nothing. (V.v.36–41)

'Nothing' marks the complete disintegration of the self when unsupported by the world. Both the word and the idea will come back insistently in *King Lear*.

Richard has kingship torn from him: an abrupt, traumatic weaning. Lear of course chooses to give away his kingdom—while specifying that he will still keep 'the name, and all th' addition to a king' (I.i.136). What he means by this is expressed in his demand that his daughters profess their love. As Goneril and Regan well understand, what he is asking for here is the confirmation of a love that is unconditional and total, that makes their own existence utterly subservient to the caring attention they lavish upon him. Their assurances may be impossible and gross, if heard as the words of one adult to another, but they also accurately express what the young child needs to feel is the case, that the nurturing figure lives only and extremely for him.

Lear the old man is very close to being a young child: his neediness, his tantrums, his self-absorption, his sense of mischief—all speak of this. 'Old fools are babes again', as Goneril puts it, who speaks as the advocate of a hard school of parenting (I.iii.19). The Fool refers to him as a child—someone who 'mad'st thy daughters thy mothers' (I.iv.172–73). And in the terrible scene with blind Gloucester, when Lear says, 'Thou know'st, the first time that we smell the air / We wawl and cry', it is as if that first smelling of the air after birth is a recent experience, a still vivid memory (IV.vi.179–80). At the start of the play, Lear may formally be putting aside the omnipotence of the King, but only, as he intends, to be embraced by the equally total assurance of support which the young child demands, as in retirement he 'crawls' toward death. We may see this as a wilfully blind denial of the loss of power which aging exacts. But it may be truer to credit Lear with some dim intuition that if he is to give up power, to accept his mortal condition, this is a process so terrifying and dismaying that he will need all Cordelia's loving support if he is to survive it. For Cordelia, he is sure, will be found to 'love us most' (I.i.51), and how much this matters is expressed in his choking disappointment when it is denied:

> I lov'd her most, and thought to set my rest
> On her kind nursery. (I.i.123–24)

'Her kind nursery' may stand well enough for what Winnicott understands by the 'holding' power of the good mother. Until this moment, as France wonderingly notes, Cordelia was Lear's 'best object' (I.i.214), his secure foothold for love in the external world. Her 'loving most' would have mirrored and confirmed his 'loving most'. (Her share of the kingdom was always to be the best.) That is, reality would wonderfully reciprocate the life of the mind.

To have this bluntly denied, to be made to confront an independent reality that is resistant to such desire, is intolerable. Lear explodes with rage and hurt: his connection with Cordelia now means a terrible vulnerability and must be utterly repudiated. Suddenly strange to him, she must become the stranger to whom all welcome is denied:

> Here I disclaim all my paternal care,
> Propinquity and property of blood,
> And as a stranger to my heart and me
> Hold thee from this for ever. The barbarous Scythian,
> Or he that makes his generation messes
> To gorge his appetite, shall to my bosom
> Be as well neighbor'd, pitied, and reliev'd,
> As thou my sometime daughter. (I.i.113–20)

Lear's imagination has, like Othello, been among the anthropophagi: in this case, those who feed upon their own children. The image of being kindly nursed is set against a horrible ingestion, an aggressive hunger that both destroys and internalises the child. Although Lear loudly thrusts such barbarous hunger away from himself, the structure of his sentence also acknowledges his secret affinity with that desire. This image of the parent devouring his children, annihilating them as separate beings, functions as the absolute denial of familial dependency, whose terrors are thereby displaced into a more manageable and more disavowable form. The image makes a ghostly reappearance at the end of the second act in relation to his other daughters, when Lear desperately asserts his vanishing omnipotence:

> I will have such revenges on you both
> That all the world shall—I will do such things—
> What they are yet I know not, but they shall be
> The terrors of the earth! (II.iv.279–82)

These lines recall (even as they shrink from recalling) the exact moment in Seneca's *Thyestes* when Atreus hatches his plan to feed Thyestes his own children.[76] If Lear is the terrified unsupported child, he is also the malignant, destructive parent of whom the child is terrified, each position amplifying the other. He threatens to banish or devour his daughters or, as he does with Goneril, to curse them with sterility or with offspring deformed in mind and body—a curse on fertility that, in the storm, becomes universal: 'all germains spill at once / That makes ingrateful man!' (III.ii.8–9).

It is easy—and in one sense obviously right—to be critical of Lear as a monster of egotism, who cannot conceive of love as a relationship between adults. Cordelia's suitors are waiting in the wings; she is about to become an adult, a married woman. Lear knows this in a notional way, but seems to understand nothing of what it means. (Unless indeed he cannot bear to understand what it means, and the love-test is his way of ensuring that he will never truly give Cordelia away: she must either put her father above all other loves, or be rendered unmarriageable, in another version of the curse on fertility.) But to settle for being critical of Lear is to slight the intolerable hurt caused by the denial of his need. In the scenes that follow, the position of being merely critical is occupied by Goneril and Regan, who continue the process that Cordelia had begun. They do so more proactively and callously, but their refusal to indulge their father is continuous with hers. His hundred knights are what he reserves to himself of his abdicated kingship, his crucial reassurance that although he no longer has power, he still or 'really' has power, that some

---

76 Seneca, *Thyestes*, lines 269–270.

part of the external world remains pliant to his will and is therefore a safe environment for him to place his love.

> My train are men of choice and rarest parts,
> That all particulars of duty know,
> And in the most exact regard support
> The worships of their name. (I.iv.263–66)

They are Lear's comfort blanket, his favourite toy. But they are 'unnecessary', and as Goneril correctly perceives, they support in Lear an unreal fantasy of power, 'these dispositions which of late transport you / From what you rightly are' (I.iv.221–22). And so Goneril and Regan whittle the knights away, down to fifty, down to twenty-five, until—'what need one?'—there is nothing left (II.iv.263). However we understand the daughters' motivation here—a mixture of distaste for disorder, pre-emptive strike against their father's anger, and a pleasure, perhaps sadistic, in feeling their own power—the effect is to bring Lear up abruptly against an external world that yields not at all to his will, and confronts him only with what he 'rightly' is:

> O sir, you are old,
> Nature in you stands on the very verge
> Of his confine. You should be rul'd and led
> By some discretion that discerns your state
> Better than you yourself. (II.iv.146–50)
>
> I pray you, father, being weak, seem so. (II.iv.201)

Lear's stupefaction at finding his messenger in the stocks is another moment in this process. As the King's emissary, Kent-as-Caius should have been immune to prosecution or punishment—yet, bewilderingly, impossibly, it is not so. This external world proves to be as unaccommodating, as hostile, as could have been feared; the former king is brought up against the extremity of utter dependency.

Lear's best hope of managing this growing perception of a hostile world lies in his relationship with the Fool, who offers support for his inner life that is both sympathising and realistic. The Fool can be played in two ways: as the boy that Lear calls him, or as little younger than Lear himself, being Lear's long-time entertainer and companion. But in either case, the Fool is simultaneously old and young. He seems to have much experience of how the world goes: but in his foolery, his doggerel songs and rhymes, his mischievous nonchalance, he evokes, without exactly inhabiting, a child's playfulness and irresponsibility. It is the Fool who most acutely recognises that Lear is still, in some important sense, a child:

> LEAR: Dost thou call me fool, boy?
> FOOL: All thy other titles thou hast given away, that thou wast born with. (I.iv.148–50)
>
> LEAR: When were you wont to be so full of songs, sirrah?
> FOOL: I have us'd it, nuncle, e'er since thou mad'st thy daughters thy mothers. (I.iv.170–73)

This is critical: but the Fool is also acknowledging where Lear really is. Making his daughters his mothers is exactly what Lear was trying to do (demanding from them a mother's unconditional love), impracticable though that had to be. Both Lear's questions to the Fool gesture at asserting the sober authority of adulthood; the Fool, however, turns each question back into a revelation of Lear's childishness. Beneath the movement of challenge and counter-challenge, we feel the rhythm of the double-act in which Lear's straight man colludes with, even looks for, the comical answer which turns adult interrogation into the play of repartee. If these exchanges are overtly antagonistic, they also carry the sense of Lear and the Fool playing together, as children play. To understand Lear is to understand that he is more of a child than an adult, or that he is a child wearing the mask of an adult (the political responsibilities which Lear wants to discard), or that he is someone in whom the child and the adult are radically confused. By offering himself as Lear's playfellow, the Fool offers permission for the Lear-child to exist and breathe and begin to know himself. (Lear hath ever but slenderly known himself.)

Like much good play, this incorporates elements of a threatening external reality: family relationships that can turn savagely destructive—

> For you know, nuncle,
> "The hedge-sparrow fed the cuckoo so long,
> That it had it head bit off by it young."
> So out went the candle, and we were left darkling. (I.iv.214–47)

—and the terror that, when support is removed, there is nothing but falling:

> Now thou art an O without a figure. I am better than thou art now, I am a Fool, thou art nothing. (I.iv.192–94)

The Fool tells Lear that he was a fool to give away his power in a world of ruthless aggression. This indeed seems to be the case: but it is also to externalise and reflect back to Lear his subjective perception of a horrifying betrayal at the heart of things. It was this that triggered his rejection of Cordelia, and is now steadily growing as first Goneril and then Regan deny him the primal comfort he craves. They tell him, in severely adult manner, that his extremity of response is unreasonable, that a life of dependency without the comfort blanket of his knights is perfectly liveable. But this is to deny the reality of his rage and fear. It is for the Fool (a person not rigorously sane) to reflect his worst fears back to him: children devour their parents, the world is a heartless and persecutory place, and the family is no refuge at all but rather the great source of affliction.

> Fathers that wear rags
> Do make their children blind,
> But fathers that bear bags
> Shall see their children kind.
> Fortune, that arrant whore,
> Ne'er turns the key to th' poor.
> But for all this, thou shalt have as many dolors for thy daughters as thou canst tell in a year. (II.iv.48–55)

The Fool tells Lear's story, as Lear increasingly fears and feels it to be. But he also tells it in the manner of a Fool: that is to say, as if in play, with a kind of playground nursery-rhyme nonchalance. As if to say: look, a child can know these things and remain a child. And also: look, look how we can make play with them, make a game of them, create word-play and double meanings out of them. And also: be reassured, I can enter into your fears, and I am not destroyed. (In a Winnicottian view of the psyche, a great part of the child's fear is that no-one could truly know what they feel without being destroyed by the experience.)

With regard to that last point, it matters that the Fool is felt to be in some sense immune from harm. As a 'licensed' being, he enjoys a measure of protection from punishment, and this extends to our sense that he is not vulnerable as others are vulnerable. This needs qualification; we are told that since Cordelia's banishment he has pined away, and in the third act it is possible, though not absolutely necessary, to play him as succumbing to the affliction of the storm. But in the first two acts he has a kind of blessed imperviousness. For all his unwavering fidelity to Lear, he is undistressed by Lear's distress; and although whipping is spoken of, we do not suppose that the Fool could be whipped, or that it would hurt him overmuch if it happened. This is reinforced by those moments when he addresses the audience directly:

> She that's a maid now, and laughs at my departure,
> Shall not be a maid long, unless things be cut shorter. (I.v.51–52)

> This prophecy Merlin shall make, for I live before his time. (III.ii.95)

A character who can thus step outside the frame of the play seems likely to be safe from what happens within it.

All these qualities in the Fool, taken together, qualify him (for a while) to tell Lear's story, to offer him the kind of support that he really needs, reflecting the Lear-child's terrors back to him as realities, yet as realities that do not overwhelm and destroy but can be made play with, or even made a play of, in which other persons could also bearably appear. If part of Lear's terror is of being mocked in an infinite humiliation, the Fool presents himself as one who can mock Lear yet remain unswervingly loyal: as if he were offering the mockery as a gift, an extension of what he provides as entertainer. There is a marvellously moving moment that suggests what this makes possible. After the confrontation with Goneril at the end of Act One, the Fool and Lear have an apparently gratuitous exchange:

> FOOL: Shalt see thy other daughter will use thee kindly, for though she's as like this as a crab's like an apple, yet I can tell what I can tell.
> LEAR: What canst tell, boy?
> FOOL: She will taste as like this as a crab does to a crab. Thou canst tell why one's nose stands i' th' middle on's face?
> LEAR: No.
> FOOL: Why, to keep one's eyes on either side's nose, that what a man cannot smell out, he may spy into.
> LEAR: I did her wrong.

The Fool has made no reference to Cordelia. Lear's ability to acknowledge, for the first time, a truth about her and about himself that stands beyond his fantasy-life, arises from within. Yet it can only arise out of the supportive environment which the Fool provides: glancing at Lear's unspoken fears and follies, showing that he has them fully in mind, yet also incorporating them within the world of playfellowship.

But for the most part, the Fool's support can do no more than hold at bay, for a time, that sense of radical vulnerability to which Goneril and Regan expose him. To be exposed in this way seems to Lear, and will soon become in the play, the stuff of psychic nightmare, paranoia made real. Rather than tolerate what is intolerable, he takes refuge in a rage that manifests itself as madness. This, Lear somewhere knows, is the only alternative to weeping, to the grief that would fully acknowledge how much is lost.

> You think I'll weep:
> No, I'll not weep.
> I have full cause of weeping, but this heart
> Shall break into a hundred thousand flaws
> Or ere I'll weep. O Fool, I shall go mad! (II.iv.282–86)

His madness emerges at first in the fantastical assertion that he is, after all, powerfully supported: the gods are his audience, they hear and understand him and will identify with his cause, wreaking vengeance on the world that hurts him through the storm that sympathises with his rage. In these passages Lear adopts the crime-and-punishment story, projecting the principal crime upon others. 'I am a man / More sinn'd against than sinning' (III.ii.59–60). Later, there is a more complete disintegration, a breaking into many flaws:

> No, they cannot touch me for coining, I am the King himself. [...] Nature's above art in that respect. There's your press-money. That fellow handles his bow like a crow-keeper; draw me a clothier's yard. Look, look, a mouse! Peace, peace, this piece of toasted cheese will do't. There's my gauntlet, I'll prove it on a giant. Bring up the brown bills. O, well flown, bird! i' th' clout, i' th' clout. (IV.vi.83–92)

Lear replaces an intolerable world with a world of his own making. Within this world he can give orders, hand out money, make judgements, issue challenges. And he is immune from prosecution or harm: 'they cannot touch me for coining' (or in the Quarto, interestingly, 'for crying'). He is still 'the King himself'. Winnicott's characterisation of such disintegration of self in the young child seems relevant; he understands this as

> a sophisticated *defence*, a defence that is an active production of chaos in defence against unintegration in the absence of maternal ego-support, that is, against the unthinkable or archaic anxiety that results from failure of holding in the stage of absolute dependence. The chaos of disintegration may be as 'bad' as the unreliability of the environment, but it has the advantage of being produced by the baby and therefore of being non-environmental. It is within the reach of the baby's omnipotence.[77]

If we follow Winnicott's lead, we may say that Lear's is the voice of one who cannot imagine that he is heard or supported by the world. The arrival of Gloucester changes things, but not greatly. As the blind man becomes increasingly present to Lear as someone who might recognise him ('Is't not the King?', IV.vi.107), and so as someone he can afford to recognise ('I know thee well enough, thy name is Gloucester', IV.vi.177), Lear's language acquires more shape and meaning, tentatively envisaging an auditor or interlocutor. There are moments when Lear seems to be fooling with Gloucester—playing fool to sorrow, in Edgar's phrase—as the Fool once fooled with him; there are moving passages of fleeting coherence. But Gloucester and Edgar cannot take in very much of what Lear is feeling; they cannot 'gather' much of Lear, as one might say, in his disintegrated state. Their cries of dismay ('O thou side-piercing sight!', 'Alack, alack the day!', IV.vi.85, 181) reach little further than the 'gesture of helpless compassion' performed by Beckett's Auditor.

It will take the more truly attentive presence of Cordelia, in the following scene, for Lear to begin to put together some more coherent sense of himself. Her great speech of pity—

> Was this a face
> To be oppos'd against the warring winds?
> To stand against the deep dread-bolted thunder?
> In the most terrible and nimble stroke
> Of quick cross lightning? to watch—poor perdu!—
> With this thin helm? ... (IV.vii.30–35)

---

77 Winnicott, 'Ego Integration in Child Development', in *The Maturational Processes and the Facilitating Environment: Studies in the Theory of Emotional Development* (London: Karnac, 1990), p.61.

—arrives in the play like water in the desert. Here at last is a place, a site of consciousness, where the immense pain of the play is being *felt*—not registered in shock and horror, but taken in as the source of grief. Her ability to imagine and support Lear's distress, without any trace of judgment or opposition, is a form, at last, of that 'kind nursery' which he looked for at the beginning. Its good effect is seconded by his discovery (which is also the play's discovery) that she is *still there for him*, that his rage has not, after all, had the fearful power to destroy her or drive her away or fill her with reproach—and therefore, crucially, that the separateness of the world can be benign as well as hostile. If Cordelia survives his hatred, then all things are possible.

The scene is one of great delicacy as well as great emotion. The delicacy lies in the sensitivity with which, little by little, the reality of the situation is admitted into Lear's consciousness. Waking from his long sleep, he sees the being whom he addresses as 'a soul in bliss', 'a spirit' (IV.vii.45, 48). No-one corrects him; 'let him alone awhile', says the wise doctor (IV.vii.50); and gradually, hesitantly, like blurry vision slowly coming into some degree of focus, he recognises the spirit as a lady, and the lady as 'my child Cordelia', whose tears, he carefully ascertains, have sensory existence—they are wet (IV.vii.68–70). The scalding tears of his self-imagination as one of the damned are replaced by, or perhaps merge with, the actual tears of his daughter. Cordelia and Kent hang upon his words with intense attention, but say little, pressing nothing upon him, rather allowing him to take in just so much of their presence and his situation as he can bear. Then the doctor intervenes:

> Be comforted, good madam, the great rage,
> You see, is kill'd in him, and yet it is danger
> To make him even o'er the time he has lost.
> Desire him to go in, trouble him no more
> Till further settling. (IV.vii.77–81)

There is danger in admitting too much external reality too soon or in the wrong way; hence the extreme delicacy involved in Lear's transition from madness to something closer to sanity. 'Pray you now forget, and forgive' both begins to acknowledge the harm he has done and simultaneously fends off such knowledge, while admitting a hope that there may be, after all, no malevolence here, no retribution. 'I am old and foolish': a truth which was unbearable from Regan's mouth, he can now—in the presence of Cordelia—bear to begin to discover for himself (IV.vii.83).

It is an infinitely delicate and, in the doctor's word, dangerous matter, this rapprochement between madness and sanity, this adjusting of the passions of the mind to the contours of the world. The danger is negotiated, though not dispelled, by Cordelia's 'holding' of Lear's grief, by her attunement to his need. But now a large question presents itself: is it Cordelia who ministers to Lear in this scene, or it is the play? And in either case, is the support too much? The Cordelia who returns to Lear is a different figure from the independent-minded woman of the opening scene; she is the devoted daughter of his imaginative need, the daughter who loves her father all, and who has 'no cause' for anger at his treatment of her. When Lear misidentifies her as 'a spirit', this catches her near-symbolic quality, as if she were indeed a projection of his deepest need. Her whole identity may now seem to be comprehended in her being-there-for-him, and if we persist in regarding her as a separate person, we may worry at how far such devotion now defines her. The total concern and loving attention she offers Lear makes her the perfectly nurturing carer which an infant needs and desires, but which no adult should expect from any relationship. Janet Adelman agonises with great precision about how to reconcile the moral beauty of the later Cordelia scenes with the challenge her subjection presents to any intelligently feminist awareness:

> Insofar as the Cordelia of 1.1 is silenced, insofar as we feel the Cordelia who returns more an as iconic presence answering Lear's terrible need than as a separate character with her own needs, Shakespeare is complicit in Lear's fantasy, rewarding him for his suffering by remaking for him the Cordelia he had wanted all along; Shakespeare too requires the sacrifice of her autonomy. This is a very painful recognition for a feminist critic, for any reader who reads as a daughter. [...] [And yet] how can we experience this play and not want Cordelia to return to Lear? And yet how can we want what Lear—what Shakespeare—does to her? It is easy enough simply to dissociate ourselves from Lear's need, to gender it male and thus escape its traces in ourselves; it is easy enough thus to mobilize anger against both the authors—literal and literary—that require Cordelia's sacrifice. And yet, if we allow the anger we mobilize to cut us off from the heart of longing embedded in Lear's suffering, do we not replicate Lear's own attempt to mobilize anger against vulnerability—this time our own? For the fantasies that determine the

shape of Cordelia's return are, I think, only in part gendered; in part they spring from the ground of an infantile experience prior to gender.[78]

Such questions go to the root, I think, even if we need not feel the scene to be entirely one of wish-fulfilment, whether for us or perhaps even for Lear. Its joy is very close to grief. Something is shifting in Lear, some of his torment is passing from him, but his return from madness feels still tentative and precarious, still acutely apprehensive of pain. As the doctor says, it is much too early to speak of healing. Will Lear *ever* be able to 'even o'er the time he has lost', or does his simplicity of spirit depend upon a simple-mindedness which speaks of damage as well as grace? We hold our breath. An external world of harsh realities—most obviously figured by the imminent war, but containing much else that will be painful to remember—is suspended, rendered insignificant for now by Cordelia's presence, but it has not gone away.

The *Bacchae* and the death of Cordelia: grief, witness, and the theatre

These great tensions around the return of Cordelia and the play's 'complicity' or otherwise in Lear's need are most fully worked through at the end of the play, in Cordelia's death. But before attempting to speak about that—and to give myself a way of doing so—I would like to make an excursion to one more great tragedy of madness: the *Bacchae* of Euripides. In particular, I want to call up its comparably shattering final scene, in which another parent holds the dead body of their child, and with immense difficulty comes to see what it is that they hold in their hands.

The action of the *Bacchae* can be briefly told. Dionysus, a young, new god, is establishing his worship in Greece. But the people of Thebes, where Zeus sired him on the princess Semele, are resistant; Semele's sisters have denied the truth of the story of his divine origin. As punishment, or perhaps as a kind of forced conversion, the god has possessed all the women of Thebes with a divine frenzy; they have left the civilised space of the city and lead a life together on the mountains that is without inhibition, outside civilised norms. Now Dionysus comes to the city

---

78 Janet Adelman, *Suffocating Mothers: Fantasies of Maternal Origin in Shakespeare's Plays* (New York: Routledge, 1992), p.125.

in person, in human form, as a foreigner who preaches the new cult. The young king, Pentheus (who is unknowingly his cousin) regards his influence as an intolerable threat to good order. He attempts to imprison the stranger and proposes to subdue the women on the mountain by force. But instead, the stranger-god possesses him with a great desire to spy on the women and watch their practices. Pentheus is induced to disguise himself, bizarrely, as a woman; he watches them from the trees, but Dionysus exposes him to them in his hiding-place as their common enemy. They joyously tear him apart, gifted with superhuman power. Chief among the women is Pentheus's mother, Agave; she returns to the city in triumph with what she believes to be the head of the lion that she has killed, but as her divine frenzy gradually fades, she recognises this as the head of her son.[79]

There could hardly be a more striking example of the challenge, and the danger, of welcoming the stranger. If there was ever a moment when Dionysus could have been admitted without overturning the norms of the city, that moment is in the past; as things stand, what he now requires is submission to his influence, with no assurance of where that influence will lead. In one sense, of course, he *must* be admitted; he is a god of power, the energies that he embodies are real. The tragic theatre of Athens takes place in the theatre of Dionysus, part of the festival in

---

79   It will be seen that the action can be read as telling a story of crime and punishment. Agave and Pentheus both denied Dionysus, and they are duly made to suffer; the destruction of Pentheus is made the instrument of Dionysus's terrible retribution upon Agave. As is the way with great tragedy, this story accounts for everything and nothing. Yes, the energies of tragedy come from somewhere larger and deeper than everyday rationality can comprehend, and to insist that such rationality is all-sufficient is an error that exposes one to disaster. But the punishment meted out is so disproportionate to the offence that it is impossible to feel, as part of our experience of the play, that justice in any sense is being done. (That Agave's original offence took place before the play began, and in dramatic terms is notional only, is relevant here.) Cadmus acknowledges their fault, but protests to Dionysus that 'your reprisals are too severe'. 'I am a god, and you insulted me', answers Dionysus, to which Cadmus responds that 'gods should not resemble men in their anger'. Euripides, *The Bacchae*, trans. by Geoffrey S. Kirk (Englewood Cliffs, NJ: Prentice-Hall, 1970), p.136. Greek gods often do, but Cadmus' insistence that human sympathies cannot be aligned with the god's-eye narrative of crime and punishment is overwhelmingly supported by the dramatic movement of the ending. The perception of justice done, or retribution exacted, or a life-lesson taught, feels like a minor matter by comparison with the real centre of our interest: Pentheus' doomed appeal to his mother, and his mother's terrible coming to mourn her son, which fills the ending sequence of the play.

his honour. But to bear true witness to Dionysus is difficult, for he blurs and dissolves distinctions, as a force impossible to categorise: foreigner yet native by birth, androgynous in manner, appearing both as god and as human, irresistibly enticing yet coldly punishing, alien and intimate, a 'terrible' god, 'but to men most gentle', as the chorus sing.[80] To seek to *apprehend* the energies of Dionysus, from some external point of vantage, would seem impossible. He easily evades imprisonment, overthrowing the buildings that seemed to contain him; when Pentheus's spies try to seize Agave, the women on the mountain—peaceful hitherto—become violent, in an awesome display of the power with which the god has inspired them. Trying to apprehend the energies of Dionysus from without transforms them from what they are in themselves into something that can only be experienced as destructive.

Hence the nature of the trap that Dionysus sets for Pentheus. The moment when the stranger-god asks Pentheus if he would like to *see* the women on the mountain is the moment Pentheus falls under his spell:

> DIONYSUS: Would you like to see them sitting close together, up in the hills?
>
> PENTHEUS: Very much indeed—I would give an untold weight of gold to do so!
>
> DIONYSUS: What, have you fallen into so great a passion for this?
>
> PENTHEUS: I should be pained to see them the worse for drink.
>
> DIONYSUS: Nevertheless you would enjoy seeing what causes you distress?
>
> PENTHEUS: Yes, you are right; but in silence, lying low under the firs.[81]

Resistance melts away; from this moment Pentheus is Dionysus' puppet, walking obediently into his trap. We can say that the god has taken his wits away, possessed him with madness; or, in terms that amount to the same thing, that he is flooded by the desire that civilisation has suppressed in him hitherto. Not that Pentheus fully acknowledges his desire; voyeur-like, he wishes to observe without participating, to witness from a place of safety. Euripides is surely glancing here at the audience of tragedy. 'You would enjoy seeing what causes you distress?' He invites us to reflect on the parallel between our situation and that of

---

80   Euripides, *The Bacchae*, p.94.
81   Ibid., p.89.

Pentheus, and on whether our position as witnesses to the action is as safely separate as it might seem.[82]

The special state of mind into which Dionysus has thrown Pentheus, in which he desires to approach a condition in which distinctions melt away, is expressed as a fantasy of maternal protection and support.

>   D<small>IONYSUS</small>: Follow, and I shall go as your escort and protector,
>   though another shall bring you back ...
>   P<small>ENTHEUS</small>:   Yes, my mother!
>   D<small>IONYSUS</small>: ... as a sight for all.
>   P<small>ENTHEUS</small>:   It is for this that I come.
>   D<small>IONYSUS</small>: You will be carried here ...
>   P<small>ENTHEUS</small>:   That is pampering me ...
>   D<small>IONYSUS</small>: ... in your mother's arms.
>   P<small>ENTHEUS</small>:   ... and you will make me really spoiled!
>   D<small>IONYSUS</small>: Yes, spoiled—in a special way.[83]

Dionysus speaks with chilling double meaning. But what moves Pentheus is the idea of being held and supported by his mother: like Lear's 'kind nursery', a blissful fantasy of regression to the ideal state of a young child. The god of tragedy has offered him what the writer 'A' in Kierkegaard's *Either/Or* sees as the essence of the tragic: when the individual renounces his claim to autonomy and acknowledges that he 'is still a child of God, of his age, of his nation, of his family, of his friends [...] he has the tragic', and thus understood, 'the tragic is infinitely gentle [...] it is a motherly love that lulls the troubled one'.[84]

---

[82] I am reminded of the moment in Tom Stoppard's *Rosencrantz and Guildenstern Are Dead* (London: Faber & Faber, 1968), when the Player asks Rosencrantz and Guildenstern if they would like to 'watch' a performance of the Rape of the Sabine Women.

> P<small>LAYER</small>: It costs little to watch, and little more if you happen to get caught up in the action, if that's your taste and times being what they are.
> R<small>OSENCRANTZ</small>: What are they?
> P<small>LAYER</small>: Indifferent.
> R<small>OSENCRANTZ</small>: Bad?
> P<small>LAYER</small>: Wicked.

Formally positioned as observers, like Pentheus they too will find themselves caught up in the action.

[83] Euripides, *The Bacchae*, p.104. (Points of ellipsis as in the English text.)

[84] Søren Kierkegaard, *Either/Or*, ed. and trans. by Howard V. Hong and Edna H. Hong (Princeton, NJ: Princeton University Press, 1987), Part I, p.145.

In the event, having opened himself to this blissful desire, maternal recognition and support is exactly what Pentheus is denied.

> First his mother started the slaughter as priestess
> and falls upon him; he hurled away the snood
> from his hair, for the wretched Agave to recognize
> and not kill him—and says, touching
> her cheek, "Look, it is I, mother, your child
> Pentheus, whom you bore in the house of Echion!
> Take pity on me, mother, and do not by reason of my
> errors murder your own child!"
> But she, discharging foam from her mouth and rolling
> her eyes all round, her mind not as it should be,
> was possessed by the Bacchic god; and her son did not persuade her.
> Grasping his left arm below the elbow
> and setting her foot against the unhappy man's ribs,
> she tore his shoulder out, not by her normal strength,
> but the god gave a special ease to her hands.[85]

Winnicott speaks of the failure of maternal support in the early months of life as inducing an unspeakable terror and anguish; he describes it as like finding oneself in a den of wild beasts. The mother who does not provide such support—who does not truly recognise the being of the child—may become, for the child, a figure of malignant power. And so Agave proves to be. The anticipation of a blissful cradling, of a 'kind nursery', encouraged and supported by the duplicitous god, turns in an instant to its terrible opposite, a tearing and rending at the hands of the mother who does not respond to her child's call. That Agave does this is part of what we may call the play's complicity with or realisation of the life of the psyche, its participation in energies beyond the patrol of sanity. Yet the passage also marks a crucial shift in the audience's location of delusion and reality. For much of the play, the energies of Dionysus are presented as overwhelmingly real: the women on the mountain seem to be introduced to a deeper mode of existence, and Pentheus' opposition seems puny and delusional. He believed he was binding the stranger, but Dionysus assures us he was deluded, and Pentheus' palace is then destroyed by fire and earthquake: the power of the drama is aligned with the power of Dionysus. But when, in the

---

85   Euripides, *The Bacchae*, pp.116–118.

messenger speech, Pentheus confronts his mother, the location of reality shifts: it is his terror that we feel, not her ecstasy: the delusion is now all with his maddened mother, visibly and disturbingly deranged, 'her mind not as it should be'.

This structural movement that the drama induces in us is duplicated in the movement that Agave must now make, as over some thirty lines her father gradually dispels her ecstasy and, as we must feel, restores her to sanity:

> CADMUS: First turn your gaze on this sky above.
>
> AGAVE: There: why did you suggest I look at it?
>
> CADMUS: Is it the same, or does it seem to you to be brighter?
>
> AGAVE: It is brighter than before and shines with a holier light.
>
> CADMUS: And is this passionate excitement still in your heart?
>
> AGAVE: I do not understand this question—and yet I am somehow becoming
> in my full senses, changed from my previous state of mind. [...]
>
> CADMUS: Whose head then, are you holding in your arms?
>
> AGAVE: A lion's—at least, so the women hunters said?
>
> CADMUS: Now consider truly—looking costs little trouble.
>
> AGAVE: Ah, what do I see? What is this I am carrying in my hands?
>
> CADMUS: Look hard at it and understand more clearly.
>
> AGAVE: What I see is grief, deep grief, and misery for me!
>
> CADMUS: It does not seem to you to resemble a lion?
>
> AGAVE: No, but it is Pentheus' head I am holding, unhappy woman![86]

It is a dreadful transition that Agave makes, and that we make with her. Cadmus acknowledges this even as he facilitates it:

> Alas! if you all realize what you have done
> you will grieve with a dreadful grief; but if to the end
> you persist in your present condition,
> though far from fortunate, you will think you are free from misfortune.[87]

---

86   Ibid., pp.127–128.
87   Ibid., p.126.

'You all' in the English registers that the Greek verbs are plural: 'you and the other women', primarily, but we may feel ourselves included, more participants in than spectators of the tragedy, engulfed by the enormous pathos of the scene, its 'dreadful grief'. Our relation to theatre is deeply implicated in this: when Cadmus asks Agave what head she holds in her hands, he uses the word *prosopon*, which more properly means face or mask, as in the mask worn by an actor in the theatre. The question of what it is that Agave holds is also a question about the potency of theatre. When she recognises the head as her son's, she uses a different word, *kara*, that can only mean head. The inherent doubleness of theatre, with its power to experience illusions or representations as realities even while knowing them for what they are, has hardened into a world of fixed and non-negotiable realities. The terrible transition that Agave makes, from ecstatic excitement to the dreadful sobriety of seeing what she holds in her hands, enacts in compressed form the transition that we are making as audience, from entering into the energies of Dionysus to contemplating their residue and aftermath. Agave is no longer filled with divine energy, but emerges into the sober, disillusioned seeing that belongs, now, indisputably to reality. Within the action of the play, these two states are incompatible: and we might say that tragedy is what results from their incompatibility. Alternatively, though, we might say that the total experience of the play holds the two states together, discounting neither. Theatre, we might then remember, is not committed to the hard binary between reality and illusion, but lives in the space or overlap between, having always the potential to offer itself as both a representation of the world and the expression of a vision.

What this leads to is the 'deep grief' which Agave sees awaiting her as her vision readjusts. Thinking back to Macbeth's inability to mourn his wife, as well as to Lear's ferocious resistance to weeping, it matters that the transition out of madness here is marked by a sustained lament. The manuscript is imperfect, but we know that the rest of Pentheus's body is brought on stage, that Agave asks whether the limbs have been fitted together in a way that is decent and proper and even beautiful (*kalōs*), and that she mourns over each body part in turn, no doubt joining the head to the rest. Most of the words are lost, but the effect must have been of a sustained openness to grief, in which what might have been unbearable is nevertheless borne. We are given something like a funeral mourning rite, a scarred and imperfect version of the normal ceremony, but for that reason (being rooted in the experience of disaster) immensely moving and, importantly, *achieved*. The body that had been torn apart is pieced back together, and the destructive mother gives way to one who mourns. The play's mourning is nominally for Pentheus, but it is more profoundly for Agave, and still more profoundly, I think, for the necessary loss of ecstasy, the necessary transition out of madness. Such mourning arises out of intimate engagement with *both* states of being, madness and sanity, the realm of psychic fantasy and the vulnerability and precarity of life in the world; it bears witness to both, holding connection between them even as it grieves over their incompatibility.

To return now to *King Lear*. In watching the *Bacchae*, we come to see clearly only after we have entered into the energies of Dionysus; Agave's transition out of madness is also ours. In the central acts of *King Lear*, comparably, we enter into Lear's madness. The storm scenes sympathise with Lear, not primarily by presenting him as an object of pathos, but by conforming the play-world—in large part—to his fears and projections. The storm in his mind is answered by a terrible storm out on the heath. He sees in Goneril and Regan monsters of ingratitude and cruelty, and, as if in response, monsters are what they then become. The narcissism by which he generalises his own situation to the condition of all mankind, is endorsed by the presence of the Gloucester sub-plot, unique among Shakespeare's tragedies. As Lear goes mad, so the play for a while goes mad, unhinged from plot or structure, in the extraordinary sequence of scenes that run from the storm to the meeting with blind Gloucester, in which the play-world is given over to a paranoid-schizoid mindscape: the mad King with his Fool, the blind man with the Bedlam beggar, hunted down by the persecuting children, mania and disintegration everywhere.

At the same time, the play-world offers continual points of resistance to this pressure of inner fantasy. If the storm in Lear's mind engulfs the heath and the cosmos, so that we feel it as a dreadful, elemental force—'Man's nature cannot carry / Th' affliction nor the fear'(III.ii.48–49)—we are also allowed to see the storm, some of the time, as a weather event that is outside Lear, bigger than him and indifferent to his sense of grievance, while he 'Strives in his little world of man to outscorn [or out-storm] / The to-and-fro conflicting wind and rain' (III.i.10–11). Wind and rain make you wet and cold, the Fool reminds us, and the Fool's dialogue continually seeks to connect Lear's tumultuous feelings with the bare facts of the situation. What happens to Gloucester is *unlike* what happens to Lear in important respects, and crucially is much less involved with an inner life: it was not Gloucester's needs that set the plot against him in motion, and the damage done to him is bodily rather than of the mind. As he himself wonderingly remarks, he remains sane and sentient throughout everything. It is possible—just—to see the Wicked Children not as 'monsters of the deep' (IV.ii.50), but as responding credibly enough to the social and familial pressures of an overbearing and unstable father, of illegitimacy, and of a political power vacuum. By the end, the energies which cast them as enlarged shadows to be feared and hated have been largely withdrawn, and they dwindle into caricatures of stage-villainy.

The play therefore does two things. By supplying Lear with a world that fits with his rage and fear and need—a world made to his mind— it bears witness to his inner life. In 'going mad' along with Lear, the play makes us *participate* in his experience. If this means distorting the world, or representing it highly selectively, it nevertheless honours Lear's cry against the cruel objectivity of Goneril and Regan: 'O, reason not the need' (II.iv.264). That Lear's children become either monsters of ingratitude or paragons of loving-kindness answers to some part of that need. But at the same time, or at least from moment to moment, the play offers points of resistance that acknowledge the separateness of an external world. And this too is the qualification of the good witness, who must stand outside passion in order to speak of it, to represent it, to afford it its place within the world.

In the *Bacchae*, the counterpointing of these two modes of being is experienced principally as a transition: we pass, like Agave, from ecstasy to sanity. The second state emerges from the first, without cancelling or superseding it, being so deeply marked by its consequences: Agave holds her son's head in her hands. Still, the grieving unlocked by this feels like an arrival, a terminus, a stable place after the turbulent energies of Dionysus: what Agave sees has no element of projection or illusion. *King Lear*, by contrast, tends to oscillation rather than transition, moments of apparent grounding in which the ground proves illusory or shifting or unstable. Poor Tom strikes Lear as 'the thing itself' (III.iv.106), but his nakedness is a disguise, and his arrival only intensifies Lear's mad fantasies. Gloucester composes himself to suicide, making his peace with the reality of his situation, but Dover Cliff is not what it seems, and Edgar works to frame his falling as a symbolic moment in a contest between devils and gods. He thrusts Gloucester back into superstitious fantasy, casting him as a figure in a romance, in the paradoxical hope of thereby reconciling him to reality. The marked theatricality of this scene, which also attends his performance of Poor Tom, plays its part in telling us that the play has not yet become entirely sober. Our experience of the last three acts of *Lear* mirrors Lear's own experience in the first two: a continual oscillation, between apprehensions of the way the world barely and nakedly is, and a convulsive reaction that mobilises all the powers of fantasy and outrage against such knowledge (knowledge which the play sometimes calls 'patience'), insisting on the counter-claims of the psyche as the more vital realities. For Lear, as we have seen, madness means, above all, *not weeping*. And for the audience too, I think, much of the play is tremendous, gripping, heart-stopping, in a way that makes pathos—grieving—peculiarly elusive or ever-deferred.

The return of Cordelia is the heart of the matter. Her presence brings Lear out of madness, calms the 'great rage' in him; she re-enters the play as the stabilising reality that the world desperately needs. And she weeps, both in report, hearing of her father's sufferings, and on stage with him. Her compassion releases a pathos that is grounded in attention to the way things are. And yet, as we have seen, she also returns like a figure from romance, the infinitely loving daughter of his need, whose presence is restoration and blessing. The emotion of the reunion scene vibrates, I think, between this sense of blessing and a more painful perception that the damage to Lear may go beyond healing, that although he can recognise Cordelia and recognise her love, there are further realities which may be (as yet? forever?) too painful for him to recognise. Cordelia weeps over Lear in this scene, and in her weeping the proportion of joy at his recovery to grief at his still-damaged condition is hard to know; a good deal depends on how the scene is played. Their next scene together exhibits the same extraordinary tension. In Lear's great speech to Cordelia, 'Come, let's away to prison', he revels in the fantasy of their living out their days together in prison, 'we two alone', praying and singing and telling old tales, endlessly re-living her forgiveness of him, sublimely distanced from and untouchable by what goes on, meaninglessly, out in the world (V.iii.8–19). We cannot hear the aching power and beauty of this poetry without believing in it: this condition of mind is a reality, and a reality infinitely desirable; to feel oneself so well supported by another is to be immune to all harm. But Shakespeare requires us also to notice that the speech is a fantasy, generated in denial of another kind of reality:

> CORDELIA: Shall we not see these daughters and these sisters?
> LEAR: No, no, no, no! Come let's away to prison ... (V.iii.7–8)

There are things that Lear does not wish to see. And there is no place for Cordelia's acid contempt in Lear's idyll of reciprocity. By the end of his speech Cordelia is, once more, weeping, unconsoled by Lear's vision, doing what Lear still cannot afford to do, grieving over the irreparable reality of damage and loss. Whereas Lear, yet again, takes his stand against weeping:

> Wipe thine eyes;
> The good-years shall devour them, flesh and fell,
> Ere they shall make us weep! (V.iii.23–25)

In the end, with Cordelia's death, it is as if Shakespeare at last puts a decisive end to this tension, this oscillation, with a violence that testifies to the strength of the impulses that must be overcome. In the old play of *Leir*, all ended well, and there are enough generic marks of romance in Shakespeare's play—the loss and restoration of identity, the reunions between parent and child, the movement of exile and return, the ascendancy of the sympathetic characters—for the first audience to expect that this play, too, would answer to their wishes. But shockingly, it is not to be: and now Lear, like Agave, must see what it is that he carries in his arms.

> She's gone for ever.
> I know when one is dead, and when one lives;
> She's dead as earth. (V.iii.260–62)

But he cannot sustain this for long; for Lear at least, the oscillation continues:

> This feather stirs, she lives! If it be so,
> It is a chance which does redeem all sorrows
> That ever I have felt. (V.iii.266–68)

which in turn gives way to:

> I might have sav'd her, now she's gone for ever! (V.iii.271)

But then, two lines later, he hears her speak, though only to him:

> What is't thou say'st? Her voice was ever soft,
> Gentle and low, an excellent thing in woman. (V.iii.273–74)

After this, his attention slides away for a while to other matters, as simply unable to take in what is before him. As Albany says:

> He knows not what he sees, and vain it is
> That we present to him.[88]

What Agave achieves, Lear can do only intermittently. The sight is too painful; Lear's sanity cannot hold. Yet this turns once more, with a last, brutal insistence on the reality, an attempt at grasping, irrevocably, the irrevocable thing itself:

> Thou'lt come no more,
> Never, never, never, never, never. (V.iii.308–09)

And this, in the Quarto, is final, the overwhelming knowledge in which Lear dies. But in the Folio text, Lear's mind turns yet again, rising up against such knowledge, and he dies very differently:

> Do you see this? Look on her! Look her lips,
> Look there, look there! (V.iii.311–12)

In the Folio text, there is for Lear no achieved transition from madness to sanity, and no ultimate admission of grieving. What he sees at the end, we must suppose, are the signs of life in Cordelia that would redeem all sorrows. For his audience, both on stage and in the theatre, this changes the nature of the pathos, but makes it no less excruciating. We know that Cordelia is dead, and that Lear cannot bear to know this for more

---

88 The Quarto reading, which gives us something more than the Folio's 'He knows not what he says' (V.iii.294).

than a few seconds at a time: it is, in truth, all but unbearable. And yet Lear demands, urgently, that witness be borne: 'Do you see this?', 'Look there, look there!' In the theatre, this has an extraordinary effect: Lear demands that we look closely at the body of the actor playing dead and asks whether we can see signs of life. Just as earlier, when he held a feather to Cordelia's lips, in Shakespeare's open-air theatre the feather may well have moved, so now, if we look hard enough at Cordelia, we may see a body that is still breathing. We know that she is dead, dead as earth, but the presence of the theatre opens up the boundary between reality and make-believe, life in the world and the life of the mind, in a way that baulks at giving automatic precedence to the former. As Winnicott said, we are poor indeed if we are only sane. There is no consolation in this, certainly no positive delusion, but it allows us to participate in Lear's experience to the very end: what is oscillation in him is co-presence in us, and we witness on our pulses that division in the nature of reality, that tension between mind and world, which without such witness could only appear as madness. This is what it is to speak (or at least to know) what we feel, not what we ought to say, if 'ought' means submission to the world's decree as to what is the case. This is what it is to find our own condition truly spoken about.

Bibliography

Adelman, Janet, *Suffocating Mothers: Fantasies of Maternal Origin in Shakespeare's Plays* (New York: Routledge, 1992).

Aeschylus, *Oresteia*, trans. by Richmond Lattimore (Chicago: University of Chicago Press, 1953).

—, *The Eumenides*, trans. by Hugh Lloyd-Jones (New Jersey: Prentice-Hall, 1970).

—, *The Suppliants*, trans. by Gail Holst-Warhaft, in *Aeschylus, 2*, ed. by David R. Slavitt and Palmer Bovie, Penn Greek Drama Series (Philadelphia: University of Pennsylvania Press, 1999), pp.103–150.

Ahmed, Sara, *Strange Encounters: Embodied Others in Post-Coloniality* (London: Routledge, 2000).

Ainsworth, Mary S. and John Bowlby, 'An Ethological Approach to Personality Development', *American Psychologist*, 46 (1991), 333–341.

Albee, Edward, *A Delicate Balance* (Harmondsworth: Penguin, 1969).

Arendt, Hannah and Günther Stern, 'Rilke's Duino Elegies', in Hannah Arendt, *Reflections on Literature and Culture*, ed. by Susannah Young-Ah Gottlieb (Redwood City, CA: Stanford University Press, 2007), https://doi.org/10.1515/9781503620148-003

Aristotle, *Poetics*, trans. by M. E. Hubbard, in *Ancient Literary Criticism: The Principal Texts in New Translations*, ed. by D. A. Russell and M. Winterbottom (Oxford: Oxford University Press, 1972), pp.85–132.

Augustine, *Confessions*, trans. by R. S. Pine-Coffin (London: Penguin, 2003).

Baudelaire, Charles, *Baudelaire: Selected Writings on Art and Artists*, trans. by P. E. Charvet (Cambridge: Cambridge University Press, 1981).

Beckett, Samuel, *The Complete Dramatic Works* (London: Faber & Faber, 1990).

Bettelheim, Bruno, *Surviving and Other Essays* (London: Thames and Hudson, 1979).

Blanchot, Maurice, *The Infinite Conversation* (Minneapolis: University of Minnesota Press, 1993).

Boyle, A. J., *Tragic Seneca: An Essay in the Theatrical Tradition* (London: Routledge, 1997).

Cavell, Stanley, *Disowning Knowledge in Seven Plays of Shakespeare* (Cambridge: Cambridge University Press, 2003), https://doi.org/10.1017/cbo9781139165129

Coetzee, J. M., 'Confession and Double Thoughts: Tolstoy, Rousseau, Dostoevsky', in *Doubling the Point: Essays and Interviews* (Cambridge, MA: Harvard University Press, 1992), pp.251–293.

Constantine, David, 'Kafka's writing and our reading', in *The Cambridge Companion to Kafka*, ed. by Julian Preece (Cambridge: Cambridge University Press, 2002), pp.9–24, https://doi.org/10.1017/ccol0521663148.002

Crimp, Martin, *Attempts on Her Life* (London: Faber & Faber, 2007).

Critchley, Simon, 'I Want to Die, I Hate My Life—Phaedra's Malaise', in *Rethinking Tragedy*, ed. by Rita Felski (Baltimore: Johns Hopkins University Press, 2008), pp.170–198, https://doi.org/10.56021/9780801887390

Cusk, Rachel, *Aftermath: On Marriage and Separation* (London: Faber & Faber, 2012).

Derrida, Jacques, *Memoirs of the Blind: The Self-Portrait and Other Ruins*, trans. by Pascale-Anne Brault and Michael Naas (Chicago and London: University of Chicago Press, 1993).

Dimock, Wai Chee, 'After Troy: Homer, Euripides, Total War', in *Rethinking Tragedy*, ed. by Rita Felski (Baltimore: Johns Hopkins University Press, 2008), pp.66–81, https://doi.org/10.56021/9780801887390

Dostoevsky, Fyodor, *Brothers Karamazov*, trans. by David Magarshack (Harmondsworth: Penguin, 1958).

Douglas, Mary, *Purity and Danger: An Analysis of Concept of Pollution and Taboo* (London: Routledge, 2002), https://doi.org/10.4324/9780203361832

Eliot, T. S., *The Family Reunion*, ed. by Nevil Coghill (London: Faber & Faber, 1969).

Euripides, *The Bacchae*, trans. by Geoffrey S. Kirk (Englewood Cliffs, NJ: Prentice-Hall, 1970).

—, *Hippolytus*, trans. by Rachel Kitzinger, in *The Greek Plays: Sixteen Plays by Aeschylus, Sophocles, and Euripides*, ed. by Mary Lefkowitz and James Romm (New York: Modern Library, 2016), pp.533–583.

Farber, Yaël, *Molora: Based on the Oresteia by Aeschylus* (London: Oberon Books, 2008).

—, *Theatre as Witness: Three Testimonial Plays from South Africa* (London: Oberon Books, 2008).

—, 'MoLoRa: The Independent Interview with Yael Farber', *Indy Week*, 17 March 2010, https://indyweek.com/culture/archives-culture/molora-independent-interview-yael-farber/

Felman, Shoshana and Dori Laub, *Testimony: Crises of Witnessing in Literature, Psychoanalysis and History* (New York and London: Routledge, 1992).

Fonagy, Peter and Elizabeth Allison, 'The Role of Mentalizing and Epistemic Trust in the Therapeutic Relationship', *Psychotherapy*, 51 (2014), 372–380, https://doi.org/10.1037/a0036505

—, Gyorgy Gergely, and Elliot L. Jurist, *Affect Regulation, Mentalization and the Development of the Self* (London: Routledge, 2002), https://doi.org/10.4324/9780429471643

Fosha, Diana, 'Dyadic regulation and experiential work with emotion and relatedness in trauma and disordered attachment', in *Healing Trauma: Attachment, Trauma, the Brain and the Mind*, ed. by M. F. Solomon and D. J. Siegel (New York: Norton, 2003), pp.221–281.

—, *The Transforming Power of Affect: A Model for Accelerated Change* (New York: Basic Books, 2000).

Freud, Sigmund, 'Mourning and Melancholia', in *The Penguin Freud Reader*, ed. by Adam Phillips (London: Penguin, 2006), pp.310–326.

—, 'On the Introduction of Narcissism', in *The Penguin Freud Reader*, ed. by Adam Phillips (London: Penguin, 2006), pp.358–390.

—, 'The "Uncanny"', trans. by James Strachey, in *Art and Literature*, ed. by Albert Dickson, Penguin Freud Library, vol. XIV (London: Penguin, 1985), pp.335–376.

Giudice, Gaspare, *Pirandello: A Biography*, trans. by Alastair Hamilton (London: Oxford University Press, 1975).

Goethe, Johann Wolfgang von, *Iphigenia in Tauris*, trans. by John Prudhoe (Manchester: Manchester University Press, 1966).

Goldhill, Simon, *Aeschylus: The Oresteia*, 2nd edn (Cambridge: Cambridge University Press, 2004), https://doi.org/10.1017/cbo9780511800269

—, *Language, Sexuality, Narrative: The Oresteia* (Cambridge: Cambridge University Press, 1984).

—, 'The Great Dionysia and civic ideology', in *Nothing to Do with Dionysos?: Athenian Drama in Its Social Context*, ed. by John J. Winkler and Froma Zeitlin (Princeton, NJ: Princeton University Press, 1998).

Goldmann, Lucien, *The Hidden God: A Study of Tragic Vision in the 'Pensées' of Pascal and the Tragedies of Racine* (London: Verso, 2016).

Hammond, Paul, *The Strangeness of Tragedy* (Oxford: Oxford University Press, 2009), https://doi.org/10.1093/acprof:oso/9780199572601.001.0001

Homer, *The Iliad*, 2 vols, trans. by A. T. Murray (London: William Heinemann, 1976).

—, *The Odyssey*, trans. by Richmond Lattimore (New York: HarperPerennial, 1991).

Ibsen, Henrik, *The Master Builder*, in *Plays: One. Ghosts, The Wild Duck, The Master Builder*, trans. by Michael Meyer (London: Eyre Methuen, 1980), pp.217–319.

—, *The Wild Duck*, in *Plays: One. Ghosts, The Wild Duck, The Master Builder*, trans. by Michael Meyer (London: Eyre Methuen, 1980), pp.99–216.

Johnson, Samuel, *Johnson on Shakespeare*, ed. by Arthur Sherbo, vols vii-viii in *The Yale Edition of the Works of Samuel Johnson*, ed. John H. Middendorf, et al. (New Haven and London: Yale University Press, 1958–2018).

Kane, Sarah, *Complete Plays* (London: Methuen, 2001).

Kafka, Franz, *The Trial*, trans. by Willa Muir and Edwin Muir (Harmondsworth: Penguin, 1974).

Kierkegaard, Søren, *Either/Or*, ed. and trans. by Howard V. Hong and Edna H. Hong (Princeton, NJ: Princeton University Press, 1987).

Knowlson, James, *Damned to Fame: The Life of Samuel Beckett* (London: Bloomsbury, 1996).

Kyd, Thomas, *The Spanish Tragedy*, ed. by J. R. Mulryne (London: A & C Black, 1989).

LaCapra, Dominick, *Writing History, Writing Trauma* (Baltimore, MD, and London: Johns Hopkins University Press, 2001).

Lamb, Charles, 'On the Tragedies of Shakespeare, considered with reference to their Fitness for Stage Representation', in *Lamb as Critic*, ed. by Roy Park (London: Routledge and Kegan Paul, 1980), pp.85–101.

Laub, Dori, 'Bearing Witness, or the Vicissitudes of Listening', in *Testimony: Crises of Witnessing in Literature, Psychoanalysis and History* (New York and London: Routledge, 1992).

Levi, Primo, *If This Is a Man / The Truce*, trans. by Stuart Woolf (London: Abacus, 1987).

Luckhurst, Roger, *The Trauma Question* (Abingdon and New York: Routledge, 2008), https://doi.org/10.4324/9780203607305

Maus, Katherine Eisaman, *Inwardness and Theater in the English Renaissance* (Chicago: University of Chicago Press, 1995).

Miller, Arthur, *Death of a Salesman* (London: Penguin, 1961).

Morrison, Toni, *Beloved* (London: Picador, 1988).

—, *Jazz* (London: Chatto & Windus, 1992).

Nussbaum, Martha C., *The Fragility of Goodness: Luck and Ethics in Greek Tragedy and Philosophy*, 2nd edn (Cambridge: Cambridge University Press, 2001), https://doi.org/10.1017/cbo9780511817915

—, *Upheavals of Thought: The Intelligence of Emotions* (Cambridge: Cambridge University Press, 2001), https://doi.org/10.1017/CBO9780511840715

Pirandello, Luigi, *Henry IV*, in *Six Characters in Search of an Author and Other Plays* (London: Penguin, 1995), pp.67–136.

—, *Six Characters in Search of an Author and Other Plays* (London: Penguin, 1995).

Phillips, Adam, *Missing Out: In Praise of the Unlived Life* (London: Penguin, 2013).

Quayson, Ato, *Tragedy and Postcolonial Literature* (Cambridge: Cambridge University Press, 2021), https://doi.org/10.1017/9781108921992

Racine, Jean, *Jean Racine: Five Plays*, trans. by Kenneth Muir (New York: Hill and Wang, 1960).

—, *Théâtre Complet*, 2 vols (Paris: Garnier-Flammarion, 1965).

Raleigh, Walter, *Selected Writings*, ed. by Gerald Hammond (Manchester: Carcanet, 1984).

Ricœur, Paul, *Time and Narrative*, 3 vols, trans. by Kathleen McLaughlin and David Pellauer (Chicago: University of Chicago Press, 1984–1990).

Rilke, Rainer Maria, *The Selected Poetry of Rainer Maria Rilke*, trans. by Stephen Mitchell (London: Picador, 1987).

Rose, Gillian, *Mourning Becomes the Law: Philosophy and Representation* (Cambridge: Cambridge University Press, 1996).

—, *Love's Work: A Reckoning with Life* (New York: New York Review of Books, 2010).

Ryan, Kay, *The Best of It: New and Selected Poems* (New York: Grove Press, 2010).

Saunders, Graham, *Love Me or Kill Me: Sarah Kane and the Theatre of Extremes* (Manchester: Manchester University Press, 2002).

Sidi, Leah, *Sarah Kane's Theatre of Psychic Life: Theatre, Thought and Mental Suffering* (London: Methuen, 2023), https://doi.org/10.5040/9781350283152

Shakespeare, William, *The New Oxford Shakespeare: The Complete Works. Modern Critical Edition*, ed. by Gary Taylor, John Jowett, Terri Bourus, and Gabriel Egan (Oxford: Oxford University Press, 2016).

—, *The Riverside Shakespeare*, 2nd edn, ed. by G. Blakemore Evans, Harry Levin, Anne Barton, Herschel Baker, Frank Kermode, Hallett D. Smith, and Marie Edel (Boston and New York: Houghton Mifflin, 1997).

Seneca, *Medea*, in *Tragedies: I*, trans. by Frank Justus Miller (London: Heinemann, 1968).

—, *Thyestes*, in *Tragedies: II*, trans. by Frank Justus Miller (London: Heinemann, 1968).

Sophocles, *Electra*, trans. by Eric Dugdale (Cambridge: Cambridge University Press, 2008).

—, *Sophocles: Oedipus Tyrannos, Oedipus at Kolonos, Antigone*, trans. by Timberlake Wertenbaker (London: Faber & Faber, 1997).

—, *The Women of Trachis*, in *Sophocles: 2*, trans. by Hugh Lloyd-Jones (Cambridge, MA: Harvard University Press, 1994).

Steiner, George, *Antigones* (Oxford: Clarendon Press, 1986).

Stoppard, Tom, *Rosencrantz and Guildenstern Are Dead* (London: Faber & Faber, 1968).

Tourneur, Cyril (attrib.), *The Revenger's Tragedy*, ed. by Lawrence J. Ross (London: Edward Arnold, 1982).

van der Kolk, Bessel, *The Body Keeps the Score* (London: Penguin, 2014).

Waddell, Margot, *Inside Lives: Psychoanalysis and the Growth of the Personality* (London: Karnac, 2002), https://doi.org/10.1002/bap.35

Weimann, Robert, *Shakespeare and the Popular Tradition in the Theater: Studies in the Social Dimension of Dramatic Form and Function* (Baltimore: Johns Hopkins University Press, 1978).

Williams, Rowan, *The Tragic Imagination* (Oxford: Oxford University Press, 2016).

Winnicott, D. W., 'Communicating and Not Communicating: leading to a study of certain opposites' [1963], in *The Maturational Processes and the Facilitating Environment: Studies in the Theory of Emotional Development* (London: Karnac, 1990), pp.179–192.

—, 'Ego Integration in Child Development' [1962], in *The Maturational Processes and the Facilitating Environment: Studies in the Theory of Emotional Development* (London: Karnac, 1990), pp.56–63.

—, *Home Is Where We Start From: Essays by a Psychoanalyst*, ed. by Clare Winnicott, Ray Shepherd, and Madeleine Davis (London: Penguin, 1990).

—, *Playing and Reality* (London: Penguin, 1974).

—, 'Primary Maternal Preoccupation' [1956], in *Through Paediatrics to Psycho-Analysis* (London: Karnac, 1992), pp.300–305.

—, 'Primitive Emotional Development' [1945], in *Collected Papers: Through Paediatrics to Psycho-Analysis* (London: Tavistock, 1958), pp.145–156.

—, *The Child, the Family, and the Outside World* (London: Penguin, 1964).

Yeats, W. B., 'The Tragic Theatre', in *Essays and Introductions* (London: Macmillan, 1961), pp.238–245.

Zapkin, Philip, 'Ubuntu Theater: Building a Human World in Yaël Farber's *Molora*', *PMLA*, 136 (2021), 386–400, https://doi.org/10.1632/S0030812921000213

Index

Adelman, Janet 164, 210
Aeschylus 17–19, 31, 41, 45–48, 130–131, 137
  Oresteia 9, 18, 47–48, 80, 96–97, 100, 105, 107–109, 111, 114–115, 129–130, 135–137
  Suppliant Women 41
Ahmed, Sara 40
Albee, Edward 17, 42, 44–46
Aristotle 100–101, 117
Augustine 117

Baudelaire, Charles 52
Beckett, Samuel 3, 58, 99, 139–143, 145, 153, 164, 190, 208
  Endgame 99, 143
  Happy Days 143
  Krapp's Last Tape 144
  Not I 139–145, 153
Blanchot, Maurice 41
Bowlby, John 4–5

Cavell, Stanley 10
Coetzee, J. M. 36–37
Coleridge, Samuel Taylor 48
Constantine, David 124
crime and punishment story 9, 13, 93–96, 98, 100–102, 104–106, 109–110, 113–115, 117–118, 126–130, 134, 137–138, 185, 212
Crimp, Martin 70, 72–74
Cusk, Rachel 6

Derrida, Jacques 52–53, 57, 91
Dimock, Wai Chee 31
Dostoevsky, Fyodor 37, 102–103
Douglas, Mary 16

Eliot, T. S. 28
endlessness 34, 112, 114, 117, 125, 185, 191–194, 221–222

Euripides 1, 28, 31, 115–117, 119, 167, 211, 213
  Bacchae 167, 211–212, 215, 218–219
  Hecuba 27, 31, 72, 74, 101
  Hippolytus 1–2, 12–13, 28–29, 36–37, 101, 110, 116–117, 119
  The Trojan Women 31, 101

Farber, Yaël 114–115, 129–131, 133–135, 137
Fonagy, Peter 4–5, 152
Fosha, Diana 5
Freudian, Sigmund 161, 167
Freud, Sigmund 83, 158, 169, 181, 192, 198
Furies 18–19, 47–49, 96–97, 100, 104, 107, 110, 130–132, 136

grieving. *See* mourning

heroic as contested category 14, 51, 59–61, 67, 71, 74–77, 83, 183
Homer 35–36, 75, 114

Ibsen, Henrik 3, 9, 51, 60, 77–78, 80–81, 91, 139, 180–182
  The Master Builder 75, 81, 84, 139, 180, 182
  The Wild Duck 75, 77, 80–81, 83–84

Job 98
Johnson, Samuel 15–16, 38
justice. *See* crime and punishment story

Kafka, Franz 13–14, 114, 120–121, 123–125, 128–129, 132
Kane, Sarah 3, 15, 139–140, 145, 148–150
  4.48 Psychosis 139–140, 145, 147, 150–152
  Blasted 15
Kierkegaard, Søren 214

kingship 35, 55, 185, 199–200, 202
Kyd, Thomas 112

LaCapra, Dominick 10
Lamb, Charles 60, 63
Laub, Dori 7, 9, 73–74, 80
Levi, Primo 8, 160, 165

madness 1, 9, 17–20, 24, 29, 40, 44, 46, 110, 112–113, 120, 139–141, 143, 145, 152–153, 165–170, 175–176, 179–183, 189, 193–194, 197–198, 200, 204, 207, 209–211, 213, 217–220, 222–223
Miller, Arthur 76–77
Morrison, Toni 40–41, 134
mother-child relationship 4, 11, 17–18, 27, 30, 43, 47–48, 57–58, 67, 69, 92, 107, 131–132, 135–136, 139, 152, 157–159, 161–166, 169, 171, 176–178, 180, 182, 187–188, 198–201, 204, 208, 212, 214–216, 218
   Beckett's Auditor 164
   Cleopatra 91–92
   Gertrude 164–166
   in *Bacchae* 214–215, 217
   in *Henry IV* 171, 176
   in Kierkegaard 214
   in *King Lear* 200–201, 209
   in *Molora* 135
   in *Othello* 157–158
   Lady Macbeth 186–187
   Mrs Solness 182
   Phaedra's Nurse 2, 11
mourning 7, 10, 20, 27–28, 32–33, 35, 55–56, 65, 67, 87, 90, 108, 112–113, 140, 160, 162, 164, 182, 191–194, 197, 199, 207, 209–212, 216–222

Nussbaum, Martha 6, 101

object relations theory 5, 158, 167–168
omnipotence of thoughts 83, 181
Ovid 55, 109, 111

parody 64, 72, 74, 110–112, 120, 127, 137
Pirandello, Luigi 3, 53–54, 56–57, 139, 167, 169–170, 172, 177, 179–180
   Henry IV 139, 167, 169–172, 176, 178–180, 182
   Six Characters in Search of an Author 53
playing 1, 6, 16, 80, 113, 123, 129, 131, 164, 167, 169, 172–173, 197, 204, 208, 223

Quayson, Ato 161–162

Racine, Jean 3, 114–117, 119–120
reporting 3, 12, 15, 24–27, 29–30, 49, 53, 57, 66–67, 70, 73, 85–90, 153, 166, 182, 220
Revenger's Tragedy, The 111–112
revenge tragedy 96, 105–106, 110, 112
Ricoeur, Paul 25, 52, 91, 190
Rilke, Rainer Maria 162–163
Rose, Gillian 20, 191–193
Ryan, Kay 52

seeing and being seen 2–6, 8–10, 12, 14–21, 23–24, 26–31, 33–34, 36–37, 39, 48–49, 51–54, 56–61, 63–66, 68–70, 72–77, 81–85, 88, 90–93, 102, 104, 110, 112, 114–116, 118, 120, 124–126, 128–129, 133, 135, 137–144, 148, 151, 153–155, 157–158, 161–162, 164, 166, 169, 171, 179, 182–184, 190, 193, 195, 197, 211, 213–214, 217–219, 223
Seneca 110–111, 116–117, 202
   Medea 6, 110
   Phaedra 1–3, 7, 11–14, 17–18, 29, 101, 110, 116–117, 119
   Thyestes 111, 202
Shakespeare, William 3, 7–8, 10, 14, 17, 19, 21, 24, 26, 38, 51, 54, 56, 58–62, 64, 66–67, 69, 75, 85, 87, 95, 104, 109–113, 141, 152–153, 164–165, 185–186, 193, 198–199, 210, 218, 221, 223
   Antony and Cleopatra 51, 59, 85–92

Coriolanus 17, 29, 51, 57–60, 62, 66–69, 73–75, 148
Hamlet 4, 9–10, 14–15, 17, 23–29, 32, 34, 36, 39–41, 53, 60, 62, 65–66, 69, 74–75, 78, 93–96, 98–100, 102, 112, 123, 139–141, 152, 161, 164–167, 169, 174, 183, 194, 196
Henry V 59
Julius Caesar 57, 185
King Lear 10, 17, 19, 23, 26, 29, 53, 60–62, 95, 106, 139–140, 161, 167, 197–198, 200–211, 214, 217–223
Macbeth 14, 17–19, 61–62, 69, 75, 83, 95–97, 103, 139, 182–197, 217
Measure for Measure 100
Othello 3, 10, 14, 17, 19, 36–40, 61, 69, 95, 100, 103, 105, 107, 128, 139, 152–159, 161, 177, 195, 201
Richard II 7, 35, 57, 188, 199
Titus Andronicus 54, 109–111
Troilus and Cressida 51, 63–66, 68
The Winter's Tale 188
Sophocles 31, 97–98, 107
  Antigone 30, 32–34, 36, 47
  Electra 107–109
  Oedipus at Colonus 48
  Oedipus the King 98
  Women of Trachis 101
Spanish Tragedy, The 112, 193
Stoppard, Tom 10, 214
stories

Desdemona and Othello's story 8, 17, 19, 38–40, 95, 100, 105, 153–159, 161, 177, 195
narrative and time 9, 51–52, 87, 117, 145, 171, 173, 175, 190
telling another's story 4, 6, 15, 17, 23, 25–27, 30, 32, 34, 36, 41, 53, 56, 67–68, 71, 76, 81–83, 86, 91, 93–94, 102, 114–115, 121, 166–167, 183, 191, 197, 205
telling one's own story 6, 8, 23, 29, 35, 37–38, 65, 119, 140–141, 154–155, 160

weeping 28–29, 32–38, 45, 58–60, 69, 87, 132, 154, 207, 209, 217, 220–221
Weimann, Robert 3
welcoming the stranger 16–18, 23, 32, 38–48, 62, 68, 70, 180, 201, 212–213, 215
  A Delicate Balance 42–46
  Bacchae 212
  Eumenides 47–49
  Othello 38–39
  Suppliant Women 40–42
Williams, Rowan 48
Winnicott, D. W. 4, 10, 17, 158–159, 161, 164–165, 167–169, 179, 190, 196, 198–199, 201, 207–208, 215, 223
witnessing. *See* seeing and being seen

Yeats, W. B. 27

About the Team

Alessandra Tosi was the managing editor for this book.

Annie Hine proof-read this manuscript and compiled the index.

Jeevanjot Kaur Nagpal designed the cover. The cover was produced in InDesign using the Fontin font.

Annie typeset the book in InDesign and produced the paperback and hardback editions. The main text font is Tex Gyre Pagella and the heading font is Californian FB. Cameron Craig produced the PDF edition.

The conversion to the HTML edition was performed with epublius, an open-source software which is freely available on our GitHub page at https://github.com/OpenBookPublishers

Jeremy Bowman created the EPUB.

This book was peer-reviewed by Dr. Nicholas Ray, University of Leeds, and an anonymous referee. Experts in their field, our readers give their time freely to help ensure the academic rigour of our books. We are grateful for their generous and invaluable contributions.

This book need not end here...

Share

All our books — including the one you have just read — are free to access online so that students, researchers and members of the public who can't afford a printed edition will have access to the same ideas. This title will be accessed online by hundreds of readers each month across the globe: why not share the link so that someone you know is one of them?

This book and additional content is available at
https://doi.org/10.11647/OBP.0435

Donate

Open Book Publishers is an award-winning, scholar-led, not-for-profit press making knowledge freely available one book at a time. We don't charge authors to publish with us: instead, our work is supported by our library members and by donations from people who believe that research shouldn't be locked behind paywalls.

Join the effort to free knowledge by supporting us at
https://www.openbookpublishers.com/support-us

We invite you to connect with us on our socials!

BLUESKY	MASTODON	LINKEDIN
@openbookpublish.bsky.social	@OpenBookPublish@hcommons.social	open-book-publishers

Read more at the Open Book Publishers Blog
https://blogs.openbookpublishers.com

You may also be interested in:

Love and its Critics
From the Song of Songs to Shakespeare and Milton's Eden
Michael Bryson and Arpi Movsesian
https://doi.org/10.11647/OBP.0117

Characters in Film and Other Media
Theory, Analysis, Interpretation
Jens Eder (author) and Stephen Lowry (translator)
https://doi.org/10.11647/OBP.0283

Troubled People, Troubled World
Psychotherapy, Ethics and Society
Michael Briant
https://doi.org/10.11647/OBP.0416

Fiesco's Conspiracy at Genoa
Friedrich Schiller (author), John Guthrie (introduction by), and Flora Kimmich (translator)
https://doi.org/10.11647/OBP.0058

www.ingramcontent.com/pod-product-compliance
Lightning Source LLC
Chambersburg PA
CBHW050522170426
43201CB00013B/2046